Yom Kippur

Readings

Yom Kippur Readings

Readings

INSPIRATION
INFORMATION
CONTEMPLATION

Edited by Rabbi Dov Peretz Elkins

With Section Introductions from
Arthur Green's *These Are the Words*

JEWISH LIGHTS Publishing
Woodstock, Vermont

Yom Kippur Readings:
Inspiration, Information and Contemplation

2010 Quality Paperback Edition, First Printing

© 2005 by Dov Peretz Elkins
Pages 332–335 constitute a continuation of this copyright page.

Library of Congress Cataloging-in-Publication Data
Yom Kippur readings : inspiration, information, and contemplation / edited by Dov Peretz Elkins.
p. cm.
Includes bibliographical references.
ISBN 1-58023-271-X (hardcover)
1. Yom Kippur—Meditations. I. Elkins, Dov Peretz.
BM695.A8Y658 2005
296.7'2—dc22   2005017209

ISBN 978-1-58023-438-2 (quality paperback)

10 9 8 7 6 5 4 3 2 1

Cover design: Tim Holtz
Cover art: S-2, "Gates of Jerusalem," 1963 original color lithograph by Shraga Weil. Published by The Safrai Fine Art Gallery, Jerusalem, Israel. Copyright Safrai Gallery.

Manufactured in the United States of America

Published by Jewish Lights Publishing
A Division of LongHill Partners, Inc.
Sunset Farm Offices, Route 4, P.O. Box 237
Woodstock, VT 05091
Tel: (802) 457-4000   Fax: (802) 457-4004
www.jewishlights.com

Contents

Acknowledgments

Many people have encouraged me to continue the work I began decades ago in trying to enrich and enhance the experience of High Holy Day worship. A major milestone was reached when my two-volume set, *Moments of Transcendence*, was published in 1992. Since then hundreds of friends have told me how valuable that collection was to them in their intellectual and spiritual preparing for the Days of Awe. Many even have developed the custom of taking the books along with them to services, and at a lull in the worship experience, opening one of the books to find spiritual nourishment there that the *mahzor* may not have provided at the moment.

Now, some thirteen years later, that set has become in part out-of-date, and the need was seen for a new, fresh collection of illuminating material on the liturgy of Rosh Hashanah and Yom Kippur. At first I thought of having *Moments* reprinted, but Stuart M. Matlins, editor in chief and publisher of Jewish Lights, persuaded me to do an entirely new collection. His experience and wisdom easily prevailed, happily, I can say. I am delighted that Stuart has shepherded this volume from its inception, bringing keen insight and years of successful publishing experience to bear, to make this volume much better through his vision and perspicacious determination. It is an honor for me to join the distinguished pantheon of Jewish Lights authors who are in the forefront of the movement to bring crisp spiritual writings to the English-reading world. People like Rabbis Arthur Green, Larry Kushner, Larry Hoffman, and Neil Gillman have transformed the landscape of popular theological writing in the decade and more that Jewish Lights has been bringing their ideas to a wide-ranging group of readers.

I am deeply indebted to Emily Wichland, editorial vice president, and Lauren Seidman, editor, at Jewish Lights, for their diligent assistance, and to all the talented and devoted staff of Jewish Lights, for their assistance in making this book (and, with God's help, its companion for Rosh Hashanah next year), something that will grace Jewish homes, schools, and synagogues in the summer, fall, and perhaps all year round.

Special appreciation is due two gifted rabbinical students who served as research assistants in the compilation of this volume—Steve Schwarzman and Rachel Devora Kahn-Troster. I would never have made the necessary deadlines without their fastidious, capable, and persistent labors.

No book of mine was ever written or edited without the loving support of my beloved wife, Maxine. And finally, the members of my congregation at The Jewish Center of Princeton deserve warm thanks for hearing and appreciating many of the words in this compilation during my conducting of High Holy Day services from 1992 to the present.

It is my hope that having these holy words between the covers of a book will now broaden that congregation to newer and larger communities of spiritual seekers.

Introduction

Ask anyone what is the most holy day of the Jewish calendar, and the answer will most likely be: Yom Kippur, the Day of Atonement. It surely attracts more people to synagogue worship than any other Jewish holiday. While didactic theologians will argue that Shabbat is more important—and I agree with that view—it is Yom Kippur that holds the most special place in the mind and imagination of the average Jew.

Yom Kippur contains great meaning and high drama. It begins with the solemn nullification of vows, with the haunting ancient melody of *Kol Nidre*, repeated three times by the prayer leader, and carries the worshiper for another twenty-five hours of almost uninterrupted prayer, study, and meditation. It includes the Torah and Haftarah readings of sending the scapegoat into the wilderness as a surrogate for our sins; the dramatic confession of the High Priest who, in a series of declarations of guilt, absolves his own failures and those of his fellow priests as well as those of the entire Household of Israel; the remarkable contrasting nonritually focused sermon of the eloquent Isaiah on his Jerusalem soapbox telling the people who smugly fast and pat themselves on the back for their humble penance that the true fast is feeding the hungry and caring for the orphan and the widow; the innumerable *piyyutim* (medieval liturgical poetry) that embellish the liturgy with themes of sin, regret, repentance, faith, hope, and renewal; the unique chant of the biblical book of Jonah that lends itself to dozens of fascinating interpretations; the *N'eilah* service—the symbolic closing of the gates of *Teshuvah* as the sun begins to set in the sky; and finally the moving *Havdalah* ritual, the triumphant blast of the Shofar signaling the end of the long day of prayer and repentance; and finally that long-awaited "Next Year in Jerusalem!"

While the day is solemn, awe-filled, and holy, it is also long and has the potential to be confusing and empty of spirituality for many who attend out of obligation, custom, family pressure, or other non-religious reasons. The readings in this book are designed to fill that gap of meaninglessness for those who crave meaning; and to provide a deeper level of spiritual intimacy with God for those who find the day meaningful but not enough so.

In it we have provided a selection of readings from a wide realm of sources—ancient, medieval, modern, Jewish, and non-Jewish. They are designed to uplift, inspire, and inform. In some cases they will add to the understanding of the purpose of the day. In others they will offer a new or different perspective on a certain prayer or poem that the worshiper may not have thought of before. In all cases we hope that each reading will expose a new prism of light on the day that brings new hope and renewed confidence that next year will be a better one than the one just completed.

It is our intention to offer the lay and scholarly public a variety of stimulating thoughts and ideas that will make of this most sacred day of Yom Kippur one that is ever more memorable and influential in our daily lives.

Rabbi Dov Peretz Elkins

FIRST REFLECTIONS

Many of the great liturgical compositions of the synagogue, both poetic and musical, have been written for Yom Kippur. It is generally considered to be a full day of prayer. In traditional synagogues, there may be just a brief break between the *mussaf* and *minhah* services. The leaders of prayer and many others are dressed in white, symbolizing innocence, and the *aron kodesh* and Torah scrolls are also covered in white, as they are throughout the penitential season. The length and repetitious quality of the prayer services on Yom Kippur have a cathartic effect, and by the end of the fast, following the appearance of three stars in the evening sky, we are filled with a sense of both exhaustion and cleansing.

RABBI ARTHUR GREEN, *THESE ARE THE WORDS*

And You Shall Afflict Your Souls....

Yom Kippur is in many ways the essence of Judaism. Perhaps no holy day better than Yom Kippur symbolizes Judaism's belief that there can be no intermediary between God and each of us. It is for this reason that Judaism lacks a professional class of people who intercede to God on our behalf. The job of facing God is ours alone.

Judaism emphasizes that life is a tablet for us to write on as we wish. We can use our life to be people of character by performing mitzvot throughout our lives, or give in to moments of rage, anger, selfishness and egocentricity. From Yom Kippur's perspective the choice is ours and ours alone.

Yom Kippur demands of us that we face God directly and be adult enough to account to the "Judge of Judges" for our actions, be they of an individual or of a collective nature. Yom Kippur teaches us that only we can correct our faults.

These tasks are not easy, nor is the day easy. Yom Kippur's fast pushes us to the limit. It is hard to go from Sundown to Sundown without food or water. How quickly even the strongest man realizes how frail he is in the eyes of God.

Yet as hard as the fast is, and it is never easy, the day's spiritual message is even harder. To examine the totality of one's life, to realize that all of us are fallible means that we must not only demand that we improve but be willing to demand that we forgive others who seek to improve. Forgiveness (*teshuvah*) in Judaism, however, comes with a price. It is only granted to those who sincerely desire to recognize their errors, to repent, to change their ways, and to begin again. No easy task, but then Yom Kippur is not meant to be an easy day.

Rabbi Peter Tarlow

A *Techine* for Yom Kippur

O God, creator of Heaven and Earth, creator of humankind and of all living things, grant me the power to feel as others feel, the power to listen and to hear, to behold and truly see, to touch and be touched.

Keep fresh within me the memory of my own suffering and the suffering of *clal yisrael* (the whole community), not in order to stimulate eternal paranoia, but rather that I may better understand the suffering of strangers; and may that understanding lead me to do everything in my power to alleviate and to prevent such suffering.

When I see streams of refugees bearing the pathetic belongings they have salvaged from ruined homes, may I recall the wanderings of the people of Israel and may I vow never to be the cause of loss and homelessness.

Enable me to be like Yourself—to feed the hungry, clothe the naked, tend the sick, comfort the bereaved. Guide me in the ways of *tikkun olam*, of mending the world. As I delight in a loving marriage of true minds, may I never forget the thousands of women battered and beaten by their spouses. As I rejoice in the bliss of my children and grandchildren, may I never forget the pleading eyes and swollen bellies of starving infants deprived of physical and emotional nourishment. May my woman's capacities for concern, compassion, and caring never be dulled by complacency or personal contentment. May my feelings always lead me to act.

Grant me the wisdom to discern what is right and what is wrong and inspire me with the courage to speak out whenever I see injustice, without shame or fear of personal retribution. Enable me to feel pity even for my enemies. Grant me the will and the ability to be a peacemaker, so that the day may soon come when all people will live in friendship and your tabernacle of peace will be spread over all the dwellers on earth. Amen.

God and God of our ancestors, forgive me my sins of pride and conceit, my obtuseness to the needs, desires, and ambitions of others, my lack of empathy, my ignorance and obliviousness to all that is going on in the world save what is directly related to my own experience and that of the Jewish people. Forgive us our arrogance and narrowness of vision; forgive us our readiness to inflict pain on those who have hurt us. Make us whole, make us holy.

Alice Shalvi

Is This the Fast I Have Chosen?—It Wasn't My Turn

A teacher in Minnesota asked his class, "How many of you had breakfast this morning?" As he expected, only a few of them raised their hands. So he continued. "How many of you skipped breakfast this morning because you don't like breakfast?" Lots of hands went up. "And how many of you skipped breakfast because you didn't have time for it?" Many other hands went up. He was pretty sure by then that the remaining children hadn't eaten, but he didn't want to ask them about poverty. So he asked, "How many of you skipped breakfast because your family just doesn't usually eat breakfast?" A few more hands were raised. Then he noticed a small boy in the middle of the classroom, whose hand had not gone up. Thinking the boy hadn't understood, he asked, "And why didn't you eat breakfast this morning?" The boy replied, his face serious, "It wasn't my turn."

Irving Cramer

What Is Life Without *Teshuvah?*

Rebbe Shmelke of Nikolsburg once described the true meaning of *teshuvah*, the true greatness of *teshuvah*, the indispensability of the process of growth which *teshuvah* implies; when he said that life is all about *teshuvah*—about change.

He said: If I had a choice, I would prefer not to die. Why? Because in the next world there is no Yom Kippur. And what can the soul of a person do in the Next World without Yom Kippur? And what purpose is there to life without *teshuvah?*

The third century neo-Platonist philosopher, Plotinus, defined *teshuvah* as the task to constantly re-make yourself in the divine image, in these words:

"Withdraw into yourself and if you do not like what you see, act as a sculptor. Cut away here, smooth there, make this line lighter, this one purer. Never cease carving until there shines out from you the Godlike sphere of character."

Rabbi Dov Peretz Elkins

Returning to Ourselves

While concerned with the self, the process of *teshuvah* is not itself narcissistic. The annual call to *teshuvah* is a reminder that our time in this world is limited and that we must journey honestly, accepting that our gifts are not for us alone, but meant to be put forth in this world as a way of reconstructing the once whole, now shattered vessel whose shards, the mystics tell us, are scattered all over the universe. Returning to ourselves helps us engage in partnership with the world and with the One of all that is.

When our bodies, the sacks in which our *neshamot* are housed, begin to give way and we confront death, the psychological walls that we build for our protection also begin to give way. They make way for the soul to emerge, becoming accessible not only for self, but for everybody and everything around. Denial of our finitude would only feed the avoidance of our spiritual potential.

I am reminded of a midrash about the destruction of the Temple. The *Shekhinah* (close-dwelling presence of God, associated with the feminine), which dwelled in the Temple, went out and accompanied the prophets as they warned the people of the potential destruction for which their behavior was paving the way. Each time the prophets were rejected by the people and the *Shekhinah* saw that the people did not change, She withdrew further into the walls of the Temple. Finally, there was nowhere for her to go. The *Shekhinah* withdrew into the Holy of Holies, the core of the Temple. At that point, the Temple was destroyed.

As we build more walls for self-protection, there are fewer places for our souls to emerge. Confrontation with suffering can enable us to lower our walls and provide more space for our souls, but the ultimate liberation happens when we die, and our bodies, like the ancient Temple, turn to dust.

When a disaster befalls us, we have the option to withdraw or to attempt to transform the experience into a teacher for ourselves, our friends, our families, and our communities. Our personal disaster may not only be our gift, it may sometimes be another's gift as well. It is our obligation to discover these gifts and give them to others. A word, a thought, a touch may turn someone's life around and give meaning to their existence. And you may never know that you were responsible for that.

Debbie Friedman

God's Book of Life

We are the people of the Book and we are created in God's image; it stands to reason that our God must also have a Book. And what, then, would God's Book be like? Needless to say, it would be a paragon of perfection, no sentence obscure, no word out of place, no letter missing or superfluous. It would require no study, no commentary, no debate. It would pulsate in harmony with the heartbeat of creation.

Our Book, on the other hand, is an ungainly mess. It is full of errors and confusion, narratives of horror, contradictions, obscurity, lacunae. What would you expect? We are only human. Yet we cling tenaciously to our Book, debate its oddities, savor its imperfections, study and revere its every letter, dot and tittle. We lovingly inscribe God's name into every word until the whole Book shimmers with meaning, transforming itself into living Torah.

And it's good that we do, for every human life is just like our Book, an ungainly mess, full of random encounters, unexpected dead ends, irrevocable mistakes, comically and tragically perverse twists and turns—contradictions, obscurity, lacunae. Yet we cling tenaciously to the story of our lives, searching for purpose and connection, longing to discern and then do what is right, striving to weave coherent narratives out of the frayed fibers of experience.

And then, once a year, if we so dare, we stop clinging to the narratives of our Book and of our lives. We let go of the tenacious effort that so defines us and stand revealed before God, our sins confessed, our souls laid bare, our bodies hungry and unadorned. With the *chutzpah* of aspiring angels, we pray to be inscribed, even sealed, into God's Book, so that our lives, ever so briefly, may become a living Torah, may shimmer with meaning and pulsate with the heartbeat of creation.

G'mar hatimah tovah—this Yom Kippur, may a small piece of our souls be, if ever so briefly, inscribed, even sealed, *b'sefer ha'hayim*—into God's Book of Life.

Rabbi Rena Blumenthal

The Cab Ride

Twenty years ago, I drove a cab for a living.

When I arrived at 2:30 a.m., the building was dark except for a single light in a ground floor window. Under these circumstances, many drivers would just honk once or twice, wait a minute, then drive away.

But I had seen too many impoverished people who depended on taxis as their only means of transportation. Unless a situation smelled of danger, I always went to the door. This passenger might be someone who needs my assistance, I reasoned to myself.

So I walked to the door and knocked. "Just a minute," answered a frail, elderly voice. I could hear something being dragged across the floor.

After a long pause, the door opened. A small woman in her 80s stood before me. She was wearing a print dress and a pillbox hat with a veil pinned on it, like somebody out of a 1940s movie. By her side was a small nylon suitcase. The apartment looked as if no one had lived in it for years. All the furniture was covered with sheets.

There were no clocks on the walls, no knickknacks or utensils on the counters. In the corner was a cardboard box filled with photos and glassware.

"Would you carry my bag out to the car?" she said. I took the suitcase to the cab, then returned to assist the woman. She took my arm and we walked slowly toward the curb.

She kept thanking me for my kindness.

"It's nothing," I told her. "I just try to treat my passengers the way I would want my mother treated."

"Oh, you're such a good boy," she said.

When we got in the cab, she gave me an address, then asked, "Could you drive through downtown?"

"It's not the shortest way," I answered quickly.

"Oh, I don't mind," she said. "I'm in no hurry. I'm on my way to a hospice."

I looked in the rear-view mirror. Her eyes were glistening.

"I don't have any family left," she continued. "The doctor says I don't have very long."

I quietly reached over and shut off the meter. "What route would you like me to take?" I asked.

For the next two hours, we drove through the city. She showed me the building where she had once worked as an elevator operator. We drove through the neighborhood where she and her husband had lived when they were newlyweds. She had me pull up in front of a furniture warehouse that had once been a ballroom where she had gone dancing as a girl.

Sometimes she'd ask me to slow in front of a particular building or corner and would sit staring into the darkness, saying nothing.

As the first hint of sun was creasing the horizon, she suddenly said, "I'm tired. Let's go now."

We drove in silence to the address she had given me. It was a low building, like a small convalescent home, with a driveway that passed under a portico. Two orderlies came out to the cab as soon as we pulled up. They were solicitous and intent, watching her every move. They must have been expecting her.

I opened the trunk and took the small suitcase to the door.

The woman was already seated in a wheelchair. "How much do I owe you?" she asked, reaching into her purse.

"Nothing," I said.

"You have to make a living," she answered.

"There are other passengers," I responded.

Almost without thinking, I bent and gave her a hug. She held onto me tightly.

"You gave an old woman a little moment of joy," she said. "Thank you."

I squeezed her hand, then walked into the dim morning light.

Behind me, a door shut. It was the sound of the closing of a life.

I didn't pick up any more passengers that shift. I drove aimlessly lost in thought. For the rest of that day, I could hardly talk. What if that woman had gotten an angry driver, or one who was impatient to end his shift? What if I had refused to take the run, or had honked once, then driven away?

On a quick review, I don't think that I have done anything more important in my life.

We're conditioned to think that our lives revolve around great moments. But great moments often catch us unaware—beautifully wrapped in what others may consider a small one.

People may not remember exactly what you did, or what you said, but they will always remember how you made them feel.

Life may not be the party we hoped for, but while we are here we might as well dance. Every morning when I open my eyes, I tell myself that it is special. Every day, every minute, every breath truly is a gift from God.

As told to Rabbi Jory Lang

Preface to the *Amidah*

To pray is to take notice of the wonder, to regain a sense of the mystery that animates all beings, the divine margin in all attainments. Prayer is our humble answer to the inconceivable surprise of living. It is all we can offer in return for the mystery by which we live. Who is worthy to be present at the constant unfolding of time? Amidst the meditation of mountains, the humility of flowers—wiser than all alphabets—clouds that die constantly for the sake of His glory, we are hating, hunting, hurting. Suddenly we feel ashamed of our clashes and complaints in the face of the tacit glory in nature. It is so embarrassing to live! How strange we are in the world, and how presumptuous our doings! Only one response can maintain us: gratefulness for witnessing the wonder, for the gift of our unearned right to serve, to adore, and to fulfill. It is gratefulness which makes the soul great.

Rabbi Abraham Joshua Heschel

Introduction to the *Amidah*—God's Presence Vibrates on Our Lips

... *When we recite the* Amidah *prayer, the* Shechinah *enters into us and prays through us. That is why we begin the prayer by saying, "Oh, Lord, open my lips and I shall sing Your praise." It is God who moves our lips as we pray.*

Rabbi Pinchas Shapiro, the Koretzer Rebbe, once sat and struggled with a passage from the prophet Isaiah: "It is written, 'Lift up thy voice as a shofar'" (Isaiah 58:1).

"What could it mean?" he wondered. "How can a voice become like a shofar?"

After pondering the verse further, Rabbi Pinchas suddenly realized that God was revealing to us something about the nature of prayer.

"The shofar remains silent," he said, "and cannot emit a sound unless the breath of a [person] passes through it. When we become like a shofar, the breath of the Holy One, the divine *Shechinah,* passes through us. That is how we pray: the breath of God's Indwelling Presence vibrates on our lips. We may think we pray to God, but that is not exactly so: the prayer itself is divine."

David Patterson

Moving toward the Light of God

Propitiation of the gods, human sacrifice, this is not the way of Yom Kippur. The way of Yom Kippur is to accept our imperfection. This is what Yom Kippur is all about. We accept that to be human is to be imperfect, to be broken, and we realize that we don't have to project our brokenness onto someone else. We don't have to try to cast it out. We can fix it. We can repair it in the context of our own lives.

The way of Yom Kippur is to realize, like Isaiah, that we are all part of a whole, and that we move toward the light of God when we behave this way, when we care for each other, when we realize in our flesh and bones that our own happiness depends on the happiness of everyone else in the world. We can't enjoy our affluence while people are starving.

When we experience this sense of the world, we realize that every need in the world is our need. Nature always takes care of the next need. The forest replenishes itself, the T cells in our body strive to heal. The world is set up to heal itself. Our choice is to align ourselves with this healing or not.

Compassion heals. Loving-kindness heals. Justice heals. Meditation heals. Prayer heals. The Sabbath heals. Yom Kippur heals. All these activities reenforce each other, depend upon each other, and taken together they purify us of our delusion of separation and its attending sense of absurdity. They impart a sense of the sacred to us, an immediate sense of our connection to everyone and to everything, and the imperative for engagement with the world which flows out of this sense.

So purified, we simply take care of whatever is in front of our face. We simply answer the immediate need. It is our need.

When we are hungry we eat, and when we are tired we sleep. When someone else is hungry, we feed them. When someone else is homeless, we find shelter for them.

If we try to ignore them, we only darken our own world. Better to pick up the broken shards of our vessel and begin to piece them together again. We are all broken vessels yearning for the light.

Rabbi Alan Lew

Spiritual Flutterings

We read in Bereshit (Genesis 1:2), in the Story of Creation, *ruah elohim mirahefet al p'nei ha-mayim*. This is typically translated as: "a wind from God hovered (or swept) over the face of the water." The word that is translated as hovered or swept is *mirahefet*. *Mirahefet* is a word of ancient Hebrew poetry. It is rarely found in Torah, but we do read it in Deuteronomy (32:11) where *mirahefet* refers to a mother eagle beating her wings in place, over the nest of her young, in order to feed them. And so I translate *mirahefet* as "fluttering." So that *ruah elohim mirahefet al p'nei ha-mayim* is better understood as "a wind from God fluttered over the face of the water."

Because each of us is created *b'tzelem elohim*, in the unique image of God, each of us has our own deep and internal *mirahefet*; our own spiritual fluttering. All spiritual yearning begins in the wordless flutterings/*mirahefet* of our souls. Because *mirahefet* at its core is wordless, no matter what language we speak, we spend our lives trying to attach words to our own deep internal spiritual fluttering.

Communally, as we approach every New Year we both celebrate the beginning of the new year and review the past. Yet individually, depending on our current physical, emotional, or spiritual state, we may look forward to the fullness of this coming year or we may not. We may look at the past year as filled with promise or we may not. Certainly there are some years we have looked forward to and some years we were glad to end.

No matter what our framework for any particular year, we are always filled with wordless yearning, *mirahefet*, that flutters in us and seeks to be articulated. Part of our spiritual task at any time, and certainly at the turn of the new year, is to listen to the *mirahefet* that soul-flutters, to pay attention to its own unique patterns in each of us, to attempt to give it expression, and allow words—as best they can—to settle in so that we can let ourselves and others know the wisdom that our spiritual flutterings can give.

May this New Year give us enriching spiritual flutterings.

Rabbi Eric Weiss

KOL NIDRE—
OUR VOWS AND
PROMISES

The evening prayer on Yom Kippur is preceded by *kol nidre,* a legally-worded declaration that nullifies vows to be made in the coming year. The recitation of this formula, one of the best-known portions of all Jewish liturgy, has a long and controversial history. It was already known and debated in the Gaonic period (9th century). The original formula was retroactive, nullifying all vows made in the preceding year. Its recitation would allow one to enter Yom Kippur with a clean slate, with no forgotten or unfulfilled vow blocking one's path to atonement. But some argued that the availability of such a blanket nullification would encourage people to vow more casually, and then rely on the coming *kol nidre* as an escape from obligation. As a compromise with those who opposed *kol nidre* altogether, the rabbis changed it into an anticipatory rather than a retroactive formula.

The melody used for *kol nidre* is considered to be among the most ancient of the synagogue's repertoire. The recital is an act of high drama. It is preceded by removing two Torah scrolls from the ark, held by two elders of the congregation who take the symbolic role of court witnesses. A special formula permitting the congregation "to pray together with the transgressors" is then recited. This formula, which is also in legal language, served in some periods of Jewish history to allow forced apostates to join their Jewish brethren in Yom Kippur prayers. That formula, then the *kol nidre* proper, is each recited three times, rising from quiet chant to a great crescendo. The congregation responds by calling out Numbers 15:26: "All the Children of Israel and the strangers in their midst are forgiven, for the whole people has acted unintentionally."

All this must take place before sundown, as release from vows is not permitted on the Sabbath (Shabbat). This initial rite of forgiveness concluded, the congregation loudly praises God with the blessing *she-heheyanu*, thanks to the One who has "kept us in life, sustained us, and enabled us to reach this time." This blessing, I once heard a wise teacher say, is the very essence of Yom Kippur. Here we are—the slate wiped clean once again—ready to stand directly in God's presence with a clear and undivided attention that is possible only on Yom Kippur. This blessing is followed directly by the evening service of Yom Kippur itself.

RABBI ARTHUR GREEN, *THESE ARE THE WORDS*

Kol Nidre: Nothing Affects the Human Being More Than Music

One night, in the late 1960s ... [Rabbi Joseph B. Soloveitchik, who died April 8, 1993] reflected on music. Nothing affected the human being more than music, he said. By happenstance, a person can hear a certain melody at a time of personal difficulty or joy and then let the melody pass out of his mind, as innocently as it entered. Years later, even decades later, the same person may suddenly hear the same melody, only to be overpowered by the emotional sadness or joy he experienced when he first heard the melody, decades earlier. Music is powerful. Music doesn't forget. Emotions are never dead, only dormant. A person's link to his past is never severed. Memory never entirely recedes, and music may summon it. This is what Rabbi Soloveitchik was saying that night. And now, this great musician is gone. His clefs were the pages of the Talmud. His quarter notes were the letters of the Torah. His melody was the Divine song imbedded in the sheet music of Judaism. His power was the power to summon each Jew's link to his past, to his history, to the Patriarchs and the martyrs, the heroes and the anonymous Jews who lived their lives humbly and then, as he would put it, withdrew from the Covenantal stage. In each letter of the Torah, literally each one, he found resonance. His ... disciples ... had unveiled before their eyes strands of their own collective memory they did not know they had. This great musician played the notes of the Torah in a way that, after listening to them, one's emotions as a Jew could never die, one's link to the glorious past of the Covenantal community could never recede....

Rabbi Hillel Goldberg

Kavannah for *Kol Nidre*

Worlds are joined in this opening recitation. Upper and lower worlds are joined. The divine and the human are joined. We and they—those who have crossed the boundary to leave the we—are joined. This reveals our intention in seeking atonement; at-one-ment. We seek unification, the dissolution of barriers, the merging and unity that will culminate at the end of Yom Kippur.

Rabbi Sheila Peltz Weinberg

Can a Sinner Dare to Pray?

Knesset Yisrael, p. 12*

"Let everything that hath breath praise the Lord" (Psalms 150:6). Our Rabbis of blessed memory (Genesis Rabbah 14:9) interpret this verse to mean that man should praise his Maker for every breath he draws. For at every moment the soul wishes to leave the body, but the Holy One, blessed be He, restrains it. It follows that man becomes a new creature at every moment of his life. Man can gain encouragement from this when the thought enters his head at the time of prayer and worship, "How dare you, so base a man, full of sin and iniquity, open your mouth to praise God?" But he should then consider that at that very moment he has become a new creature and has not sinned in that moment, so now he is justified in standing in God's presence.

The novel idea is here expressed that, strictly speaking, no man is really worthy to pray to God. Yet at every moment man is, as it were, created anew by God, so that the man who now stands in prayer is not the man who had sinned.

Rabbi Dr. Louis Jacobs

Quoting God

One Yom Kippur night, when Reb Levi Yitzchak of Berditchev was reciting the prayers, he came to the verse: "And God said, 'I have forgiven according to your words.'" Upon reading these words, he interrupted the service and turned to address the congregation.

"My masters," he said. "Do not our Sages teach us that 'One who cites a quotation in the name of the person who first said it brings redemption to the world' ... ? Very well, then, let us together say something in the name of its Author: 'And God said, "I have forgiven according to your words"'!"

Hasidic tale

---

* *Knesset Yisrael* is a collection of the teachings of Israel Friedman of Ruzhyn (1797–1850; grandson of Nahum of Chernobil and of the Maggid of Meseritch, two famous masters) and his sons, who all became Hasidic masters. The above quotation appears in this book (originally published in Warsaw, 1906, p.12).

The Jew Must Stand for Something

Let me tell the story of a man who returned to the circle some sixty years ago. His name may be familiar to some of you, Arnold Schönberg, one of the great musical geniuses of this century. He was raised in an ambivalent Jewish home, and when he fell in love the only condition to the marriage was baptism. When asked at the time "What are you?" he said: "I am an atheist, unbelieving, and freethinking, as my father was." Schönberg converted. Years later, divorced and alone, he attended the synagogue with friends who brought him to hear the music of *Kol Nidre*. He was so moved by the experience that he decided to return to Jewish life.

In a ceremony at the Rue de Copernic Synagogue, Arnold Schönberg returned to the circle. His witness for the ceremony was Marc Chagall. A few years later he wrote a new *Kol Nidre*. This man, who stepped out of the circle so completely, came to understand himself as a Jew again through the power of *Kol Nidre*. Arnold Schönberg willingly divested himself of the garment which art, academism, and culture had clothed him in order to return to the condition of a simple liturgist, a poet of God. *Kol Nidre,* as written by Arnold Schönberg, was first heard publicly in Los Angeles in 1938, not in a concert hall but in a synagogue on Yom Kippur.

The narration begins. . .

Rabbi: *The Cabbala relates a legend. "In the beginning, God said: 'Let there be light.' From infinite space a flame sprang up. God scattered this light into atoms. Myriad sparks were hidden in the universe but not all of us can perceive them. The vain man who walks proudly will never notice them, but the modest and humble man whose eyes are lowered is able to see them."*

"A Light is sown for the righteous." *'Biyeshivah shel malah, uv'yeshivah shel matah.* By the authority of the court on high, and by the authority of the court below. In the name of God, we solemnly urge that every transgressor, even if unfaithful to our people out of fear or led astray by false doctrines of any kind, be liberated from his weakness or his greed. We invite him to unite himself with us in prayer tonight. A light has been sown for the righteous—a light has been sown for the *Baal Teshuvah:* the one who returns.

The choir sings: Kol Nidre. *A light has been sown for the* Baal Teshuvah.

The Rabbi responds: *We invite him to be one of us tonight.* Teshuvah. *We make our souls anew:* Kol Nidre.

The story of Arnold Schönberg has been repeated again and again during the course of Jewish history. It is the story of the Conversos who also left their imprint on the liturgy of *Kol Nidre.* The lesson to be learned from these examples is that a Jew is never too far from the circle to return and in meaning again in Jewish life. The same can be said to the many in our time who have walked away from the circle of Jewish life in America.

On the Yom Kippur we have entered into the circle, we are all *Baalei Teshuvah,* all of us have returned. *Kol Nidre* reminds us that it is not enough to stand in the circle, the Jew must stand for something. We can make our souls anew, rediscover our Jewish essence. May each of us have the courage to raise ourselves up and look into the face of the Eternal One and consider what we stand for as Jews.

Rabbi Michael S. Siegel

Our Vows Are Not Vows

The *Kol Nidre* prayer is commonly understood as a formula which releases us from foolish vows. To be sure, it cannot absolve us of any contractual agreements with business associates or promises made to loved ones, but it does annul meaningless commitments made to God in moments of well-intentioned weakness. It invalidates oaths such as: "God, get me through this crisis and I swear I'll donate half my possessions to charity, give up chocolate, and never sleep past 6 a.m." Hyperbole such as this is obliterated when we solemnly recite: "our vows are not our vows; our bonds are not bonds; and our oaths are not oaths."

Rabbi Max Arzt, the late Vice-Chancellor of the Jewish Theological Seminary ... detected another nuance of meaning in this last phrase. In his book, *Justice and Mercy,* Rabbi Arzt suggests that "*Kol Nidre* can serve us as a reminder that only by resolute will and by severe self-discipline can we hope to lessen the distance between what we are and what we ought to be."

To reinforce his point, Dr. Arzt refers us to Rabbi Moshe Mordechai

Epstein's novel interpretation of the concluding words of the prayer. In Epstein's view, *Kol Nidre* is our contrite acknowledgment that all too often the lofty resolutions we make during the High Holidays have no substance—our vows are no vows; our oaths, no oaths.

What an exercise in futility if reasonable commitments we take upon ourselves are conveniently ignored! Only by acting on our best intentions do we grow in the New Year. Only by taking our obligations to man and God seriously do we become worthy of atonement.

Rabbi Bruce Ginsburg

Blessing the Children Yom Kippur Eve

A most meaningful tradition of the High Holy Day season is the blessing given by parents to their children just before they leave for *Kol Nidre* services. Throughout the ages, generations of Jewish parents have placed their hands on their children's heads and implored God's mercy, love and guidance for the year to come.

"May the Lord make you like Ephraim and as Menasheh" (for boys).

"May the Lord make you like Sarah, Rebekah, Rachel and Leah" (for girls).

May it be the will of our God in Heaven to place love and reverence in your heart. May you fear God all the days of your life so that you not sin. May God implant in you the desire to study Torah and observe commandments. May your eyes look straight ahead and not be distracted by vanities, your mouth speak wisdom, and may your heart be filled with righteousness. May your hands always be involved in the accomplishment of worthwhile endeavors and may your feet ever be ready to do God's bidding.

May the Almighty grant you righteous children who will also occupy themselves with Torah and Mitzvot all the days of their lives. May God grant you sustenance and livelihood, obtained morally, received graciously and shared abundantly, and may you never have to depend on the charity of others. May your professions always allow you time to serve God and to care for God's world.

May you be inscribed and sealed in the Book of Good and Long Life together with all the righteous of the world.

Traditional

Prayer of the Hidden Jews

This prayer has long been associated with the Hidden Jews—the Jews in Spain who converted to Christianity during the Inquisition and kept their Jewish life secret in order to survive. This prayer allowed them to pray as Jews by forgiving the vows they had made to another religion, another system of beliefs. What a deep resonance this interpretation has for gay and lesbian Jews who are living hidden, secret lives! For those in the closet about their gay identity in their Jewish communities and those in the closet about their Jewish lives in the gay community, this prayer recognizes the pain of hidden and split identities and offers the hope for integration and healing.

Adina Abramowitz

Kol Nidre: Drawn into Heaven's Womb

There was an exhibit of kites recently called "Pictures in the Sky." One hundred artists from around the world were asked to design kites—varied in color, shape, design. All of them could fly. Each kite portrayed the unique talents, maybe even the very soul, of its artist. The exhibit informed its viewers that people of the Far East see kites as visible manifestations of the soul of the earthbound owner.

This evening, *Kol Nidre* night, we stand poised between heaven and earth, and we measure the success of the flight of our lives. We think of how we shake our shoulders against the wind, and assess what binds us to earth; what enables us to climb heaven's steps; what draws us into heaven's womb.

Rabbi Deborah R. Prinz

Kol Nidrei: Why Three Times?

The *Kol Nidrei* is chanted three times, though only once in some Reform congregations. The threefold repetition most likely derives from the ancient practice of reciting all official proclamations three times. A beautiful midrash [Jewish legend], however, explains this practice in a different way. The first time, says the midrash, *Kol Nidrei* is chanted in a quiet, awe-filled voice, like that of a servant entering a [ruler's] chamber for the first time. The second repetition is a bit louder, symbolic of the servant approaching the royal throne. The third time, the *Kol Nidrei* is sung in full voice, as a subject in the presence of the [ruler], confident of the ruler's mercy and forgiveness.

Rabbi Daniel B. Syme

Whose Vows—Ours or God's?

The kabbalists say that God is praying for release from God's vow ... i.e., God promised to redeem us from the long exile, and yet another year has gone by and we are still not redeemed.

So Jews come to *shul* and God comes to *shul*, and it's the night of Yom Kippur, and God opens by asking that *God* will do better in the year ahead, that God's vows to exile the people for sin will be recanted, and that therefore God's promises to us can be fulfilled. Thus, the profound emotion that people show regarding *Kol Nidre*, even though *Kol Nidre* is actually nothing other than a dry legal formulation, results from God's recitation of *Kol Nidre*, and from the hope that this will be the year of our redemption.

Traditional

Who Are the *Avaryanim?* Permission to Pray with the Iberians (?)

An interesting theory has been advanced in regard to the phrase we are about to chant before the *Kol Nidre*—"We hereby declare it permissible to pray with '*Ha-Avaryanim.*' The word "*Avaryanim*" is usually translated from the Hebrew root "*Avar*"—to transgress; and it thus would mean to be able to pray together with all the sinners who are here tonight—namely, all of us.

However, an historian has proposed a novel interpretation—translating the Hebrew word "*Avaryanim*" not as sinners, but as "Iberians."

The suggestion, thus, is that the phrase "*anu matirin lehipalel im ha-avaryanim*"—referred originally to Iberians—conversos who returned openly to the Jewish community after 1492.

In any case, we permit the community to now recite *Kol Nidre,* and absolve all of us of sins for which we have truly repented.

Rabbi Leon T. Rosenblum

Forgiveness on *Kol Nidrei*

One Yom Kippur Eve Rabbi Levi Yitzchak of Berditchev delayed the start of *Kol Nidrei.* His demeanor was one of worry and distress, and to his followers this indicated that he knew that it was not a propitious moment for attaining forgiveness for the many sins Jews had committed. Rabbi Levi Yitzchak scanned the assembled worshipers and then said, "I don't see Berel, the tailor."

"Berel is not here," someone said.

"Then go fetch him!" the Rabbi said. "We cannot begin *Kol Nidrei* without Berel."

The congregation was bewildered, because Berel was hardly a personage whose presence warranted delay of services for the entire congregation. When Berel finally appeared, Rabbi Levi Yitzchak asked, "Why weren't you in *shul,* Berel?"

"Because I have nothing to do anymore with God. He has been unfair to me, and I have no way of taking my complaints against Him to court, so all I can do is protest. That is why I am not davening."

"Tell me your complaints against God," Rabbi Levi Yitzchak said. "Perhaps I can settle things for you."

"Very well," Berel said. "Two weeks ago the *poritz* [feudal lord] sent for me, and said that he wanted me to sew him a *peltz* (fur coat) for the winter. I took my sewing box to the *poritz*'s mansion, and he gave me the skins for the coat. When the coat was finished, there were a few skins left. Now the *poritz* had given me all the skins to use for the coat, and if I was skillful enough to complete the coat and still have some left over, they were properly mine. Furthermore, I have a daughter to marry off, and I need every cent I can get, and as far as the *poritz* was concerned, the skins could have all gone into the coat. I therefore put the leftover skins in my bag and left.

"After I had walked back to town, having gone several kilometers, a horseman came after me. 'Berel!' he said, 'The *poritz* wants you back right away.' I panicked, figuring that the *poritz* had counted the skins in his coat and had discovered that I had not used them all, but had not returned the excess. This could lead to my imprisonment in his dungeon for life. I dropped my bag and mounted the horse, back to the mansion.

"When I came in the *poritz* said, 'Berel, the coat is beautiful, but you did not sew on a hook for hanging up the coat. That is not how you finish a job, Berel.'

"I raised my eyes to heaven in gratitude, and I sewed on a hook. I retraced my steps, but alas! My bag was gone. It was clear to me that this was the work of God, who considered my taking the extra skins as stealing, but this was not so. The *poritz* had not asked for an accounting. He gave me the skins to make the coat, which I did. The extra skins were legitimately mine, and God was wrong in taking them from me. I then decided that if that was how He acts toward me, I am no longer going to do His will.

"I came home and sat down to eat without washing my hands and without saying a berachah. That night I did not daven, nor the following days. On Rosh Hashanah I did not go to hear the blowing of the *shofar* [ram's horn]. If God can be so unjust toward me, I will have nothing to do with Him. That is why I did not come to *shul* for *Kol Nidrei*."

Rabbi Levi Yitzchak said, "But Berel, it is Yom Kippur, a time for forgiveness. Can't you find it in your heart to forgive God? After all, on Yom Kippur God forgives everyone's sins."

Berel thought for a moment, then said, "Very well. I will forgive Him, but only if He in turn forgives everyone's sins without exception, regardless of how severe they may have been."

Rabbi Levi Yitzchak was overjoyed. He lifted his eyes toward heaven. "Master of the Universe," he said, "do You hear? Berel says he will forgive You, but only if You forgive everyone's sins. I, Levi Yitzchak the son of Sarah Soshi, Rabbi of Berditchev, decree that this is an equitable settlement. You are forgiven, and all transgressions that Jews have committed during the entire year must be forgiven.

"Now let us say *Kol Nidrei*," Rabbi Levi Yitzchak said.

Rabbi Abraham J. Twerski

SIN

The "good and evil inclinations" are the forces within each person that lead us to do good and evil, according to the psychology of the early rabbis. Sometimes these forces are personified and depicted as quarreling with one another inside us, each arguing that we should follow its path.

The Torah speaks only of the evil inclination, in passages (Genesis 6:5; 8:21) where God sadly concludes that the creation of humans was regrettable since their inclinations turn only to evil. The rabbinic tradition, apparently unwilling to affirm the pessimism of these passages, created a parallel "good urge," with the human soul a *tabula rasa* upon which the forces of good and evil fight out their battles. For the Kabbalists (Kabbalah), who believe there are demonic forces in the universe that threaten the Divine Presence, the good and evil urges become the internalized representations of these mighty forces that act on the cosmic as well as the personal scale.

An alternative psychology to that of good and evil inclinations is found in the midrashic and mystical notions of *kelipah* and *pri* or "shell" and "fruit." Here the mind or soul is compared to a delicate fruit that needs to develop a hard shell around itself for protection. The truest self lies within. This is the "fruit," not subject to evil or corruption. But the *kelipah,* which was originally seen as a protective device, may turn evil or even demonic and keep the inner self from expression. Here the psychological model is that of the good inner self seeking to escape (yet still needing) its shell, rather than the neutral self before the two warring forces.

RABBI ARTHUR GREEN, *THESE ARE THE WORDS*

The Capture and Release of the *Yetzer Ha-Ra*

I have a problem. Everybody should have such problems. Last week I received two post cards. One was addressed to me and one to my husband and as some of you know we have different last names. Each card was redeemable for a half pound of free coffee at a new coffee store which opened up in Evanston. My *Yetzer Ha-Ra*, my evil inclination, said in a greasy voice, " Go and get one half pound one week and take Jay's card and get another half pound another week. They won't recognize you." But my *Yetzer Ha-Tov*, my good inclination—why is it that the evil inclination always comes first in these stories?—my good inclination added, "You know they just want you to be introduced to their coffee. They don't mean for you to get a pound." The *Yetzer Ha-Ra* chimed in, "Yea, but who would know???" This may not sound like evil as in "twentieth century evil," but it's still the *Yetzer*. I remain ambivalent.

The rabbinic insight into our ambivalent nature appears in the Mishna where the rabbis discuss tomorrow's Torah portion. Tomorrow we will read how two goats will be chosen to be sacrificed for Yom Kippur. The Rabbis go on to tell how each must be the same size, color and price. By lottery one is chosen to be sacrificed to God and the other to Azazel—the fallen Angel of Evil.

We humans have no lottery to help us distinguish between good and evil. No place or person is exempt from corruption. No place or person is devoid of holy sparks. It requires wisdom to live with ambivalence.

It says in the Zohar that when God came to create the world and to reveal what was hidden in the depths, light emerged from darkness—both were wrapped in one another. So it is that from good—evil comes forth—like the *Yetzer Ha-Ra* and the *Yetzer Ha-Tov*—the evil and good impulse. All are intertwined. In fact, the rabbis felt that evil was a necessary part of the world. Even in the Holy of Holies, the special sanctuary in the Temple where only the High Priest was allowed, do we find that ambivalence....

And that leads me to a story from the Talmud....

The Israelites returned from Babylonian exile to find the Holy Temple destroyed, burned. Even in the sanctuary no one was safe; the priest's sons were found dead. But the *Yetzer Ha-Ra*—the Evil Inclination—still breathed in that most holy of places.

Ezra and the other leaders prayed: "Please God, You who brought this evil spirit into being so that we could receive a reward by resisting it—we want neither it nor the reward!

"Erase the *Yetzer* from every heart in Israel. Although it is good for us to triumph over the evil inclination, it is better to have no evil at all."

In response to their prayers, the heavens opened and a note fluttered to the earth from above. On it—one word: *Emet.* Truth.

For three days and three nights they fasted. They prayed with such *kavana* [intention] that all of a sudden, the *Yetzer Ha-Ra* came charging out of the Holy of Holies like a fiery lion.

"Catch it," the people cried and they tried to seize the beast but only managed to get—a single hair. Evil is hard to grasp. The creature bellowed so loudly that its cry was heard a thousand miles away.

Eventually they did manage to capture the *Yetzer Ha-Ra* and, according to Zechariah's instructions, they put it in a lead pot, and sealed it.

For three days they held it captive. But during this time, the chickens stopped laying eggs. Not one egg could be found for the sick in all of Palestine. From this the people learned that the suffocation of the *Yetzer* would simultaneously smother the *Chalya Olma,* the libidinal energies indispensable for civilization. The destruction of the *Yetzer* would be the destruction of the world. There was no recourse but to release it.

"Perhaps we can pray to the heavens for *Rachame Apalga,* 'half mercy,'" said the people. "Let there be lust—but let it be restricted to one's own spouse—let there be ambition and aggressiveness but let it be restricted to noble and peaceful ends; let there be anger, but let it be limited to righteous indignation."

The plan was abandoned. "*Palga birkiah lo yahave,*" said the sages. "Halves are not granted from heaven."

So they lifted the lid of the pot, blinded the creature and set it free. Once again it roamed the world but its power, so they say, was greatly diminished.

The *Yetzer Ha-Ra* rests its slimy self at our doors. We struggle not to answer its knock. It takes wisdom to live with ambivalence.

Susan Stone

Is Reciting *Al Het* Reason to Rejoice?

Arriving at a certain town once before Rosh Hashanah, the Baal Shem Tov asked the local people who led the congregation in prayer during the Days of Awe, and was told that the *rav* of the town acted as *shaliah tzibbur* [prayer leader] himself.

"And how does he conduct himself during the prayers?" the tzaddik asked them.

In the course of their reply, they told him that on the Day of Atonement their *rav* had the unusual custom of singing the lengthy confession to jolly melodies.

The Baal Shem Tov at once called for this man. On asking him the meaning of his custom, he was answered as follows: "If the lowliest of a king's servants, whose task it is to rake away the filth from the gutters of the royal courtyard, *loves his king*, then as he works he sings with joy out of the sheer pleasure he derives from making him happy."

"If this is what you have in mind while you are at prayer," said the *tzaddik*, "would that my lot be at one with yours!"

Rabbi Shlomo Y. Zevin

Don't Be Judgmental

It was outside Schwartz's bakery on Fairfax Ave. that I first saw him do it while I waited in my car for my wife to finish Shabbos shopping. As I watched the *erev Shabbat* [Sabbath evening] crowd go by, my attention was drawn to a poorly dressed young woman pushing an old market wagon, filled with bundles of rags, paper bags, and whatever else goes into living hand to mouth.

A small child sat cushioned in the wagon, and another kid walked alongside her. Passengers in poverty.

Coming from the opposite direction was this man whom I recognized. As he passed her, he turned around suddenly and called out something to get her attention. I didn't hear what. When she turned, he pretended to be picking up some money. Green it was, how much wasn't meant for me to know.

He motioned that she had dropped it, and quickly put it in the child's lap and was gone.

It was less than a month later, while I waited at the checkout counter at Ralph's market, that I saw that man again. He was standing behind an *alte bubbie* [old grandmother] who was counting out her pennies to pay for her milk and bread.

He didn't see me, but I saw him as he bent down and came up holding a twenty in his hand, all the while saying that the *bubbie* had dropped it. She said "no," it wasn't hers. Everybody in line urged her to take it, and she did.

Now when anyone is lucky enough to see an act of kindness, it makes for good feelings. Trouble was that I never liked this man until now.

God gave two eyes to see. The right one to see the good in others, and the left to see the fault in ourselves.

I see better now.

Rabbi Howard Weiss

Bold, Humble, Daring

Today we stand before the Mirror of All
to see ourselves as we are.
We come with no gifts, no bribes, no illusions, no excuses.
We stand without defense and wait to be filled.
What will fill us?
Remorse, certainly. So much error and needless pain.
And joy: remembered moments of love and right doing.
We are too complex for single-sided emotions.
And we are too simple to be excused by our complexity.
Let us be bold enough to see,
humble enough to feel,
daring enough to turn and
embrace the way of justice, mercy, and simplicity.

Rabbi Rami M. Shapiro

Dibbur Peh ... Leshon Ha-ra—Even If True, Gossip Is Still a Sin

"Miriam and Aaron began speaking against Moses because of the dark-skinned woman he had married." [Numbers 12:1]

In *Behalotcha,* we read of Miriam's loose tongue and God's quick punishment: "When the cloud left its place over the Tent, Miriam was leprous, white as snow" [Numbers 12:10].

Who isn't aware that slander and libel are condemned? But try to tell a magazine specializing in gossip that parading the mistakes and sins of others is forbidden!

Maimonides, in his Laws of Knowledge, Ch. 7, Law 1, cites the verse: "You shall not be a talebearer among your people [Lev. 19:16]," pointing out that the second part of the verse: "You shall not stand upon the blood of your brother," proves that gossip can "destroy the world." He cites the example of Doeg the Edomite, who reported to King Saul that David, whom Saul saw as his competitor and nemesis, had been granted sanctuary in the priestly city of Nov. Doeg spoke the truth, but his tale resulted in the slaughter of 85 priests as well as every man, woman, child and beast in the well-meaning but unfortunate city of Nov [I Samuel Ch. 22].

Maimonides distinguishes between three categories of gossip, each of which is Biblically condemned: *rekhilut* (talebearing), which he interprets to refer to even innocuous, but unnecessary, information about a third party; *lashon hara* which is negative but true information; and *motzi shem ra,* which is negative and untrue.

Take, for example, the complimentary comment, "Bob's son just finished law school." If said to a man whose own son was thrown out of law school, the words could be as sharp as a knife in the heart. Our tradition tells us that the malady translated as "leprosy" is the punishment for slander, the crime and the punishment linked linguistically because the word for "leper"—*metzora*—and the word for slander *motzi shem ra*—share a common sound, as if one were the echo of the other.

In analyzing the text describing Miriam's sin, we learn a great deal about the Biblical attitude toward gossip. All that is revealed by the text is that *something* was said concerning the Kushite woman. Rashi (loc. cit.) quotes the Sifri, which brings down the words of R. Natan who explains that Miriam happened to be next to Moses' wife Tzipporah when Moses was informed that two men in the camp, Eldad and Medad, had begun to prophesy. Commiserating with the wives of Eldad and Medad, Tziporah shared her fear that their husbands might leave them as her husband had left her. Tziporah sees the burden of prophecy as including the cessation of marital relations; her husband's dedication to God having severed his ties with his wife.

Armed with this bit of intimacy, Miriam pulls along Aaron, and the gossip about Moses gets rolling, though the text merely hints at what transpired. This is why Rashi fills us in with the missing pieces, including the idea that a "Kushite woman" is synonymous with "beauty." Hence, according to Rashi, the Kushite is Tziporah and Miriam broadcasts her sister-in-law's feelings, subtly adding that Moses has become estranged from a beautiful and good woman.

An alternative interpretation by Joseph ben Kaspi [1279–1340] understands the verse to be a literal reference to Moses having taken a second wife, a Kushite, and this is why Miriam and Aaron are gossiping.

Common to both readings is the fact that nowhere is there the remotest suggestion that Miriam and Aaron are spreading untruths. Whatever they said about Moses is fact: either he left Tziporah or he took a second wife—neither of which is Biblically forbidden—yet this talk leads to Miriam's flesh turning leprous, a terrible condition for a person earlier described as a prophetess.

The clue to Miriam's sin is found in her motive. In the following verse, we read that Miriam and Aaron go on to say: "Is it to Moses exclusively that God speaks? Doesn't he also speak to us?" [Numbers 12:2].

Now we understand what they're driving at. Miriam is jealous of her brother Moses. By first cutting her brother down to size, she may be able to prove that he's not the only prophet in the desert. Talking about Tziporah might have been utterly innocuous, but in this context blackening Moses' reputation was part of an attempt to whiten her own—another reason why a talebearer suffers a disease that make's one's skin as white as snow.

Rabbi Yisrael Salanter, founder of the Mussar movement in the 19th century, illustrated the attraction of slander this way: If I want to appear bigger than someone, I can either climb a ladder and keep reaching for higher branches, or I can push my competitor into a pit so deep he'll never crawl out. The latter is the function of slander.

After the question, "doesn't he also speak to us?" God clarified the difference between the prophecies of Miriam and the prophecies of

Moses: "If someone among you experiences divine prophecy, then when I make Myself known to him in a vision, I will speak to him in a dream. This is not true with My servant Moses, who is like a trusted servant throughout My house. With him I speak face to face. How can you not be afraid to speak against My servant?" [Numbers 11:6–8]

In God's defense of Moses, there is no reference to the Kushite woman; that isn't the real issue. What is at stake is the positioning and the purpose of a seemingly innocent remark.

The laws of kosher food—what one may or may not put into one's mouth—have always been easier to keep than the laws of kosher talk—what one may or may not allow out of one's mouth. Perhaps this principle is one reason why Maimonides quotes the dictum of the sages that idol worship, incest and murder remove a person from this world and the next, and that *"loshon ha-ra"* is equivalent to all three.

Avoiding gossip can thus be a matter of life and death for at least three people: the gossiper, the one who hears it, and the one the gossip is about.

Rabbi Shlomo Riskin

Gossip: A Chronic Infectious Disease

Those who listen to slanderous gossip are just as guilty as the talebearers. Repeated use of the evil tongue is like a silk thread made strong by hundreds of strands. The foul sin of talebearing often results in a chain of transgressions.

Leprosy was regarded as a punishment for slander, because the two resemble each other: they are both slightly noticeable at the outset, and then develop into a chronic, infectious disease. Furthermore, the slanderer separates husband from wife, brother from brother, and friend from friend; he is therefore afflicted with the disease which separates him from society.

One sinful Jew can do harm to all his people, who are like a single body sensitive to the pain felt by any of its parts.

Hafetz Hayim (Rabbi Yisrael Meir HaKohen, 1838–1932)

Al Het: The Need for Community

Recently, a new edition of Alexis de Tocqueville's masterpiece, *Democracy in America*, was re-issued, and a *New York Times* reviewer said this about the mid-nineteenth-century Frenchman's book, which was written after a visit to America:

> It is Tocqueville's enduring observations about the American character ... that most impress the contemporary reader. Americans' obsession with progress and self-improvement, our materialism, pragmatism and faith in the future: all are intelligently described and analyzed. The resulting portrait is an oddly melancholy one, a portrait of a people both idealistic and selfish, a people both liberated by and isolated by their own individualism.

In Tocqueville's words: "Thus not only does democracy make every man forget his ancestors, but it hides his descendants and separates his contemporaries from him; it throws him back forever upon himself alone and threatens in the end to confine him entirely within the solitude of his own heart. "

Over a century ago, Tocqueville captured one of America's most serious problems: rampant individualism. *Al Het* reminds us, in its plural formulation, that we live as a community, in our glory and in our shame, and when we forget that, we lose everything.

Rabbi Dov Peretz Elkins

Ashamnu ... Bagadnu ... —Neither Repentance Nor Confession

Rabbi Simhah Bunam of Pshis'cha taught that if one thinks in his heart in the moment of reciting *Ashamnu:* How pleasant it will be for the Blessed Holy One to forgive me; or, in the moment of reciting *Bagadnu:* After we are forgiven, we will be able to receive many good rewards; in this kind of prayer there is neither Repentance nor Confession.

Rabbi Simhah is making the point that often in our prayers we think ahead of the positive results that will accrue after the prayer, or confession. Such a prayer is selfish, insincere, and lacking humility, says Rabbi Simhah, and hence will not be heard on High.

Rabbi Dov Peretz Elkins

The Power of Words

Words, the power of words, is all important. Words can inspire. Words can destroy. There is an insightful Midrash which says, "These are the words." Read *Devarim* and also *devorim*, wasps. Words can console us, words can cajole us. Words can tear like wasps at our very flesh.

Rabbi Seymour J. Cohen

Can You Cross the River?

Rabbi Pinhas ben Yair was going to the House of Study, but the river Ginnai was too strong for him.

He said to it.

Ginnai, Ginnai, why do you keep me from the House of Study? It parted before him, and he passed.

His disciples said to him: Could we pass too?

He said to them: One who knows in the heart that he has never injured any human being in Israel can pass without harm.

Talmud Yerushalmi, Demai 22a

Recognize Our Own Flaws

The Rabbi of Lelov always said to his students:

One cannot be redeemed until one recognizes the flaws in the soul and tries to mend them.... Whoever permits no recognition of one's flaws ... permits no redemption. We can be redeemed to the extent to which we recognize ourselves.

Hasidic tale

Yetzer Ha-Ra—For the Sin of the Evil Impulse

Judaism basically looks upon human nature in a positive vein, unlike other religious traditions which see humans as having been created inherently evil.

Yet, Judaism is not Pollyannaish. It recognizes what it calls our *Yetzer Ha-Ra*, our proclivity to do evil; our tendency to be selfish and neurotic. The aim is by performing *mitzvot* [good deeds] and studying Torah, to help our *Yetzer Ha-Tov*, our good impulse, win over the *Yetzer Ha-Ra* in the battle for our soul.

Many writers have recognized our dual nature. Dostoevsky, writing in his novel *A Raw Youth*, describes the human being's "faculty of cherishing in his soul the loftiest ideal side by side with his greatest baseness, and all quite sincerely."

Likewise, the prominent psychiatrist and best-selling author, M. Scott Peck, in his book, *The Road Less Traveled*, wrote that "We all have a healthy self and a sick self."

Rabbi Hayim Vital, sixteenth-century author on Jewish ethics, wrote that in addition to God having implanted within us a good impulse, God also placed the *Yetzer Ha-Ra*, but that the *Yetzer Ha-Ra* is encased in a shell, and it's extremely difficult to reach it.

This is our human dilemma. To change for the better from our worst parts to our best; from our *Yetzer Ha-Ra* to our *Yetzer Ha-Tov*.

It's easier to accomplish this formidable task when we recognize its difficulty. Thus, we include in the *Al Het* litany the prayer for forgiveness for the times when our worst part got the better of us.

Rabbi Dov Peretz Elkins and Rabbi Stephen Chaim Listfield

Lashon Ha-Ra—Traditional Sources

1) "For lack of wood, fire is extinguished. Without a talebearer, strife is stilled" (Proverbs 26:20).

Message: Unless gossip is "fueled," it dies down and is forgotten.

2) "The gossiper stands in Syria and kills in Rome" (Yerushalmi, Peah 1:1).

Message: Gossip's reach and power are far and wide.

3) "Your friend has a friend, and your friend's friend has a friend, so be cautious in your speech."

Message: Gossip spreads quickly. You tell one "trustworthy" person, and that "trustworthy" person tells his/her "trustworthy" person, and before you know it ...

4) "A person who honors the tongue and uses it to speak words of Torah and mitzvot will be rewarded, but one who speaks slander and gossip brings much sorrow to the world" (*Tzenah Ure'ena* on Lev. 14: 1–2).

Message: A good strategy for overcoming the tendency to gossip is to be preoccupied with positive words, such as Torah and mitzvot.

5) "One may discount the value of words. After all, they can be neither seen nor touched. However, so it is with the wind, which can be neither seen nor touched. Yet it is capable of destroying entire worlds" (Anonymous).

Message: It is a common tendency, and easy to underestimate the potential damage of speech. Yet we must not, for its power for destruction is beyond our wildest imagination.

6) "There is hardly a day when we are spared from *leshon ha'ra*" (Baba Batra 164b).

Message: Gossip and slander are ubiquitous and pernicious; beware of speaking or listening to them.

7) "The Talmud equates speaking *leshon ha-ra* with flagrant atheism, with adultery, and with murder. In act, it is worse than murder since it simultaneously destroys three people: the one who relates the gossip, the one who listens to it, and the one it concerns."

Rabbi Pinchas Peli

Lashon Ha-Ra—Be Careful of Unnecessary Words!

The story is told about the Hafetz Hayim (Rabbi Yisrael Meir Kagan HaKohen, early 20th century) who once visited a generous donor to his Yeshiva. During their conversation the wealthy entrepreneur was busy writing a telegram to a business associate.

After a few minutes of conversation, it seemed that the discussion was leading in the direction such that *leshon ha-ra* might ensue. At that point the Hafetz Hayim noticed that the businessman had rewritten the telegram several times, and commented to him about his having written out every word with great care.

The businessman replied that indeed he had taken great care in composing the telegram, since "every unnecessary word here will cost me extra expenses." The Hafetz Hayim replied: "If only everyone was as careful as this when choosing what to say! Don't they know that every unnecessary word they speak will cost them dearly in the World To Come?"

The *midrash* says: "Refrain from evil talk and live a life of shalom."

Derekh Eretz Zuta

On Justice, for All Children

O God, forgive our rich nation where small babies die of cold quite legally.

O God, forgive our rich nation where small children suffer from hunger quite legally.

O God, forgive our rich nation where toddlers and school-children die from guns sold quite legally.

O God, forgive our rich nation that lets children be the poorest group of citizens quite legally.

O God, forgive our rich nation that lets the rich continue to get more at the expense of the poor quite legally.

O God, forgive our rich nation which thinks security rests in missiles rather than in mothers, and in bombs rather than in babies.

O God, forgive our rich nation for not giving You sufficient thanks by giving to others their daily bread.

O God, help us never to confuse what is quite legal with what is just and right in Your sight.

Marian Wright Edelman

Lashon Ha-ra: Judaism Is, Above All, a Love of Language

In a marvelous flourish of rabbinic fantasy, R. Yosi ben Zimra has God address the tongue directly. "What else could I have done to rein you in, O tongue of deceit? Though all human limbs are erect, I made you to lie flat. Though all limbs are external and visible, I concealed you inside the body. Moreover, I enclosed you behind two walls, one of bone (the teeth) and one of flesh (the lips)." In other words, the very anatomy of the organ betrays the Creator's anxiety about its physiology!

What motivates this tirade against loose and hurtful language? It is the rabbinic conviction that the ability to speak makes humankind most God-like. What was it that God blew into Adam's nostrils at the moment of creation which brought him to life (Genesis 2:7)? For the Hebrew phrase "*le-nefesh hayya*—living being," the oldest Aramaic translation we have, Onkelos, suggests "a being that speaks." The added specificity underscores the nature of the endowment. Like God, humankind was to be the only living creature to enjoy the extraordinary power to create through words. Human speech is a faint echo of the language of God, and to abuse and corrupt it is to assault the essence of our being. It is for this reason that the long and oft-respected public confessional on Yom Kippur, the "*al het*," devotes at least one quarter of its lists of transgressions to acts of verbal violence.

Judaism is, above all, a love of language, witness the rabbinic efforts to sanctify it. The way we address each other foreshadows the way we will treat each other. The words of the gifted Russian poet Osip Mandelstam, sent to Siberia by Stalin in the 1930s and murdered by the Nazis in 1941, haunt me: "The word is flesh and bread. It shares the fate of bread and flesh: suffering."

Rabbi Ismar Schorsch

Ve-Khof Et Yitzrenu Le-Hishtabed Lakh—Direct Our Impulses [*Yetzer*] ...

YETZER (Gen. 6:5; 8:21): This Hebrew term (from *yatzor,* to create) implies human creativity and refers to a person's imaginative drive. More than inclination, lust, impulse, urge, drive (as the term is variously rendered), the Hebrew term *yetzer* denotes human design and purpose, involving ingenuity, resourcefulness and motivation.

Human *yetzer* is deemed by our talmudic sages as a positive force, existentially indispensable and morally neutral. The sages speak of "two" kinds of *yetzer*—a "good" one *(tov)* and a "bad" one *(ra)*—

both operating and wrestling within one's conscience. This metaphor of duality and constant battle between the *yetzer-tov* and *yetzer-ra* dramatizes the complexity and intensity of the human moral dilemma. Ultimately, however, it is by the power of our free will that we can employ our *yetzer,* or creative energy, either constructively, for good and beneficial purposes, or destructively, for evil and futile goals. Metaphorically, the righteous have the *yetzer* under their grip; the wicked are within the grip of their *yetzer.* The virtuous ones rule over their drives; the wicked ones let their drives rule over them.

Rabbi Zvi Yehuda

We Humans Are Cracked Vessels: *Ashamnu, Bagadnu, Gazalnu*—We Have Sinned, We Have Dealt Treacherously ...

One of the great statesmen of this century, Ambassador George F. Kennan, in his book, *Around the Cragged Hill* (1993, p. 17), describes in eloquent and insightful terms the pitfalls of the human predicament, which lead us to the failures described so completely in the *Vidui,* the Confessional we are about to recite. Says Kennan:

> "Man, to the degree that he tries to shape his behavior to the requirements of civilization, is unquestionably a cracked vessel. His nature is the scene of a never-ending and never quite resolvable conflict between two very profound impulses. One of these, built into him from birth and not a matter of his own choice, is something he shares with the animals: namely, the imperative impulse to preserve and proliferate his own kind, with all the powerful compulsions that engenders. The other is a need ... to redeem life, at least partially, of its essentially animalistic origins by lending to it such attributes as order, dignity, beauty, and charity ... and the capacity for compassion. A central feature of the human predicament is the conflict between these so frequently conflicting impulses—a conflict for which man's own soul constitutes the field of battle."

D.P.E.

Sweetening the Evil

Rabbi Larry Kushner describes the Hassidic understanding of *teshuvah* as "sweetening the evil in yourself." "We go down into ourselves with a flashlight," he says, "looking for the evil we have intended or done—not to excise it as some alien growth, but rather to discover the holy spark within it. We begin not by rejecting the evil but by acknowledging it as something we meant to do. This is the only way we can truly raise and redeem it."

Rabbi Nachman of Breslov taught that most sins involve food, money, or sex. How do we sin around food? Some of us nurture ourselves and comfort our anxieties by eating when we should realize we don't need to; some of us try too hard to nurture others by feeding them, not recognizing when they don't need to eat. But aren't the desires to nurture and to be nurtured holy?

How do we sin around money? For some of us, the desire for personal wealth comes first from the need to assure the well-being of our families, but then no amount of wealth seems to provide enough assurance, and money itself becomes our primary goal, to the exclusion of so much else. But isn't the desire to support our families holy?

How do we sin around sex? Some of us are so starved for intimacy and for transcendence that we rush ahead in all kinds of destructive directions, unmindful of the needs of our long-term partners. But isn't the desire for intimacy and for transcendence holy?

All of these sins come originally from the pure and holy sparks of divine motivation—the desires to nurture and to be nurtured, to support those we love, to find intimacy, and to reach transcendence. If we can recognize the holy sparks within our sins, and we can have a clear vision of the world and of those around us, we can raise these sparks and redeem them. In this way not only do we atone for our sins, but we also gain access to new forces of holiness in our lives. The Baal Shem Tov interpreted the verse: "Turn aside from evil and do good" to mean: "Turn the evil into good." This is what we are about, here, today.

Rob Goldston and Ruth Goldston, adapted from
Rabbi Lawrence Kushner

Ashamnu—A to Z

Assumed the worst in others and the best of ourselves,
Betrayed the trust others have placed in us,
Confused that which is essential with that which is not,
Destroyed ourselves with needless abuses,
Enjoyed the downfall of our adversaries with glee,
Felt superior to others by means of ability, wealth, or power,
Given less than our full selves to our community and our
     world,
Hastened to decry responsibility for our own actions,
Instigated animosity among others,
Junked our world with trash, showing no regard for the
     environment,
Kindled misplaced passions,
Lied to cover our vanities,
Missed opportunities to better ourselves,
Negated the validity of others in an effort to aggrandize
     ourselves,
Observed persons in need, and ignored what we saw,
Perverted the blessings of our lives into dangerous obsessions
     and mere possessions,
Quietly slipped into lives defined by moral decay,
Refused ourselves and others our love,
Seduced ourselves with the lie that "no one will get hurt,"
Trivialized the power we represent in God's universe,
Unleashed hurtful words,
Valued strangers more than our family and friends,
Wished ill upon others,
Xeroxed in violation of copyright and trademark,
Yielded to temptation,
Zestfully pursued happiness to the exclusion of goodness.

Rabbi David Greenspoon and Steve Kerbel

The Consequences of Sin and the Meaning of Evil

[*The late Rabbi Mordecai M. Kaplan, one of the 20th century's greatest
American Jewish philosophers, discusses the idea of sin and punishment*

in his diaries. In an entry dated July 11, 1929, this is what Kaplan writes after listening to a lecture at a convention of the (Conservative) organization of rabbis, The Rabbinical Assembly. The selection is from Prof. Mel Scult, Kaplan's biographer.]

"... He made a point of retaining the fear concept of God. He repeated almost verbatim the statements I have so often come across by Christian preachers protesting against the tendency to identify God with love only and urging that we should behold in the consequences of sin the punitive aspects of God's dealings. To me the very idea of a punishing God is perfectly abhorrent. All punishment is nothing but revenge and therefore belongs to the same class of evils as sin, suffering, cruelty, disease and death. I might as well think of God as deliberately *sinning* or committing cruelty as to attribute to him the will to punish. God is not concerned in seeing to it that the consequences of sin shall be suffering. The consequences of sin are part of the sin which caused them, and like the sin itself possible in the universe because the domain of chance and accident still occupies a tremendous part of that universe and has not yet come under the dominion of God who is synonymous with whatever there is of order, purpose, intelligence and love in the universe."

[As we recite the *Al Het*, perhaps we can focus more on our capacity to change and improve, instead of the fear of punishment, which might be less productive.]

D.P.E.

Let Them Fix Their Errors

Recently I listened to an audiotape on American history called "General Lee's Last Years." The story is told that toward the end of the Civil War, Confederate General Alfred P. Hill wanted General Lee to court-martial a certain junior general, as the man had caused several calamitous situations.

Lee answered, "General Hill, this man in question is not a professional general. He is a lawyer. He was pressed into the service of our cause, and he is doing the best he can. I am willing to help him correct his errors; but I will not punish him as you suggest."

Hearing this in the car recently, I said to myself, "That's the story of the Jews who come on the High Holy Days.... They are not professionals in the service of the Lord.... Their training and expertise lie elsewhere. Yet they volunteer in the service of God, they are here, in *shul,* trying to do their best."

The task of Yom Kippur should be to help them see a better way. We must not criticize or berate ourselves, even if we and the community fall short. We are doing what we can.... We recite *Al Het* to help ourselves see and correct our errors, not to berate ourselves. In the end, what we should hope for is to emerge with a cleaner soul, a clearer purpose, and a more noble resolve—to do better next year.

Rabbi Stephen Chaim Listfield

Al Chet

I wrote this piece the evening after the funeral of Dr. Steven Z. Miller z'l, a physician who was killed in a plane crash with several colleagues while on his way to a medical conference. As I listened to the eulogies it occurred to me that in a lot of ways Steve was the kind of person that my daughter Shira (who was run over and killed almost 4 years before) would have become had she lived past the age of 20 and into middle age.

Funerals outside of the normal life cycle turn the customary pat theological nostrums about death into mockery and torment. Really, what we need from God is some sort of apology, or at least an acknowledgment of the wrongness of what has happened. Obviously no such thing will be forthcoming unless we ghostwrite them, which is what I have presumed to do here.

This piece is dedicated to the blessed memories of Shira Palmer-Sherman and Steven Z. Miller.

I am *Adonai,* your god, the god of your ancestors, Abraham, Isaac, Jacob, Sarah, Rebecca, Rachel and Leah. I have brought you out of Egypt to become a great nation, mighty, numerous and prosperous. In your midst, in each generation, I give you men and women of exceptional intelligence and compassion, who are loved and respected by all who know them. They shall be for you an example of the type of people I want you to become.

And then I make them die before their time.

For the sin I have sinned against you by letting them die too soon, I ask you, my people, to forgive me, although I know you never will.

Andrew Sherman

The Body/Mind Connection

A large portion of the *hata'im*/sins listed refer to a part of the body (mouth, lips, tongue, eyes, throat, neck) for two reasons. First, our bodies need to know the nature of our wrongs. We need to experience the pain of our behavior viscerally before we are willing to change. Our confession and acknowledgment cannot remain a purely intellectual activity. We must feel, in our guts, the ill we cause ourselves and others, or we will not be motivated to really change. Second, most of the *hata'im* derive from forgetting our connection to the whole. We imagine that we can act as if there were no consequences, as if we were loose limbs and eyes and mouths divorced from a larger body, the body of our fellow human beings, the body of organic life on earth, the body of all life. Most *hata'im* derive from our separation and isolation from past and future. Most *hata'im* spring from the illusion of separateness. We think we can get away with it. But there is no getting away. There is no forgetfulness. All is remembered. All is related.

Rabbi Sheila Peltz Weinberg

What We Have Lost

We have taller buildings, but shorter tempers; wider freeways, but narrower viewpoints; we spend more, but have less; we buy more, but enjoy it less.

We have bigger houses and smaller families; more conveniences, but less time; we have more degrees, but less common sense; more knowledge, but less judgment; more experts, but more problems; more medicine, but less wellness.

We spend too recklessly, laugh too little, drive too fast, get too angry too quickly, stay up too late, get up too tired, read too seldom, watch TV too much, and pray too seldom.

We have multiplied our possessions, but reduced our values.

We talk too much, love too seldom and lie too often.

We've learned how to make a living, but not a life; we've added years to life, not life to years.

We've been all the way to the moon and back, but have trouble crossing the street to meet the new neighbor.

We've conquered outer space, but not inner space; we've done larger things, but not better things; we've cleaned up the air, but polluted the soul; we've split the atom, but not our prejudice; we write more, but learn less; plan more, but accomplish less.

We've learned to rush, but not to wait; we have higher incomes, but lower morals; more food but less appeasement; more acquaintances, but fewer friends; more effort but less success.

We build more computers to hold more information, to produce more copies than ever, but have less communication; we've become long on quantity, but short on quality.

These are the times of fast foods and slow digestion; tall men and short character; steep profits and shallow relationships.

These are the times of world peace, but domestic warfare; more leisure and less fun; more kinds of food, but less nutrition.

These are days of two incomes, but more divorce; of fancier houses, but broken homes.

These are days of quick trips, disposable diapers, throwaway morality, one-night stands, and pills that do everything from cheer, to quiet, to kill.

It is a time when there is much in the show window, and nothing in the stockroom.

Author Unknown

Sins of the Tongue— ... *B'Dibbur Peh,* ... *B'Siah Siftotenu,* ... *B'Leshon Ha-Ra*

[*Eleven of the 44 sins in* Al Het *have to do with sins of speech.*]

What is noble can be expressed in any tongue.
What is ignoble should be said in no tongue.

Maimonides

If a horse with four legs can sometimes stumble,
how much more a human with only one tongue.

Sholom Aleichem

Gossip

Eleven of the 44 sins listed in the *Al Het* litany deal with sins of speech. The Torah commands:

> "Do not be a tale bearer among your people. Do not profit by the blood of your fellow: I am the Lord" (Leviticus 19:16).

The first part of this verse says "*lo telekh rakhil*," and is widely interpreted to mean: do not be a talebearer. A *rokhel* is a merchant, one presumed to be privy to secrets and gossip. And if you do, it is as if you are bringing about bloodshed, for gossip is as terrible as a sword.

Based on Yehudah ben Attar, 17th–18th c. Morocco

No Time for Sin

I do not want my students to avoid sin merely because they have controlled the urge to sin. I want them to avoid sin because they have no time for sin.

Hasidic teaching

Ve-al Dibbur Peh ... Sins of the Tongue

A Father's Message to His Two-Year-Old Son:

It perplexes me that you still aren't talking. But it's not an entirely bad thing. After all, you have never yet told a lie. You have never yet used a bad word. You have never yet uttered an insult or hurt anyone's feelings. You have never yet spread malicious gossip.

Once you start talking, you'll feel the urge almost daily to engage in one or another of these forms of wrongful speech. And—trust me on this, Caleb—it's an urge fiendishly difficult to resist. But resist you must, and part of my job is to help you learn how. Our tradition places so much emphasis on the importance of avoiding malignant talk. "Who is the man who desires life, and yearns for many days to enjoy prosperity?" asks King David in the 34th Psalm. "Then guard your tongue from evil and your lips from speaking lies."

I know that nothing will influence the words that come out of your mouth more than the words that come out of your parents' mouths. So we are careful about what we say and how we talk in your presence. The Talmud teaches, "What a child says in the street is the words of his father or mother." Eventually you will meet people, maybe even other kids, who resort to crude language or cutting putdowns when they don't get their way. I cannot shield you from such speech forever, but I can try to make sure you never hear it at home.

Jeff Jacoby

An Interview with God

"Come in," God said. "So, you would like to interview me?"

"If you have the time," I said. God smiled and said:

"My time is eternity and is enough to do everything. What questions do you have in mind to ask me?"

"What surprises you most about humankind?"

God answered: "That they get bored of being children, are in a rush to grow up, and then long to be children again. That they lose their health to make money and then lose their money to restore their health. That by thinking anxiously about the future, they forget the present, such that they live neither for the present nor the future. That they live as if they will never die, and they die as if they had never lived …"

God's hands took mine and we were silent for while, and then I asked …

"As a parent, what are some of life's lessons you want your children to learn?"

God replied with a smile:

"To learn that they cannot make anyone love them. What they can do is to let themselves be loved. To learn that what is most valuable is not what they have in their lives, but who they have in their lives. To learn that it is not good to compare themselves to others. All will be judged individually on their own merits, not as a group on a comparison basis! To learn that a rich person is not the one who has the most, but is one who needs the least. To learn that it only takes a few seconds to open profound wounds in persons we love, and that it takes many years to heal them. To learn to forgive by practicing forgiveness. To learn that there are persons that love them dearly, but simply do not know how to express or show their feelings. To learn that money can buy everything but happiness. To learn that two people can look at the same thing and see it totally differently. To learn that a true friend is someone who knows everything about them … and likes them anyway. To learn that it is not always enough that they be forgiven by others, but that they have to forgive themselves."

I sat there for awhile enjoying the moment. I thanked God for the time and for all that God has done for me and my family, and God replied, "Anytime. I'm here 24 hours a day. All you have to do is ask for me, and I'll answer."

Author Unknown

Watch Out for the "Little" Sins

Do not say that one need only repent of sinful deeds such as robbery and theft. Just as one needs to repent of these sins involving act, so one needs to investigate and repent of any evil dispositions (*dayot*) in one's character that one may have— for example: a hot temper, hatred, jealousy, quarreling, scoffing, eager pursuit of wealth or honors, greediness in eating, and so on.

Rambam (12th century, Spain & Egypt)
(*Mishneh Torah, Hilkhot Teshuvah* 7:3)

Marshall Petain, the [erstwhile] great French hero, made a compact with the Nazis. General Charles de Gaulle explained this kind of treason: 'The years had gnawed away at his character.' We have strength enough to resist the large temptations. The little hypocrisies, the minor duplicities are a different matter.

Rabbi Morris Adler

Al Het for Our Age of Violence

Al het she-hatanu … For the sins we have committed before You in not curbing violence.

For the sin we have committed in not strongly encouraging our legislators to exercise their responsibility, to pass gun control laws, and curb the wanton use of firearms.

For the sin we have committed in emptying our mental hospitals and not at the same time providing services and help for those prone to violence.

For the sin we have committed in not adequately addressing the scourge of child abuse, hence perpetuating the cycle of violence.

For the sin we have committed in allowing our children to watch 8,000 acts of murder and violence on television while yet in elementary school.

For the sin we have committed in allowing our children to watch professional wrestling with its emphasis on violence, sadism and sex.

For the sin we have committed in not really treating domestic violence as violence.

For the sin we have committed in not treating the violence of date rape as rape.

For the sin we have committed in not treating police brutality as brutality.

For the sin we have committed in paying only lip service to stopping racism, a disease that fosters violence.

For the sin we have committed in not promoting respect for each person, thus giving aid and encouragement to hate groups and the violence they perpetrate.

V'al Kulam [And for them all] ...

Rabbi Daniel A. Jezer

God's Questions

1. God won't ask what kind of car you drove, but will ask how many people you drove who didn't have transportation

2. God won't ask the square footage of your house, but will ask how many people you welcomed into your home

3. God won't ask about the fancy clothes you had in your closet, but will ask how many of those clothes helped the needy

4. God won't ask about your social status, but will ask what kind of class you displayed

5. God won't ask how many material possessions you had, but will ask if they dictated your life

6. God won't ask what your highest salary was, but will ask if you compromised your character to obtain that salary

7. God won't ask how much overtime you worked, but will ask if you worked overtime for your family and loved ones

8. God won't ask how many promotions you received, but will ask how you promoted others

9. God won't ask what your job title was, but will ask if you performed your job to the best of your ability

10. God won't ask what you did to help yourself, but will ask what you did to help others

11. God won't ask how many friends you had, but will ask how many people to whom you were a true friend

12. God won't ask what you did to protect your rights, but will ask what you did to protect the rights of others

13. God won't ask in what neighborhood you lived, but will ask how you treated your neighbors

14. God won't ask about the color of your skin, but will ask about the content of your character

15. God won't ask how many times your deeds matched your words, but will ask how many times they didn't

Author Unknown

Al Het—Is It Possible to Change?

Dr. Alexander Bukovich and Dr. Francine Bennett are both scientists who work in the field of neuro-circuitry brain disorders at the structural neuroscience lab at McLean Hospital, which I believe is in Boston. With the help of computer-assisted microscopes and nuclear probes, they came to important conclusions about schizophrenia. But one finding of theirs is of value to everyone, not only schizophrenic patients, and it's of value especially on Yom Kippur. What they found is that the brain does not cease to develop somewhere in utero; in other words, we labor under a misconception when we think that who we are biologically and what we are mentally capable of, has been determined even before we enter this world. In fact, says Dr. Bennett, brain development continues through adolescence and even into middle age (NPR interview).

Now, I am a middle-aged person, and these two scientists are telling me that my mind is not fixed into any one pattern of thought, that I am still capable of growing mentally, and that as my brain cells continue to develop I can do different things and behave differently than I have before. In other words, I can change—I'm not locked in to old behaviors. I can be different than how I have been this past year, and in fact different from what I have been my whole life—if I choose to be different.

Yom Kippur calls upon us to act upon what we have learned about ourselves on Rosh Hashanah, when we took a *din ve-heshbon*, a personal scrutiny of ourselves. Yom Kippur calls upon us to turn that newly acquired self-knowledge into action—to retain what we are doing right and to change what we have been doing wrong.

The findings of these two scientists insist that, if we say, "I cannot change, this is me, and this is who I am, I have been this way too long to change now, you'll just have to accept me as I am," Bukovich and Bennett say, "That's a lie." Change, real basic change, is still possible. If we don't change, it means that we don't want to change, that perhaps deep down we don't believe that that particular behavior is wrong. We believe it is justified, or we're entitled to behave that way because of the injustices done to us. "That's me and that's just who I am" is another way of saying, "I believe I'm right, but its hard for me to convince anyone of that, so I fall back to claiming that there's nothing I can do about that. But the truth is that I love acting that way, I'm pleased with myself when I act that way, that's really how I want to be."

So, whether it's losing weight, or reading a book, or learning how to speak rather than yell, or getting out into the world and doing something for others—don't say, "I can't!" Say, "I don't want to." Or, better still, say, "Yes, I will, I can; why not change?"

Rabbi Moshe Levin

Ashamnu—We Have Sinned

We have sinned in many ways.
Some of these sins were apparent.
Many of them were hidden.

So well hidden were they,
That often we thought they were virtues.
The roster is so long—
It reads like an unabridged, Alphabetic dictionary.
We have sinned by Alibiing our Absence
From where the Action was;
by Bigotry, Blatant and Concealed;
by Complacency towards the Concerns of the Community;
by Delinquency in our Duties
by Debates and Discussions
that were Empty and Endless—
in the very midst of Emergency—
and Engendered Futility and Failure.
We have sinned by the Gaudiness
of our House of Worship
By the Insincerity of our Jewishness
which was Juvenile and Joyless.
We have sinned from A to Z, and from Z to A
We have sinned with Apathy,
And we have sinned with Zeal.
When Zest was needed we responded with Apathy,
When Apathy was called for we were uncommonly Zealous.
We pray to You, O Lord, this day
Grant us a new Understanding and a new Wisdom,
New Values and a new Vision; And a new alphabet
That will be much more pleasing to You.

Rabbi Noah Golinkin

Al Het ... B'timhon Levav—For the Sin ... of Confusion of Values

One day Nasrudin was out walking and found a man sitting on the side of the road crying.

"What is the matter, my friend," asked Nasrudin. "Why are you crying?"

"I'm crying because I am so poor," wailed the man. "I have no money and everything I own is in this little bag."

"Ah-ha!," said Nasrudin, who immediately grabbed the bag and ran as fast as he could until he was out of sight.

"Now I have nothing at all," cried the poor man, weeping still harder as he trudged along the road in the direction Nasrudin had gone. A mile away he found his bag sitting in the middle of the road, and he immediately became ecstatic. "Thank God," he cried out. "I have all my possessions back. Thank you, thank you."

"How curious!" exclaimed Nasrudin, appearing out of the bushes by the side of the road. "How curious that the same bag that made you weep now makes you ecstatic."

Happiness is relative, and so is wealth and poverty. Mostly it is in the attitude of the possessor. When we confuse our values, we attribute our happiness and our depression to the amount of cash in our bank account, or the list of our possessions. It is these same possessions which have the power to make us happy or sad, but in the end, it is our own decision how we view them. It is not the world we see, said a wise person, but how we see the world.

D.P.E.

Sins Are Parts of Us Yet to Complete

When I was young, I had an unfailing indicator of my spiritual health. Whenever I recited the *Al Het*, the confession of sins on Yom Kippur, the more alive I was both religiously and ethically, the more sins I was able to recognize for the past year.

From the opening admission of wrongdoings committed "unwillingly and willingly" and "by hardening the heart" to the closing misdeeds done through "breach of trust" and "confused hearts," so many of them applied to me. I saw that not just obvious acts, but also much subtler attitudes and feeling, were being judged.

But as I stood before a loving but all-knowing Judge, my self-deceptions fell away. I could admit the truth and I could work to change my life.

As I matured, however, I began to see that by focusing on my misdeeds, I was missing a deeper truth in Judaism. The greater issue was not just turning from sin, but rather becoming a full human being. The focus on wrongdoing allowed me to overlook all the standard good actions, the routinized daily behaviors which fell short of what I could, and should, be doing.

The issue was not just misdeeds, therefore, but mediocrity. Could I change? Could I grow? The Days of Awe challenged me to reshape myself, to improve relationships, to become a more vital person.

Rabbi Irving Greenberg

How Do We Abolish Sin?

A wise Indian elder once described his inner struggle.

He reported that inside him are two powerful dogs. One of them is kind and good. The other is mean and evil. These two dogs fight each other all the time.

Someone once asked the Indian elder which of the two dogs wins? He replied: The one that wins is the one that I feed the most.

Each of us has the choice: which part of our being do we "feed" the most? The good and the kind; or the mean and the cruel? Whichever we feed the most will win.

For having fed the mean and cruel dog a bit too much during the past year, we now recite the *Al Het*.

Based on a teaching of Rabbi Michael Gold

... *B'Dibbur Peh*—Leprosy of Irresponsible Speech

Speaking and thinking ill of another person, construing their actions in the worst possible way, gossiping and spreading rumors which harm the reputation of another person—these activities are so widespread among our contemporaries that they no longer attract our notice at all. Yet they strike at the core of the kind of world Judaism is trying to establish. Those practices provoke a cynical disregard of human decency; they cultivate our suspicion of each other and our assumption that others are speaking ill of us behind our backs just as we are of them.

In Hebrew, such speech is called *lashon ha-ra* (literally, "an evil tongue"). *Lashon ha-ra* is the practice of speaking *about* other people, rather than speaking *to* them. It involves transforming a living, complex human being into a caricature—an object of evil, or sloth, or competition. In speaking ill of others, we participate in their dehumanization, initiating a process whose end is uncontainable.

In the words of the Rabbis, "A loose tongue is like an arrow. Once it is shot, there is no holding it back." The Midrash notes that five times, the word "Torah," teaching, is used to refer to *tzara'at*. From this superfluous repetition, the sages derive that "one who utters evil reports is considered in violation of the entire five books of the Torah."

A marvelous tale is told of a wandering merchant who came into a town square, offering to sell the elixir of life. Of course, large crowds would surround him, each person eager to purchase eternal youth. When pressed, the merchant would bring out the Book of Psalms, and show them the verse "Who desires life? Keep your tongue from evil and your lips from guile."

In an age awash in corrosive mistrust, a lack of confidence in our public leaders, and an alienating sense of loneliness and isolation, there is little hope of establishing real community until we learn to speak a new language—one of responsibility, kindness and compassion.

Rather than spreading rumors to make others look bad, we can devise empathic explanations for why someone might have acted in a disappointing way. Rather than repeating a racist joke (including remarks about JAPs, "*shikses*," "*shgotzim*" and "*shvartzes*"), we can focus attention on the shared humanity of all people. Rather than speaking *about* other people, we can speak *to* them, out of love and a desire to live in a shared community together. By learning to channel and control our speech, we will transform our world from one of isolation and cynicism to one of community and trust. Isn't that what the rule of God is all about?

Rabbi Bradley Shavit Artson

Al Het ... B'timhon Levav—By Confusion of Values, by Spoiling Our Planet

When you enter the land and plant any tree for food, you shall regard its fruit as forbidden. Three years it shall be forbidden for you, not to be eaten. In the fourth year all its fruit shall be set aside for jubilation before God; and only in the fifth year may you use its fruit, that its yield to you may be increased. (Leviticus 19:23–25)

Chapter 19 of Leviticus, which is called the Holiness Code, includes the commandments that are the basis for creating a civil and compassionate society. One concerns delaying the harvesting of newly-planted fruit trees.

What does this have to do with our lives today? This commandment teaches that we must nurture a sense of delayed gratification and develop a commitment to developing a long-term perspective. When we set out communal goals, how long a time frame do we give ourselves to harvest "new fruit"? Do we rush to harvest the early success, or do we let it grow and ripen until we "pluck it from its branch"?

In thinking about these questions, we might learn from some Native Americans who, when they begin a new enterprise, often ask, "What effect will this have seven generations from now?" Imagine asking such a question when planning a new familial or communal initiative.

Rabbi Lori Forman

... *B'timhon Levav*—By Confusion of Values

One day a hasid came to the Rabbi; he was rich, but a miser. The Rabbi took him by the hand and led him to the window. "Look out there," he said. And the rich man looked into the street.

"What do you see?" asked the Rabbi.

"People," answers the rich man. Again the Rabbi takes him by the hand, and this time leads him to the mirror.

"What do you see now?" he says. "Now I see myself," answers the rich man.

Then the Rabbi says: "Behold—in the window there is glass, and in the mirror there is glass. But the glass of the mirror is covered with a little silver, and no sooner is the silver added than you cease to see others but see only yourself."

S. Ansky

Alternative *Al Het*

For the sin of dismissing God's sacred time as inconvenient

And for the sin of filling our days without leaving room for God

For the sin of insisting on our rights while ignoring our responsibilities

And for the sin of insisting that Judaism is only about feeling good

For the sin of justifying our behavior because it's what everyone else does

And for the sin of profaning the sacred and sanctifying the profane

For the sin of dismissing God's sacred time as inconvenient

For all these sins, O God of forgiveness, forgive us, pardon us, grant us atonement.

For the sin of believing Judaism has no meaning without first seeking meaning in Judaism

And for the sin of reducing Judaism to chicken soup and matzah balls

For the sin of abandoning our Israeli brothers and sisters when they need us most

And for the sin of our silence in the face of media distortion of Israel's position

For the sin of seeking God without using the roadmap God gave all Jews

And for the sin of seeking a plain-wrap God who has no expectations of us

For all these sins, O God of forgiveness, forgive us, pardon us, grant us atonement.

For the sin of reading the paper every morning but not making time for Torah

And for the sin of excluding ourselves from the community of Israel that says twice daily *Sh'ma Yisrael*

For the sin of insisting on a quality Jewish education for our children, but not for ourselves

And for the sin of feeding our own intellectual hunger while our Jewish learning stopped at age 13

For the sin of talking to God without also listening

And for the sin of having walked so far from God we've forgotten what true awe is

For all these sins, O God of forgiveness, forgive us, pardon us, grant us atonement.

Rabbi Diane Cohen

Al Het—Yom Kippur, a Loving Laundromat

I hate doing laundry and with four kids that's a lot to hate.

After thirteen years of practice I've got it down to a science. First I have the kids bring all the laundry down to the basement. Then we sort out the small stuff like socks and underwear. I always do those first because there are the most in demand. Now you really have to love someone to touch their dirty underwear and turn their smelly socks right side out.

For me, washing my children's clothing is the perfect Yom Kippur metaphor.

During the 40 days preceding Yom Kippur we are asked to renew ourselves through introspection. The result is the realization that we are far from clean and pure.

We have made mistakes.

We have insulted and gossiped. We have cheated (if only a little). We have cursed and looked down on others. We were selfish.

If, after 40 days of self-examination, I haven't seen places for growth and improvement, then Judaism doesn't just say I'm not a good Jew. Judaism says I'm not even a good human being! For it's only through recognizing our mistakes that we grow and develop our humanity.

Do you think God likes doing laundry? Perhaps not.

But just as a parent launders his children's clothes, so does God wipe out our stains. All the parent needs and all God needs is for the child to bring his clothing down to the basement where the washing machine is waiting. That is the recognition that the clothing is indeed soiled—that we are not without blemish.

In exchange for the recognition of our mistakes and the commitment to change, we receive clean clothing. Clean clothing is a second, third, fourth, fifth (or more) chance to continue to be spiritual.

Love is laundering your children's dirty laundry.

Love is forgiving.

Love is cleansing.

On Yom Kippur God's Laundromat is open, but God can't clean …

Unless we realize our clothing is dirty.

Rabbi Yehoshua Rubin

FORGIVENESS

The Mishnah makes it clear that the purification of Yom Kippur is effective only for transgressions against God. Sins against our fellow person require that person's forgiveness. Since Jews do not want to go through Yom Kippur with the burden of sin still upon them, it is customary before or on Yom Kippur for us to ask forgiveness of one another.

RABBI ARTHUR GREEN, *THESE ARE THE WORDS*

What Forgiveness Is

Forgiveness is a by-product of an on-going healing process. Many of us grew up believing that forgiveness was an act to be performed or an attitude to possess, and the reason that we could not forgive was that we were not trying hard enough. But what really keeps us from forgiving the people who hurt us is that we have not yet healed the wounds they inflicted.

Forgiveness is the gift at the end of the healing process. We find it waiting for us when we reach a point where we stop expecting "them" to pay for what they did or make it up to us in some way.

Forgiveness is an *internal* process. It happens within us. It is a feeling of wellness and freedom and acceptance. Those feelings can be ours at any time, as long as we *want* to heal and are willing to try.

Forgiveness is a sign of positive self-esteem. It is no longer building our identity around something that happened to us in the past, realizing that there is more to us and more we can do. The past is put into its proper perspective, and we realize that the injuries and injustices are just a part of our life and just a part of who we are rather than all of us.

The religions in which we were raised presented forgiveness as a moral obligation. To be considered "good" and worthy, we were supposed to "turn the other cheek" and forgive our enemies. We believe, however, that *forgiveness is instead our moral right*—a right to *stop* being hurt by events that were unfair in the first place. We claim the right to stop hurting when we can finally say, "I'm tired of the pain, and I want to be healed." At that moment, forgiveness becomes a *possibility*—although it may not become a reality for quite some time.

Forgiveness is letting go of the intense emotions attached to incidents from our past. We still remember what happened, but we no longer feel intensely angry; frightened, bitter, resentful, or damaged because of it. Forgiveness becomes an option once pain from the past stops dictating how we live our life today and we realize that what once happened to us does not have to determine what will happen to us in the future.

Forgiveness is recognizing that we no longer *need* our grudges and resentments, our hatred and self-pity. We do not need them as an excuse for getting less out of life than we want or deserve. We do not need them as a weapon to punish the people who hurt us or keep other people from getting close enough to hurt us again. We do not need them as an identity. We are more than a victim of injury and injustice.

Forgiveness is no longer wanting to punish the people who hurt us. It is no longer wanting to get even or to have them suffer as much as we did. It is realizing that we can never truly "even the score," and it is the inner peace we feel when we stop trying to.

Forgiveness is accepting that nothing we do to punish *them* will heal *us*. It is becoming aware of what we did because we were hurt and how these attitudes and behaviors have also hurt us. It is deciding that we have simply done enough hiding and hurting and hating and that we do not want to do those things anymore.

Forgiveness is freeing up and putting to better use the energy once consumed by holding grudges, harboring resentments, and nursing unhealed wounds. It is rediscovering the strengths we always had and relocating our limitless capacity to understand and accept other people and ourselves. It is breaking the cycle of pain and abuse, ceasing to create new victims by hurting others as we ourselves were hurt.

Forgiveness is moving on. It is recognizing that we have better things to do with our life and then doing them.

Dr. Sidney B. Simon and Suzanne Simon

Forgiving as an Essential Human Attribute—To Make Peace with Ourselves, and with Others, to Move Forward with Hope

The eminent psychologist, Erik Erikson, discussed the concept of "*bashert*" [intended one] from a different perspective. In his classic work *Childhood and Society*, Erikson describes the struggle between what he calls "ego integrity and despair" in our passage to full maturity.

Ego integrity, he writes, is "an experience which conveys some world order and spiritual sense no matter how dearly paid for. It is the acceptance of one's one-and-only life cycle as something that had to be, and that, by necessity, permitted of no substitutions...."

The narrator of the Joseph story did not, of course, have access to Erikson, yet Joseph's words—"you intended me harm, God intended it for good"—anticipate by several millennia Erikson's concept of ego integrity. Joseph is able to forgive his brothers and effect reconciliation with them because he can say that "this was the way things had to be."

The struggle between accepting those things over which we have limited or no control, or raging against them, is at the heart of the human quest for meaning.

There is ample evidence in the text that Joseph has to work at accepting what happened to him; this is, after all, a man who named one of his sons Menasheh, which is interpreted to mean, "God has made me forget my hardship and my parental home"!

However, it is Joseph's ability to understand—more importantly, to accept—the events of his life that allows him to discover the meaning he wants them to have. He is able to look back on the road he has traveled and see the hand of God.

The Joseph story thus offers us a more subtle model of the interaction between human effort and divine intervention than we find elsewhere in the Torah. We find there no supernatural miracles, divine revelations or covenantal rituals.

Instead, we are offered the opportunity to impose meaning on the often random events of life. By so doing, we create a context in which our response to life's difficulties becomes an affirmation of the wholeness of life—life's integrity—rather than an acceptance of despair. It is this affirmation that enables us to fulfill those most essential human attributes: the ability to forgive, to make peace with ourselves and with others, and to move forward with hope.

Rabbi Richard Hirsh

Sweetening the Evil in Yourself

We go down into ourselves with a flashlight, looking for the evil we have intended or done—not to excise it as some alien growth, but rather to discover the holy spark within it. We begin not by rejecting the evil but by acknowledging it as something we meant to do. This is the only way we can truly raise and redeem it.

We lose our temper because we want things to be better right away. We gaze with lustful eyes because we have forgotten how to love the ones we want to love. We hoard material possessions because we imagine they will help us live more fully. We turn a deaf ear, for we fear the pain of listening would kill us. We waste time, because we are not sure how to enter a loving relationship. We even tolerate a society that murders, because we are convinced it is the best way to save more life. At the bottom of such behavior is something that was once holy. And during times of holiness, communion, and light our personal and collective perversions creep out of the cellar, begging to be healed, freed, and redeemed.

Rabbi Yaakov Yosef of Polnoye taught: The essence of the finest *teshuvah* [the returning to one's Source in Heaven] is that "deliberate sins are transformed into merits," for one turns evil into good, as I heard from my teacher [the Baal Shem Tov], who interpreted the "Turn aside from evil and do good" to mean: "Turn the evil into good."

The conclusion of true *teshuvah*, returning to our Source in Heaven, is not self-rejection or remorse, but the healing that comes from telling ourselves the truth about our real intentions and, finally, self-acceptance. This does not mean that we are now proud of who we were or what we did, but it does mean that we have taken what we did back into ourselves, acknowledged it as part of ourselves. We have found its original motive, realized how it became disfigured, perhaps beyond recognition, made real apologies, done our best to repair the injury, but we no longer try to reject who we have been and therefore who we are, for even that is an expression of the Holy One of Being.

We do not simply repudiate the evil we have done and sincerely mean never to do again; that is easy (we do it all the time). We receive whatever evils we have intended and done back into ourselves as our own deliberate creations. We cherish them as long-banished children finally taken home again. And thereby transform them and ourselves. When we say the *vidui*, the confession, we don't hit ourselves; we hold ourselves.

Rabbi Lawrence Kushner

Forgive Yourself

I was recently having coffee with someone who had been a friend for many years. Every time we get together, we begin by recounting the story of our lives, as if we were telling some sacred narrative. At one point, we began to wonder how life would have been different *if we only* ... We looked at each other and instantly recognized that we had it all wrong. We were wrong to regret any part of the story. The "good" decisions and the "bad" decisions were all the "right" decisions because they led us down a path that was filled with meaning. There were so many lessons learned from the mistakes, so much growth from the bad experiences that we honestly wouldn't change a moment. "Should have" and "could have" were futile phrases that did not recognize that all is for a reason and that we did the best we could at the time. "It's not enough to forgive others," I said. "We must forgive ourselves." For the next several hours, we retold the "sacred narrative," this time recounting the lessons in the turns in the road. "That's what 'repentance' means in Hebrew," I said. "The word for repentance is *teshuvah* and it means to turn toward the right path, the path that leads to an understanding of God."

She smiled. "Then let's turn from accusation toward understanding. In the turning, we can head for the goodness of God. Let's take 'should' and 'could' out of our vocabulary."

As we chatted, we became more inspired to understand the choices we had made and began the process toward self-forgiveness. Together, we wrote this prayer:

> God, thank You for helping me see
> That each phase of my life is perfect
> That I have arrived,
> That I've always been where I need to be
> Living perfect moments ...
> With Your help, I relinquish my need to judge.
> Embrace my heart as it beats, even as it bleeds.
> Help me grow with love, acceptance, and curiosity.
> Thank You for lighting my way.
> For gently illuminating a path in the darkness ...

Let it now be and always be
Yet another exquisite phase.
For the crimes against myself, I am sorry.
For all my slips and slides, I forgive myself.

At every stage in my life, I did what I knew how to do. If I would have known better, I would have done better. But every day I must remember to be kinder to myself and more forgiving of my imperfections, because, at every point along the way, I am blessed. Everything I have done and seen has made me who I am in this moment. It's OK to have been me. I forgive.

Rabbi Karyn D. Kedar

Let's Forgive Each Other—Unlocking the Gates of Forgiveness: A Personal Prayer

Ribbono Shel Olam, Master of the universe—the universe beyond me and the universe within me—I want to learn how to cease punishing myself and torturing myself with unhappy memories that stab me when I wake and when I sleep; with self-accusation that comes back to me brazenly or in disguise; with guilt and reproach that attack me frontally or strike at me from ambush where I cannot detect them. I want to learn who I am, at least as much as I know and understand the processes by which I earn my bread. For in my ignorance of myself the whole tragedy of the world lies exposed. If I could but find my way back to myself, I would learn to make peace with myself, and others who are in my plight could learn to make peace with one another. If I could learn to forgive myself I might learn, and others might learn, to forgive each other. I know how painfully difficult this is. I know that the quest for inner peace is agonizing, but all that is precious is bought with anguish.

Help me to unlock the gates of self-forgiveness, the gates of salvation, even as the prisoner goes forth when the time of punishment is past. Amen.

Author Unknown

Vidui—An Annotated Report

In loving memory of Shira Palmer-Sherman, z'l.

I cry—not a romance novelist's single crystalline tear, falling unheeded down a flawless cheek, but with sheets of saltwater, streaking down my face as a heavy rain streaks down a car's windshield. The tears are accompanied by their ever-present, even less glamorous hand-maiden, snot; I look like a small boy who's just lost a soccer game, all mucous and grime. Crumpled tissues have become my spoor.

I rage—I am a fire barely encased in skin; sometimes I sear my would-be comforters. I throw chairs, I throw words, I wish death on Arafat, most Palestinians, many Republicans, any driver who cuts me off, all traffic lights when they turn red. I don't know if I really mean it.

I lie—I go to *shul* every week and listen to words that I do not believe, about a world that I wish were true but know is not. Sometimes the music seduces me into singing, sometimes the rhythm of the words seduces me into chanting—but then the meaning betrays my weakness and I am abandoned. *Hodu l'Adonai ki tov* indeed—how about *hodu l'Adonai ki* ineffectual? *Ki* distracted? *Ki* bad? My Orthodox friends sprinkle so many "God willings" about that sometimes I think God was too busy with his other clients, seeing to it that their dentist appointments didn't conflict with their kids' soccer games, to remember to check on Shira crossing the street.

I trust—I am sending Miriam off to Harvard, where she wants to go, where she belongs, where her sister died. Miriam is as smart as Shira, less ethereal, more rooted, altogether less likely to be a sacrifice to the bloodthirsty gods of traffic who roam Harvard Square. Still, she is the only child I have left, and if she were to die so would I.

I love—Andy and Miriam are my life. Shira is gone, but they are not.

I am bounded and saved by words—words attack me. After she died the Hebrew letters of Shira's name whirled around me but I could not catch them. They were her song, my song, and they teased me and vanished. Words offend me. They are put together into stupid sentences by well-meaning idiots, promising, asserting, demanding. Words save me. They distance me from pain, they give me control, they allow me to mold them, to hide myself in them, to redeem myself through them.

I am—My hand is my hand, as solid and eternal as it ever was. My daughter is gone, but I am not. I do not understand this, but I know it to be true.

I do not ask for forgiveness, and I do not forgive.

Joanne Palmer

Pardon Our Iniquity and Our Sin (Exodus 34:9)— Can We Pardon Without Apology?

A major part of the Yom Kippur Liturgy is that God is a compassionate, forgiving God, restoring the people Israel to God's grace and special relationship. We say this each time we recite the Thirteen Attributes of God's Mercy (*Sh'losh Esray Middot*) in the service.

As God forgives us, so are we to forgive each other. But under what circumstances? According to Maimonides and other authorities, forgiveness comes only *after* regret and apologies have been made. The perpetrator must be genuinely sorry, and ask forgiveness of his/her neighbor. We know that Yom Kippur cleanses us of our sins against God, but we must confront directly our failures against our friends and family by *asking* for their forgiveness. Without that regret and apology, forgiveness cannot be expected.

In the following story we have no evidence of such regret or apology, but it is nevertheless a tale of deep pathos, and gives a vivid example of how powerful the force of forgiveness can be. It may be that the offender in this story did ask forgiveness, but in any case, the offended party was able to rise above the expected, normal reaction, and offer forgiveness in exceeding measure—beyond the call of duty.

"George Romney (the English painter, not the former Governor of Michigan) achieved widespread recognition for his paintings, but couldn't handle his success. He left home, deserting his wife and children. For 36 years he remained in London, having no contact with his wife and family. Finally, a debilitating illness robbed him of his power to paint. Suddenly, remembering his wife, he went back to her. She took him in without complaint and cared for him tenderly until he died. Romney's biographer says, 'That act of forgiveness was more significant than any canvas George Romney ever painted'" (*Pulpit Resources*).

This story may be an effective educational jumping-off point for a discussion of the meaning of true repentance; when it is proper and when too much to expect for one to ask, or receive, forgiveness. Is forgiveness appropriate when one desperately needs the forgiver for a special favor? Is it a mitzvah to forgive someone who doesn't deserve it, under special circumstances? These and other important questions regarding *Teshuvah* can be discussed based on this true event.

Rabbi Dov Peretz Elkins

Forgiveness in Hebrew Scriptures

I said, "I will confess my transgressions to the Lord." And you forgave the guilt of my sin.

Psalm 32:5

So Moses returned to the Lord and said, "Alas, this people has sinned a great sin; they have made for themselves gods of gold. But now, if you will only forgive their sin—but if not, blot me out of the book you have written."

Exodus 32:31–32

The Lord passed before (Moses) and proclaimed, "The Lord, the Lord, a God merciful. And gracious ... forgiving iniquity and transgression and sin ..."

Exodus 34:6–7

... Forgive the sin of your people Israel, and bring them again to the land that you gave to their ancestors.

I Kings 8:34

... If my people who are called by my name humble themselves, pray, seek my face and turn from their wicked ways, then I will hear from heaven, and will forgive their sin and heal their land.

II Chronicles 7:14

Have mercy on me, O God, according to your steadfast love; according
to your abundant mercy. Blot out my transgressions.

Psalm 79:9

Help us, O God of our salvation, for the glory of your name; deliver us,
and forgive our sins ...

Psalm 79:9

For you, O Lord, are good and forgiving, abounding in steadfast love
to all who call on you.

Psalm 86:5

One who forgives an affront fosters friendship, but one who dwells on
disputes will alienate a friend.

Proverbs 17:9

If you, Lord, should mark iniquities, Lord, who could stand? But there
is forgiveness with you, so that you may be revered.

Psalm 130:3–4

I have swept away your transgressions like a cloud, and your sins like
mist; return to me, for I have redeemed you.

Isaiah 44:22

… Let them return to the Lord, that he may have mercy on them, and
to our God, for he will abundantly pardon.

Isaiah 55:7

… For they shall all know me, from the least of them to the greatest,
says the Lord; for I will forgive their iniquity, and remember their sin
no more.

Jeremiah 31:34

I will cleanse them from all the guilt of their sin against me, and I will
forgive all the guilt of their sin and rebellion against me.

Jeremiah 33:8

... The iniquity of Israel shall be sought, and there shall be none; and the sins of Judah, and none shall be found; for I will pardon the remnant that I have spared.

Jeremiah 50:20

Who is a God like you, pardoning iniquity and passing over the transgression of the remnant of your possession? He does not retain his anger forever, because he delights in showing clemency.

Micah 7:18

Forgiving Debts

There once was a province that owed taxes to the king, and eventually he came to collect them. When he was within ten miles, the nobility of the province went out to greet him with praise; in response, he cancelled a third of their tax. When he was within five miles, the middle-class people of the province came out and offered praise; so he freed them of another third. When he entered into the province, all the people—men, women and children—came out and praised him; so he forgave them the whole sum. The king said to them: "Let bygones be bygones; from now on we will begin our accounting anew." Similarly, on the eve of Rosh Hashanah, the leaders of the congregation fast, and God absolves them of a third of their iniquities. From Rosh Hashanah until Yom Kippur, private individuals fast, and the Holy One, blessed be God, absolves them of a third of their sins. On Yom Kippur, everyone fasts—men, women, and children—and God says to Israel: "Let bygones be bygones; from now on we will begin our accounting anew."

Leviticus Rabbah 30:7

Sources on Forgiveness

1. Leviticus 19:17–18: Do not hate your kinsfolk in your heart. Definitely reprove [*hokhe'ah tokhee'ah*] your kinsman but incur no guilt because of him. Do not take vengeance or bear a grudge against your countrymen. Love your fellow as yourself: I am the Lord.

2. Babylonian Talmud, Yoma 23a: It was taught: What is taking vengeance and what is bearing a grudge? If A said to B, "Lend me your sickle," and B replied, "No," and the next day B says to A "Lend me your ax," and A replies, "I will not lend it to you, just as you would not lend me your sickle"—that is revenge. And what is bearing a grudge? If C says to D, "Lend me your ax," and D says "No," and the next day D asks C: "Lend me your garment," and C says, "Here it is. I am not like you who would not lend me [what I asked for]"—that is bearing a grudge.

3. Babylonian Talmud, Pesahim 113b: "Do not hate your kinsfolk in your heart." But if you see a person do something improper [unseemly, scandalous = *d'var ervah*], it is permitted to hate him, and Rabbi Nachman, son of Yitzhak, said, it is commanded to hate him, as it says in Scripture: "To fear the Lord is to hate evil" (Proverbs 8:13).

4. Babylonian Talmud, Arakhin 16b: "Do not hate your kinsfolk in your heart." You might think that means that you may not hit him, you may not slap him, and you may not curse him, [and so therefore] the Torah says, "Do not hate your kinsfolk in your heart," meaning that it is about hatred within one's heart that the verse speaks.

It was taught: Rabbi Tarton said: I wonder whether there is anyone in this generation who accepts reproof, for if one says to another: "Remove the mote from between your eyes," he would answer: "Remove the beam from between your eyes!" Rabbi Eleazar ben Azariah said: I wonder if there is anyone in this generation who knows how to reprove ...

How far shall reproof be administered? Rav said: Until [the reprover] is beaten [for his words of reproof]. Samuel said: Until he is cursed. Rabbi Yohanan said: Until he is himself rebuked ...

It was taught: Rabbi Eliezer the great said: If the Holy One, blessed be He, wished to enter in judgment with Abraham, Isaac, or Jacob, not [even] they could stand before His reproof! ...

5. Mishnah, Bava Kamma 8:7: Even though he [the assailant] gives him [the victim of an assault the monetary compensation due him], he is not forgiven until he asks forgiveness from him [his victim] ... And how do we know that the one of whom forgiveness is asked should not be cruel? For it says, "And Abraham prayed to *God,* and *God* healed Avimelekh" (Genesis 20:17) [after Avimelekh asked for-

giveness for taking Sarah for the night, not knowing that she was married to Abraham].

6. Babylonian Talmud, Rosh Hashanah 17a: Rava said: He who forges his right [to exact punishment] is forgiven all his iniquities, as Scripture says "[The Lord] forgives iniquity and passes by transgression" (Micah 7: 18): Who is forgiven iniquity? The one who passes by transgression [against himself].

7. Maimonides, Mishneh Torah, Law of Ethics (De'ot) 7:7–8: It is proper for a person to forego his rights [to recompense or punishment of another] with regard to anything in the world, for everything, according to those who understand things, is ultimately vanity and nothingness and not worthy of vengeance ...[A person wronged] should erase the matter from his heart and not bear a grudge, for as long as he bears a grudge and remembers it, perhaps he will ultimately come to wreak vengeance. Therefore the Torah took a strong stand against bearing a grudge such that a person must erase the wrong from his heart and not remember it at all. And this is the correct attitude to have so that it is possible to sustain civilization and the interaction of people with each other.

8. *Moments of Transcendence*, Dov Peretz Elkins, ed., Vol II, p.103: Professor Abraham Joshua Heschel, visiting in Germany in the 1950s, was asked the question when would the Jews forgive the Nazis? Rabbi Heschel told the following story: "There once was a rabbi traveling on a train through Russia. He was shabbily dressed and small in stature and was sitting in a railroad car studying the Mishnah. Two Poles began to make fun of him and deride him. They cursed him, and the rabbi did not reply to them, continuing to study the Mishnah. They then took his suitcase and threw it on the floor. The rabbi maintained his composure, did not rebuke them, gathered all of his belongings, and put them back in the suitcase. They continued to revile him.

"When they reached the town where the rabbi was going, a large crowd was waiting for some important dignitary. The two Poles discovered to their amazement that the little old Jew whom they were taunting was an esteemed and revered rabbi. They later asked him to forgive them for their taunts and jeers. The rabbi said, 'You are asking the rabbi to forgive you, not the little old Jew who was in the railroad car. You have to ask him to forgive you. He is the one you injured by your insults and your jeers.'"

That was Dr. Heschel's answer to the Germans that day. Only the victims can forgive. We do not have a proxy vote to forgive in their stead.

9. Babylonian Talmud, Yoma 87a: Rabbi Jose bar Hanina said: One who asks pardon of his neighbor need do so more than three times ... And if he [against whom he had sinned] has died, he should bring ten persons, have them stand by his grave, and, in their presence say: "I have sinned to the Lord, God of Israel, and to So-and so, whom I have hurt in this way." [Furthermore, if the perpetrator owes the victim money, says the Talmud, he or she must pay it to the victim's heirs. If the perpetrator does not know whether the victim had any heirs, he or she must leave the money in the hands of the court and go through the process of admission described above.]

Collected by Rabbi Elliot N. Dorff

Adonai, Adonai—The Thirteen Attributes of God's Mercy: Why Is the Ineffable Name Repeated?

Among all the ancient, medieval and modem commentaries, that of Rashi best summarizes the Talmudic comments and captures the plain meaning and essence of the text, as well as the homiletical comments of the ancient rabbis.

Regarding the repetition of God's Ineffable Name (*Yod Heh Vav Heh*—recited only once a year, on Yom Kippur, in the Holy of Holies, in its pristine form), Rashi explains that it indicates that God is a merciful God both *before* and *after* one sins. The expectation is that the sinner will repent and change. God's mercy, however, is eternal, and does not alter in the face of potential or actual sin.

The two words for God's name are pronounced *"Adonai,"* or "Lord," which is the name of God which reflects the merciful attribute displayed by God, rather than *Elohim*, which displays God's attribute of justice. The third of the Thirteen Attributes, *El*, according to Rashi, is specifically in the singular form, implying justice *and* mercy, instead of *Elohim* which might convey its normal meaning of strict justice—out of place in this collection of Attributes of Mercy.

Rabbi Dov Peretz Elkins

All in the Family

We can do violence to life in many ways. Many years ago, I was invited to hear a well-known rabbi speak about forgiveness at a Yom Kippur service. Yom Kippur is the Day of Atonement, when Jews everywhere reflect on the year just past, repent their shortcomings and unkindness, and hope for the forgiveness of God. But the rabbi did not speak about God's forgiveness.

Instead, he walked out into the congregation, took his infant daughter from his wife, and, carrying her in his arms, stepped up to the bimah or podium. The little girl was perhaps a year old and she was adorable. From her father's arms she smiled at the congregation. Every heart melted. Turning toward her daddy, she patted him on the cheek with her tiny hands. He smiled fondly at her and with his customary dignity began a rather traditional Yom Kippur sermon, talking about the meaning of the holiday.

The baby girl, feeling his attention shift away from her, reached forward and grabbed his nose. Gently he freed himself and continued the sermon. After a few minutes, she took his tie and put it in her mouth. The entire congregation chuckled. The rabbi rescued his tie and smiled at his child. She put her tiny arms around his neck. Looking at it over the top of her head, he said, "Think about it. Is there anything she can do that you could not forgive her for?" Throughout the room people began to nod in recognition, thinking perhaps of their own children and grandchildren. Just then, she reached up and grabbed his eyeglasses. Everyone laughed out loud.

Retrieving his eyeglasses and settling them on his nose, the rabbi laughed as well. Still smiling, he waited for silence. When it came, he asked, "And when does that stop? When does it get hard to forgive? At three? At seven? At fourteen? At thirty-five? How old does someone have to be before you forget that everyone is a child of God?"

Back then, God's forgiveness was something easily understandable to me, but personally I found forgiveness difficult. I had thought of it as a lowering of standards rather than a family relationship.

Rachel Naomi Remen, MD

Forgive and Forget!

Back in an intro to Psychology class in college, I remember reading a book called *The Mind of a Mnemonist*. Written by the Russian psychologist Alexandr Luria, it is about a man called "S" who has an extraordinary memory. Show him a page of several hundred random numbers, and he can instantly remember them in order. Read an entire opera libretto to him in Italian, and he instantly remembers the whole thing. And he doesn't even understand Italian. And go up to him 15 years later—and he still remembers the entire libretto word for word.

So you would think that his life was fantastic, right? This is a man who never forgot where he put his car keys or his glasses, never forgot anyone's birthday or anniversary—wouldn't you give anything to have that kind of memory? But actually, this man would have done anything to have his special talent removed. Because to him, it was more of a curse than a blessing.

His attention to every little detail made it difficult for him to follow even a simple conversation. When he would see people he knew, he would never recognize them, because he always remembered them exactly how they looked the last time he saw them. His mind was so cluttered up with things he wished he could forget—things he preferred not to know, or not to notice. He lived a reclusive life, withdrawn from society.

This book reminds us that, as vital as it is to remember, it is just as important to be able to forget.

The people who have the strongest memories are not always at an advantage. Especially those who use their gifts of memories to catalogue each and every indignity they've suffered—each and every time someone has slighted them, or been disloyal, or broken a promise.

Rosh HaShanah and Yom Kippur are our annual opportunities to clear out our memories.

This also means: it's the time to let go of the memories that are holding us back from becoming the people we ought to be.

In our prayers today, we refer to God as "*zokher ha-nishkahot,*" "the one who remembers all that is forgotten." And no human being should have to bear that terrible burden.

Rabbi Robert Scheinberg

Getting Rid of the Mud

We have a custom at weddings. Before you go to the wedding canopy, there is the veiling of the bride. At the veiling of the bride, I usually gather together all the blood relatives into a room, to ask them each to forgive each other, because it's impossible to grow up in a family, with siblings and parents, without having some secret anger. And you don't want people to have to go into the next phase of life with all this karmic load. So that is why bringing in those people is so important. That way they can forgive each other and really bless each other. It is a very powerful thing. On one occasion, a young girl was present while we were doing this forgiveness, and she wanted to know how to do it. I tell you, it was a wonderful thing that she asked this question. She really wanted to know how to do it. It was as if nobody had ever showed her how to do forgiving. So I said to her, "Could you imagine that you have a beautiful shiny white dress on, and here comes this big clump of mud and dirties it? You would want to clean it off, wouldn't you?" "Oh, yes," she said. "Could you imagine then, instead of the mud being on the outside on your dress, the mud is on your heart?" "Uh huh." "And being angry with people and not forgiving them is like mud on your heart." "I sure want to get rid of that," she said. "OK, how are you going to go about doing that?" I suggested that she close her eyes, raise up her hands in her imagination, and draw down some golden light and let it flow over that mud on her heart until it was all washed away. In this way she really understood forgiving.

Do you understand how important it is, just as with this child, to respond decently when somebody says, "You ought to … ," and starts giving you advice and you want to say, "I've been trying to do it myself. You don't have to scold me—show me how to do it"?

This is the issue in all spiritual direction work.

Rabbi Zalman Schachter-Shalomi

Day of Reconciliations

No day in the Hebrew calendar is as well known—or as dreaded—as Yom Kippur. The vast majority of the Jewish people observes this holiday in one form or another, either through fasting and praying, or by abstaining from work (even the United States Supreme Court will for the first time in its history recess tomorrow in deference to its Jewish members). And yet, despite its widespread acknowledgment, most Jews look forward to Yom Kippur much as a 50-plus male approaches a colonoscopy: something I really have to do, but not something I can get too excited about. It doesn't have to be that way.

Yom Kippur presents an opportunity for renewal that can actually fill us with a special energy and enthusiasm. It all depends on our state of mind. Interestingly, while we popularly call the day "Yom Kippur," the Torah refers to it as *Yom Hakippurim*, in the plural form. I suggest that *kippurim* is best translated not as atonements, but rather as reconciliations. This is the day to effect a reconciling of all our many relationships; to renew, repair and recharge our connection with all those who are precious to us. It is a time to review our relationship with our friends and neighbors. How many of us have ignored even our closest neighbors, or lost touch with good friends from our past? The traditional Jewish practice of asking forgiveness from those around us, even those we have neglected for years, is an amazing practice unheard of in other cultures.

The unity barometer skyrockets as Jews "find" one another and humbly express remorse for past offenses. (In that spirit, I beg your pardon for anything I have written this year which may have offended you). It is also a time to seek reconciliation with our children. No matter how out of sync we have become with our kids, no matter how large the walls have been built up between us, this is a time for renovation, for handshakes and hugs, for telling our family how much we love and need them. Pointedly, the Yom Kippur prayer book begins with a special blessing for our children. Yom Kippur is a time to strengthen the bonds with our spouse. I have a friend who says husbands are not required to ask their wives for forgiveness; they have to beg them for forgiveness. We have to tell our spouses how small and meaningless life is without them, how central they are to all we are and all we do. What better moment to renew our marriage commitment than now?

This is also a time to reconcile with our parents, to appreciate all the love and devotion they showered upon us and the mighty part they play in our lives. And if, alas, they have passed on, then the Yom

Kippur *yizkor* is our chance to communicate those powerful feelings inside us. And, of course, this is the crucial moment to reconcile with God, who created this day precisely to reconnect with His people, one at a time. It is an opportunity to make our way back. At the dramatic moment when the IDF commandos freed the Israeli hostages at Entebbe, they said but two words to them: *Nelech habayta*—let's go home. Yom Kippur is the time to go home.

Yet beyond all these wonderful reunions, there is another reconciliation which must occur on this day, and that is the reconciliation between me and myself. The Biblical phrase *Yom Ha-Kippurim* can also read as "a day like Purim." While no two holidays seem more diametrically dissimilar, Yom Kippur and Purim are, in fact, mirror images. On one, our bodies are pampered and pleasured in celebration to God; on the other, it is our souls which soar beyond mortal bounds. There is another connection: The dramatic moment of Purim comes when Esther unmasks herself before the king and reveals who and what she is, where her loyalties lie and with whom she will cast her lot. On Yom Kippur, too, we all unmask before the King. The facades and pretenses are stripped away, and our lives and deeds are laid bare before our Creator. We live in a world with too much blame, and not enough shame. Whenever something goes wrong, we immediately point a finger at someone else. It's never we who are at fault, but always "they," the other guy, the powers that be, the system. On this day, we muster up the courage and the truth to examine ourselves and admit that most of our problems emanate not from outside us, but from within. We are the source of our failings, and only we can make it right again.

During the confessional prayer of Yom Kippur, the most-recited plea of the day, we beat our own breast, not that of our neighbor. We enumerate our misdeeds and miscalculations and acknowledge that we, like Jonah in the Yom Kippur reading, cannot escape from God, nor from ourselves. If we recognize the chance we have to repair our wounded relationships, then *Yom Ha-Kippurim*, the Day of Reconciliations, can be the most eagerly anticipated day of the year.

Rabbi Stewart Weiss

HEAR, O ISRAEL: GOD, LOVE AND LEARNING

The *shema'*, or the proclamation "Hear O Israel, the Lord our God, the Lord is One," stands at the center of Jewish worship. The most essential declaration of Jewish faith is learned early in childhood. Pious Jews hope that it will be the last phrase they utter before they die. "His soul went out with the word 'One'" is often found in descriptions of martyrs' deaths.

The *shema'* actually consists of three Biblical passages: Deuteronomy 6:4–9 and 11:13–21 and Numbers 15:37–41. The daily recitation of these passages is considered a Biblically ordained precept ("You shall speak of them ... when you lie down and when you rise up" [Deuteronomy 6:7]). Although surrounded by prayers, the *shema'* itself is not a prayer. It is addressed to one's fellow Jews, and perhaps also to some broader notion of "Israel" (*yisra'el*). It proclaims God's Oneness, the obligation to love and serve God through the commandments, a warning that satiety due to too much worldly prosperity may lead one to turn away from God, and a faith that righteousness is ultimately rewarded. The *shema'* concludes with an admonition to be holy and to remember that the Lord brought Israel forth from Egypt (*Mitsrayim*) in order to be our God.

It is the first declaration of the *shema'*, however, by which it is best known. The *shema'* is referred to as the proclamation of Divine Oneness. God is One, the Source of all being. There is no demonic realm outside of God, there is no profane or "secular" realm where God's presence cannot be found. God's oneness includes and embraces all; everything exists within God. This interpretation of the *shema'* is perhaps best expressed in the words of a Hasidic master (Rabbi Judah Leib Alter of Ger, 1847–1904, author of Sefat Emet):

> The proclamation of oneness that we declare each day in saying "Hear O Israel," and so forth, really needs to be understood as it truly is. That which is entirely clear to me … based on the holy writings of great Kabbalists, I am obligated to reveal to you … the meaning of "Y–H–W–H is one" is not that He is the only God, negating other gods (though this too is true!), but the meaning is deeper than that: there is no being other than Him. [This is true] even though it seems otherwise to most people.… everything that exists in the world, spiritual and physical, is God Himself. It is only because of the contraction (*tsimtsum*) that was God's will, blessed be He and His name, that holiness descended rung after rung, until actual physical things were formed out of it.
>
> These things are true without a doubt. Because of this, every person can attach himself [to God] wherever he is, through the holiness that exists within every single thing, even corporeal things. You only have to be negated in the spark of holiness. In this way you bring about ascents in the upper worlds, causing true pleasure to God. A person in such a state lacks for nothing, for he can attach himself to God through whatever place he is. This is the foundation of all the mystical formulations in the world.

RABBI ARTHUR GREEN, *THESE ARE THE WORDS*

Can Love Be Commanded?

"And you shall love the Lord Your God with all your heart, with all your soul and with all your might."

Obedience may be commanded, but love must be freely given. God may command us to be just, or to observe given rituals, but how can love be mandated? Can those who have suffered be blamed for finding God unlovable?

A close look at the grammar of the first paragraph of the *Sh'ma* can help us understand this paradox. The verb "*v'ahavta*" is not an imperative, although it is invariably rendered as such by the translators. Rather, it refers to future action. We are not commanded to love God. The statement is, rather, one of prophecy. The time will come when we will love God of our own volition, even if we have difficulty doing so now.

Many of us have anger towards God because of our hurts, and the hurts of others. But there are answers to our questions, and we should not despair of ever learning them. Isaiah teaches us "that the earth will be as full of the knowledge of the Lord, as the waters cover the sea."

Rabbi Kenneth L. Cohen

When Words Enter the Heart

"And these words which I command you this day shall be *upon* your heart." The verse does not say: *"in* your heart." For there are times when the heart is shut. But the words lie upon the heart, and when the heart opens in holy hours, they sink deep down into it.

Rabbi Mendl of Kotzk

Who Will Recite the *Shema* with Our Grandchildren?

While Laban was off shearing his sheep, Jacob gathered his family and his flocks and made his way out of Aram. The time had come for him to leave the household of his father-in-law/uncle Laban and make his way back to Canaan. Jacob was also motivated by the reality that

Laban, who was deceitful, dishonest, and cunning, was a negative influence upon Jacob's children.

Laban, however, was not about to allow Jacob to run. He pursues his son-in-law and overtakes him. The Torah records Laban's complaint: "You ran off with my children and grandchildren without giving me a chance to kiss them good-bye."

Every grandparent can appreciate the sentiment voiced by Laban. Grandchildren are precious. I have come to believe that had God told Abraham to sacrifice his grandson, he might well have rebelled at that command. The Book of Ruth concludes with the verses that Naomi took Ruth's child "to her bosom and became nurse unto it." We understand the picture of Naomi, the devoted grandmother, whether she be called Bubbie, Granny, or Savta.

The Psalmist's great promise is "The Lord will bless you out of Jerusalem and may you see children to your children, and may there be peace Unto Israel." Grandparenthood is special, and we wonder, was Laban wronged by Jacob? Was it fair for Jacob to have removed Laban's grandchildren from his life?

The answer depends on the influence of the grandparent upon the family. Laban was a cheat and a deceiver, and Jacob was correct in distancing the family from this negative force. Most grandparents are not like that.

There is a story of an elderly Jew in Odessa who had kept the faith even during the darkest days of Soviet anti-Semitism. The Israeli emissary wanted to arrange for his *aliyah,* but the man refused. His reason? "I have one daughter, and she married a Gentile [not at all uncommon in the Soviet Union], and they have one son. Every evening, I hold this child on my lap and say the *Shema* with him. If I go to Israel, there will be no one with whom he will be able to recite the *Shema.*"

The ultimate test is what role does the grandparent play in the life of the child. Thankfully, few of us as grandparents are transmitting negative values to our grandchildren. We are not Labans.

What we do see ourselves as doing is entertaining our grandchildren: taking them shopping, going to the movies or the ball game. These are important and enjoyable activities which we should do with our grandchildren. There is, however, much more for us to do. We should adapt Naomi's model and try to be a source of Jewish values and Jewish life. We should take them not only to the movies but also to Synagogue; we not only should go shopping with them, but also review their Hebrew lessons. Above all, to the extent that our means allow it, we should help them get to Israel while they are in their teens. We should be a major support in the process of making them more informed—and thereby better—Jews.

Then, we can hope to see fulfilled in our lives the hope of the Psalmist: to be blessed with the joy of seeing our children's children growing into good Jews and decent human beings. May we all know that pleasure.

Rabbi Arnold M. Goodman

Shema Yisrael

Lieutenant Dan approached Rabbi Shlomo Carlebach after an out-door concert he had given for thousands of Israeli soldiers soon after the Yom Kippur War.

"I want to tell you a story," he said, "so that you can tell it often at your concerts. It is a story that must be shared with Jews all over the world." He paused, waiting for Shlomo's reaction.

Shlomo put his arm around the soldier's shoulder and led him away from the crowd. They stopped near some boulders on the side of a road. Shlomo saw the soldier's body quiver and realized he was crying.

"I want you to know," Lieutenant Dan sobbed, "that I had pretty much regained my composure in the past few days, but your songs reawakened some emotion that started me off once again."

Shlomo gripped his shoulder more vigorously, trying to calm him, as he waited for him to begin speaking.

"During the war I fought in Sinai. The captain of my platoon was very religious," mumbled Dan. "His name was Avner. As we fought, side by side, he chanted, *'Shema Yisrael Adonai Elohaynu Adonai Ehad!'* (Hear O Israel, the Lord our God, the Lord is One.)

"I was very annoyed with his chanting, because I was the typical secular, nonobservant Jew. You see, I did not believe that there was a God. In fact, I had even raised my two children to believe that the concept of God is the biggest hoax and that the Jewish people are no more holy than any other people.

"During the fighting, I was positioned behind Captain Avner. I heard his continuous, persistent chanting. As soon as he finished *E-chad*, he began all over again with *Shema*. Raising his arm, motioning the soldiers to follow him into battle, he repeated over and over, *'Shema Yisrael Adonai Elohaynu Adonai Ehad.'*

"I think I was the only one in the platoon who was annoyed by his chanting. Can you imagine, day after day, hour after hour, minute after minute, the sound of *Shema Yisrael?* I literally felt that the chanting would drive me out of my mind. I could not endure his foolish praying.

"Finally, I could not contain myself any longer. At the top of my voice, I shrieked, 'Why don't you stop chanting *Shema Yisrael?* You are driving me crazy! You know that I don't believe the way you do. Why can't you just lead this platoon with neutral words of encouragement like *naylekh* [let's go] or *halah* [forward]!'

"Avner didn't pay too much attention to my shrieking at first, but at last he said patiently, 'Know that the two of us have different ways of fighting. You remember, of course, King David's message to Goliath the Philistine, "You come at me with a sword, but I come in the name of the Lord"? Do me a favor. You fight your way and I'll fight my way.'

"The fighting on the battlefield intensified. I never stopped pleading with Avner to stop chanting and he never changed his answer: You fight your way and I'll fight my way.

"The more the fighting intensified, the louder Avner chanted. It seemed that the rhythm of his chant kept pace with the exploding bombs in the distance.

"On the fourth day of the battle, I thought that Avner had finally heard my pleas to stop chanting. He had advanced a short distance ahead of me when I realized why his chanting had stopped. He was lying on the sand of the Sinai desert, blood gushing from his mouth but still breathing. I ran forward and felt his chest. His breathing was painfully difficult. He opened his eyes, and I grasped his hand in mine.

"Choking, I said, 'Dearest friend, please forgive me for arguing with you, for insisting that your chanting was annoying me. I would do anything to retract those words.'

"As the tears streamed down my cheeks, I saw that he was trying to speak. I asked him if there was anything I could do for him. I laid my ear close to his mouth. He asked me to swear that I would chant *Shema Yisrael* in his place!

"I swore to him that I would fight chanting *Shema Yisrael*. I don't know if he heard me, for he died a moment later. I lay beside him for a while, thinking about the holiness of the moment, realizing what *Shema Yisrael* really meant. It was as if he had bequeathed me his message from Heaven, a message that suddenly turned on a light in my head. I knew then that there is only One God.

"So with as much energy as I had denied God, I took it upon myself to proclaim Him. That night as I lay under the stars, trying to sleep, for the battle had turned in favor of Israel, I thought about my children. I had neglected to teach them what every Jewish father is supposed to teach his children. As soon as the rays of dawn appeared in the desert sky, I ran toward the regiment commander. Breathless, I shouted, 'I must go home for twenty-four hours. It's a matter of life and death.'

"I was so agitated, that he did not even question me. He just nodded his head and waved his hand in the general direction of Israel.

"All the way home, I chanted Captain Avner's melody '*Shema Yisrael Adonai Elohaynu Adonai Ehad.*'

"I burst into my house blurting out, "I want you to know, children, *Shema Yisrael Adonai Elohaynu Adonai Ehad*. There is only one God. The Jewish people are a holy people."

"The next day, I returned to my unit. The war ended with Israel's victory. Since then, I have more than fulfilled my vow. My family and I have become observant, and we try to inspire others to follow our example.

"By repeating my story on the concert stage, you can teach the whole world to chant *Shema Yisrael.*"

Dr. Annette Labovitz and Rabbi Eugene Labovitz

Radiance and Light—*Pirkei Avot* 2:13

Rabbi Shimon said: Be careful [*zahir*] in reciting the *Shema* and in prayer. When you pray, do not make your prayer a routine, but rather [a plea for] mercy and grace before God, as it is said: " … for God is gracious and merciful, slow to anger and great in love, and repents of evil" (Joel 2:13). And do not consider yourself wicked.

Be careful:

The Hebrew word *"zahir"* (careful) also means "shining" or "glowing." For one should shine after reciting the *Shema* and praying. The Creator, the blessed Holy One, will then shower upon us radiance and light. (See *Avot* 2:1.)

Rav Chaim Heikel of Amdor

Shema: God's Oneness

God, You are the completeness of everything.

TIKKUNEI ZOHAR 17B

This description of God, which comes from the mystical writings in Judaism, is far from concrete. Nor is it anthropomorphic—e.g., God is not decribed as being a king or a father or a shepherd. We are used to thinking about God metaphorically because otherwise we are left in the realm of the abstract which is difficult for many of us to grasp. Yet, let us think about this notion that God is the completeness of everything. What could this mean? It is common for us to see the work as disjointed pieces that don't always fit together neatly. This sense of disjunction may be a fact of modern life. Nonetheless, we also seek a sense of wholeness. Perhaps when we experience the coming together of our disjointed lives into a whole cloth we have a momentary glimpse of God. May we keep ourselves open for this experience of completion.

Rabbi Lori Forman

Sh'ma

Rabbi Arthur Green, in his seminal book of Jewish theology, *Seek My Face,* writes that the first two lines of the *Sh'ma,* as we recite them in the Siddur and *Mahzor,* connote two different ideas.

The *Sh'ma* line—"Hear, O Israel, Y-H-W-H our God, Y-H-W-H is One!"—speaks of the higher unity, the unity that implies almost that nothing else in the world exists but that Oneness. We humans are but a ripple in the great ocean of the cosmic One—we are all part of the one God.

The second line—*Barukh Shem ...* —"Blessed is the name of God's glorious kingdom for ever and ever!" refers to the lower unity—the one within the many—the unity of God's kingdom here on earth. Through this vision of God we encounter the Almighty in and through the world.

On all days but Yom Kippur, we whisper the second line—implying that God and God's kingdom are one and the same. The immanence of God is hushed during the year. But on the great Sabbath, the *Shabbat Shabbaton* that is Yom Kippur, we say this verse aloud—so that the *Sh'ma* sentence, expressing God's transcendence, is balanced by helping us realize that God is not Other. As we recite *Barukh Shem* aloud—only on this night—we realize that we, here on earth, are part of the Oneness of God. The transcendent and the immanent join together aloud as we recognize both aspects of Divinity.

As we recite these two sentences now—let us feel the Oneness and Unity of God—above and part—as well as the Oneness in which we creatures of God's—are part of the ultimate Unity as well.

D.P.E.

Shema: **One Universe**

[Throughout his life Albert Einstein sought for meaning in life and an intelligible unity in the universe. In 1930 he wrote these words:]

"[I am seeking to be rooted in] a cosmic religious feeling. It is very difficult to elucidate this feeling to anyone who is entirely without it, especially as there is no anthropomorphic conception of God corresponding to it...

"The individual feels the futility of human desires and aims and the sublimity and marvelous order which reveal themselves both in nature and in the world of thought. Individual existence impresses him as a sort of prison and he wants to experience the universe as a single significant whole."

[Einstein's words help us to understand the power of the meaning of the *Sh'ma*—and the important role this one line plays in all of Jewish liturgy and Jewish theology.]

D.P.E.

Shema—The Lord Is *One*: Hear, O Israel, *Adonai* Is Our God, *Adonai* Alone

Perhaps the most famous commandment outside of the Decalogue, the *Shema*, has evolved into the Jewish Declaration of Faith.

Baal ha-Turim (14th century Spanish commentator) teaches that the Oneness of God conveyed in this verse signifies that, although the Holy One sometimes appears to us as a strict Judge and at other times as a compassionate Being, God is really one and the same God.

The call of Jewish theology, we are reminded, is not simply an admonition to refrain from idols. Rather, it challenges us to view the One Deity as a composite bearer of seemingly contradictory values—a tension that would be far less tolerable were it to be hosted by a human ruler.

Rabbi Bernard R. Gerson

Shema—And You Shall Love *Adonai* Your God....

Wherever I go—only You!
Wherever I stand—only you!
Just You, again You! always You!
You, You, You, You!
When things are good, You!
When things are bad—You!
You, You, You, You!

Rabbi Levi Yitzhak of Berditchev

Ve-Shenantam Le-Venekha—The Tradition of Study

Of the many distinguishing features of the Jewish people, perhaps none is more consistent than a commitment to learning. As the late scholar Simon Rawidowicz once pointed out, Judaism is the only tradition that pictures God studying. Even the Almighty, in this fanciful depiction, leads the way for human beings to improve their minds through learning.

When Rabbis Akiva and Tarfon had their renowned Talmudic dispute over which took precedence, study or practice, the resolution was that study took precedence, for it leads to practice. Judaism belittles study that does not change one's life, but at the same time it exalts periodic study "*lishma*," for its own sake, for no reason other than the joy of exercising one's mind and expanding one's spirit.

There are more books published on Judaism in English today than in any other language at any other time in history. Even for those who do not (yet) know Hebrew, the tradition in all its wisdom awaits. "When I pray," Rabbi Louis Finkelstein, the late Chancellor of the Jewish Theological Seminary, once said, "I speak to God. When I study, God speaks to me."

Rabbi David Wolpe

Teach Them Diligently to Your Children— Jacob and Esau

"The voice is the voice of Jacob, but the hands are the hands of Esau" (Gen. 27:22). The nations of the world entered before Abnimos the weaver. They said to him: Can we attack this nation? He said to them: Go and pass before their Houses of Study and Houses of Prayer. If you there hear children chanting, you cannot attack them. But if you do not hear children chanting, you can attack them. For thus their father assured them: "The voice is the voice of Jacob." So long as the voice of Jacob is chanting in Houses of Study and Houses of Prayer, the hands are not "the hands of Esau."

Midrash, Pesikta de-Rav Kahana, 121A

Ve-sheenantam Le-vanekha—Educate, Educate, Educate

In *Hadassah Magazine* Rabbi Arthur Hertzberg commented on the most effective method of assuring Jewish survival. His reflections are a commentary on the first paragraph of the *Shema:*

> "Educate, educate, educate. For the last century we have bet our survival on the idea that together we should fight our enemies. This has failed. We can hope to succeed only if we teach the young, and ourselves, the texts and rhetoric of the tradition. The

future, if there is to be one, is in learning 'and thou shalt teach these words diligently unto your children.' All else is vanity."

Judaism will not survive through anti-anti-Semitism, but only through Jewish knowledge. Besides a league for anti-defamation, American Jewry needs a league for pro-Judaism.

Rabbi Dov Peretz Elkins

Shema—Teach Them Well to Your Children

Moses was the greatest leader of the Jewish people. And yet he was not called a liberator or a prophet, but simply *Moshe Rabenu*, Moses Our Teacher. From earliest days, the Jewish ideal has been to enlighten and inform every Jew at every age of his or her life. The acquisition of knowledge of Jewish tradition has always been considered everyone's responsibility.

The Yiddish word for a scholar is *lamden*. It literally means "one who learns." The highest praise that can be bestowed on someone is to say *er ken lernen*, "he knows how to learn." Little wonder that Isaac Bashevis Singer said, "A Jew who doesn't learn is not a Jew."

Among the Jewish books saved from the millions burned by the Nazis was one that bears the title *The Society of Woodchoppers for the Study of Mishna in Berdichev*. The woodchoppers of Berdichev, men of a low social status, would meet regularly to study the Talmud.

Rabbi Saul Teplitz

On the Doorposts of Your House—Two Approaches to Life

Artaban, king of Persia, sent a jewel as a gift to a Rabbi. He hoped that the Rabbi would send him a precious gift in return. He was surprised and disappointed when the Rabbi sent him a *mezuzah,* which he considered to be of little value. The Rabbi, sensing the king's disappointment, said: "You sent me a valuable gift, for which I must take precautions to guard. I, however, have sent you a precious gift which will guard you and protect you, day and night." "When thou walkest, it shall lead thee, when thou liest down, it shall watch over thee" (Proverbs 6:22).

In this simple story are to be detected two approaches to life. Artaban was under the impression that riches alone assure men of happiness. The whole object of life is to acquire wealth. The more one has, the happier one will be. This was the philosophy of Artaban, and that was why he was disappointed when the Rabbi sent him a *mezuzah*, which seemed to be of insignificant value. The Rabbi, however, held that there were more important things in life than money and wealth. In the final analysis, only spiritual ideals could bring to the individual that inner peace of mind and soul, which spelled happiness.

The *mezuzah* may be of small monetary value, but it contained a parchment, on which were written great principles: The unity and love of God, the doctrine of reward and punishment, the desirability of providing youth with a religious education, the dedication of the body and soul to the service of God. These were the ideals in life to which one must aspire. By his gift of the *mezuzah*, the Rabbi intimated to Artaban, that he should take stock of his attitude to life, and give priority to spiritual values, rather than to material possessions.

Rabbi Theodore Lewis

The Quality of Our Love

The central liturgical declaration of the Jewish faith is *Shema Yisrael*. In the *Shema* we utter with total commitment, with all our heart, all our soul and all our power, our trust in the one God, Creator of all human beings. In the first paragraph of the *Shema* we read of the command to Love the Lord Your God. Richard Bach, author of *Jonathan Livingston Seagull, Illusions*, and other spiritual books, wrote: "When we come to the last moment of this lifetime, and we look back across it, the only thing that's going to matter is 'What was the quality of our love'?" Besides being commanded to love God, we are commanded to "Love our neighbor as ourselves" (Lev. 19:18). These two loves are the corps of living as a spiritual being—loving God and loving others around us. Indeed, Richard Bach's words are a sobering reminder, as the *Shema* is recited, of the deep and abiding authority of these biblical verses, reminding us of the only thing that really matters in our entire lives.

Rabbi Dov Peretz Elkins

You Shall Teach Them Diligently to Your Children—Weaving the Loom of Future Years

1993 was the centenary of the birth of the late Rabbi Abba Hillel Silver, eloquent spokesperson for world Jewry, and one of the creators of the State of Israel. At the eve of the outbreak of World War II, Rabbi Silver spoke the following message at the 36th Biennial Convention of the Union of American Hebrew Congregations, the national association of Reform synagogues, in Cincinnati, Ohio, on January 17, 1939, bringing home the point that by giving our children the values of our Tradition, they can be saved from a cruel world:

"What hands shall weave the loom of our future years? Our own hands, tender and skillful, drawing the golden strands from our own treasures of wisdom, piety, passion and dreams, which all the goodly folk from Abraham to our own day have stored for us, or shall alien hands, rude and unsympathetic, weave the web of the destiny of ourselves and our children?

"Now that many doors are closing, should we not open wide to our children the doors leading to the treasure-troves of their own people's spiritual and intellectual wealth, for their future sustenance, inspiration, solace and pride? The days ahead will be hard days for them. Until the world completes the latest stage in its economic transformation and steadies itself again, after a long, violent period of readjustment, Jews, because they are everywhere an exposed minority, easily blamed and easily victimized, will be hammered on the anvil of every world event. The days ahead will be hard days for our children, but they need not be ignoble or unrewarding days. Give them their total heritage—the copious bounty of Judaism—the Torah, the synagogue, the prayer books, the noble literature and the beautiful language of their people. Give them the millennial companionship of their kinsmen and their kinsmen's heroic faith and dreams and their matchless saga and they will be matched with their great hour. They will then come to understand what it is in our heritage that has kept us alive; what it is that laid waste the paganism of the ancient world and now finds itself again in mortal combat with another paganism which it is also destined to destroy; what it is that makes their people the brunt of attack whenever privilege, power and reaction make a major onslaught on the precious hopes of mankind, and why the ancient ideals of their people are forever the battle-cries of upstruggling humanity."

D.P.E.

Shema

Hear Israel, you are of G-d and G-d is one.

Praise the name that speaks to us through all time.

V'ahavta

So you shall love what is holy
with all your courage, with all your passion,
with all your strength.
Let the words that have come down
shine in our words and our actions.
We must teach our children to know and understand them.
We must speak about what is good
and holy within our homes
when we are working, when we are at play,
when we lie down and when we get up.
Let the work of your hands speak of goodness.
    Let it run in our blood
And glow from our doors and windows.

We should love ourselves, for we are of G-d.
We should love our neighbors as ourselves.
We should love the stranger, for we
were once strangers in the land of Egypt.
And have been strangers in all the lands of the world since.
Let love fill our hearts with its clear precious water
Heaven and earth observe how we cherish or spoil our world.
Heaven and earth watch whether we choose life or choose death.
We must choose life so our children's children may live.
Be quiet and listen to the still small
voice within that speaks in love.

Open to that voice, hear it, heed it and work for life.
Let us remember and strive to be good.
Let us remember to find what is holy
within and without.

Marge Piercy

How Fortunate Are You, Rabbi Akiva

"And you shall love the Lord your God with all your
heart, and with all your soul ... "

(DEUT.6:15)

When Rabbi Akiva was taken out to be killed by the Romans, it was the
time for the reading of *Shema Yisrael* and they kept flaying his flesh with
iron combs, yet he accepted upon himself the yoke of the rule of Heaven.

His disciples said to him:

"Are you still faithful, master?"

He said to them: "All my days I was troubled by this interpretation:
'With all your soul'—even if God takes your soul from you. I said, O
that it were in my power to fulfill this! And now that it is in my power,
shall I not fulfill it?"

He kept prolonging the "One," until his spirit left him at the word
"*Ehad*" ("One").

A voice came from Heaven and said:

"Fortunate are you, Rabbi Akiva, that your spirit has left you
at 'One.'"

Talmud, Berachot 61b

Bless God Even for Evil

One must recite a benediction for evil, just as one recites a benediction for good. For it is said: "And you shall love the Lord your God
with all your heart, and with all your soul, and with all your might"
(Deut.6:5).

"With all your heart"—even your two wills, with your will to good
and your will to evil.

"And with all your might"—for every measure that God measures out to you, thank God with all your might.

Mishnah Berakhot 9:5

Widening Our Circle of Compassion

When we recite the *Shema* we remind ourselves that our Creator is One and our Universe is one, unified humanity. The important thought that we are not separate from the rest of the Planet is brought home with great force in the touching words of the late Albert Einstein, one of the world's greatest scientists who ever lived:

> A human being is a part of the whole called by us universe, a part limited in time and space. He experiences himself, his thoughts and feelings as something separated from the rest, a kind of optical delusion of his consciousness. This delusion is a kind of prison for us, restricting us to our personal desires and to affection for a few persons nearest to us. Our task must be to free ourselves from this prison by widening our circle of compassion to embrace all living creatures and the whole of nature in its beauty.

Albert Einstein

The Calming, Nourishing Effect of *Shema Yisrael*

In a seminar held at a recent Rabbinical Assembly convention, Rabbi Naomi Levy led a session on "Female Spirituality," in which she suggested a novel interpretation of the *Shema*. She pointed out that with women now serving as Conservative rabbis and being members of the Rabbinical Assembly, new interpretations of ancient texts are opening up, from a female perspective.

She turned the participants' attention to the sounds of the word *Shema*, and how, if we recite the *Shema* very slowly, we notice some fascinating meanings.

For example, we begin by saying the first letter of the *Shema*, the Hebrew letter *shin*. SSSSHHHHHHHH. See how quieting and calming it is!

Second, the Hebrew letter *mem*. MMMMMMMMM. Sounds like Mommy, or *Ima* (Hebrew for Mom), or Mmmmmm, as in yum (as one would make a circle on their stomach). This indicates a nourishing factor of the *Shema*.

Thirdly, the Hebrew letter *ayin,* with the vowel *patach* under the *mem* before it. This sound is: Aaaahhhh! That, too, is calming, nourishing, and soothing.

So, to sum up, if we recite the word *Shema* slowly, we have: SSSSHHHHHHHHHHH; MMMMMMMMMMM; AAAAAHHH-HHHH.

What an interesting and novel interpretation. It gives the *Shema* a new dimension of interpretation!

D.P.E.

Shema: God and God's World

The soul is not always capable of experiencing a union with God. There are times when we are unable to respond to the "Hear, O Israel" with utter sincerity and complete surrender. Therefore, this passage is followed in our prayer books by the sentence, "Blessed be His glorious kingdom for ever and ever." The *Shema* affirms God's Oneness; however, the second sentence no longer speaks of God Himself but of His Kingdom. Whenever his soul is separated from God, man turns from within to without, from God to the world. Unable to experience a direct and unmediated inner union with God, man seeks to discover a divine unity in the world through secondary media—the processes of thinking, observing, reasoning; through scholarly assumptions and hypotheses. For this reason the second passage of the *Shema* is said silently through the entire year except on the Day of Atonement. On that day, all corporeality, finiteness and this-worldliness are transcended; God and the world are one; the Creator and his creatures are united. The Day of Atonement anticipates the full redemption of the world from its separation from God. Therefore, the second verse may be recited aloud and indeed triumphantly on Yom Kippur.

Samuel Hugo Bergman

I Will Love the Lord My God

A creative suggestion someone made was to try reciting the *Shema* in the first person, instead of the second person. In other words, say it as a *pledge* to God, instead of a command from God. Here is how it would sound. Notice the changes in your reaction after it is recited.

> I shall love the Lord my God with all my heart, with all my soul, and with all my might. I shall take to heart these words which You command me this day. I shall teach them diligently to my children, speaking of them when I am at home, and when I am away, when I lie down at night and when I rise up in the morning. I shall bind them as a sign upon my arm, and they shall be a reminder above my eyes. I shall inscribe them on the doorposts of my home and on my gates. (Deut. 6:4–9)

Rabbi Dov Peretz Elkins

Sh'ma: ... Ve-shenantam le-vanekha—A Jew Must Learn!

The Torah-enriched life is clearly conveyed in this account of a group of typical Jews in Ludwig Lewisohn's *This Jewish Heritage:* "After the great martyrdom and the small liberation in 1946, a little group of surviving Jews made their way westward from Siberia whither the Soviet authorities had deported them. After many months of desperate hardships, they reached the little town that had been their home and their fathers.' The town was a mass of rubble. They did not find even graves. All their kith and kin had been burned alive in the crematoriums. The synagogue was in ruins. But a stair to a cellar had been saved. Descending that stair, these Jews found a few Talmudic volumes, charred and water-soaked, but still usable in part. And they procured them a few tallow-candles, and sat down to read a page or two. There came one running then, and cried: "Jews, do you forget that you are fleeing for your lives? The Soviets are closing the frontiers, The American zone is still far off! Flee!" And one of the group waved the messenger aside: *"Shah!"* he said gravely. "Be still. *Mdarf lernen.* One must learn."

D.P.E.

Sh'ma—Teach Them Diligently to Your Children

A rabbi in Jerusalem passed an old professor on the street, and describes this conversation during the encounter:

After questions about the health of myself and family, his next question was "What are you learning?"

I thought that was lovely. *Talmud Torah keneged kulam* [the study of Torah is equivalent to them all]. I was reminded so beautifully, that in the professor's mind, study of Torah is the eternal preoccupation of the Jew.

And of course when I replied by saying: "I am studying the Talmudic Tractate Ketubot," he asked "Which chapter?" When I said "The second chapter" he started reciting some of its text by heart.

It's a nice feeling when a Jew greets you with "What are you learning?" I don't think there's any other people amongst whom that happens. If it were someone else, the question might not have been "What are you *learning*," but "What are you *earning*?"

What a people we belong to. That's why we place so much importance on reading the *Sh'ma*, and in particular the lines about teaching the Torah diligently to our children.

D.P.E.

AVINU MALKENU

The depiction of God as *melekh* or "King" was a key part of the legacy of symbols and images that ancient Israel received from the surrounding cultures. As human kings were revered as gods in the ancient Near East, so too were the gods depicted amid the trappings of royalty.

Post-Biblical Judaism continued to cherish the royal metaphor, perhaps more so than ever once historical circumstance denied the Jews earthly sovereignty. The idea that God is the only true King, and therefore that all flesh-and-blood rulers are more or less usurpers, was widely if quietly believed among Jews for a very long time. An emperor might dare call himself "king of kings," but God remained beyond him, since God was called *melekh malkhey hamelakhim*, "King over kings of kings"! The liturgy, and especially that of Rosh Hashanah and Yom Kippur, is especially enamored of royal imagery.

RABBI ARTHUR GREEN, *THESE ARE THE WORDS*

Live, Read, Grow, and Be a Mensch!

One of the lines of the *Avinu Malkenu* [Our Father, Our King] prayer asks God to help us be renewed for a good year. How do we find renewal, refreshment, and reinvigorate our spiritual lives?

Rabbi Samuel Chiel tells the story of "a remarkably brilliant man by the name of Robert Kirsch, who died at the age of fifty-eight. He was the book critic for the *Los Angeles Times*. He wrote more book reviews than any modern critic, six days a week for twenty-three years. In his spare time he also wrote a dozen books, fiction and nonfiction. Robert Kirsch was born in Brooklyn and (before his death) he summed up his career and his values in these words: 'In the end, all of it is an attempt to recapture Coney Island and the lesson I learned there: "Live, read, grow, and be a Mensch."'"

What a lovely summary of renewing life, "*Hadesh alenu shanah tovah*," "Live, read, grow, and be a Mensch!"

D.P.E.

Avinu Malkenu, Kotvaynu Be-Sefer Z'khuyot— Don't Just Ask—Tell God: Send Me!

A man once cried to God, "Lord, the world is in such a mess—everything seems wrong.

"Why don't you send someone to help and change the world?" The voice of *Adonai* answered, "I did send someone. I sent you."

We pray for life, we ask God for a year of health and happiness. But don't just ask. Tell the Almighty, tell the world, tell yourself: Send me!

Rabbi Gerald I. Wolpe

Avinu Malkenu—A Tenacious Link

Rabbi Mark Mallach tells a moving story about his family's experience with *Avinu Malkenu*. His wife was born in the Former Soviet Union, in the city of Chernovitz.

It was 1975, Rabbi Mallach and his wife, Genya, had just moved from Israel to America, and they were living with his late parents, in Bowie, Maryland. That Rosh Hashanah they went to *shul*, where he became a Bar Mitzvah. For Genya, as a recent émigré from the FSU, it was the first Rosh Hashanah service in her life

They came to the point in the service when the *Avinu Malkenu* would be recited for the first time, and they all rose. As the *Hazzan* came to the concluding stanza, and began that ever so familiar melody to the conclusion of *Avinu Malkenu,* he felt a shuddering motion against his right shoulder. He looked over at Genya—tears were streaming down her cheeks, uncontrollably. He did not know why, nor could he ask at that moment.

Later, he asked. Here is what she told him. It seems, back in Chernovitz, her home town, whenever the family would gather for family occasions with the entire extended family, birthdays, etc., at some time during the meal, someone would turn to their Aunt Esther and ask her to sing. And they would always request that she sing the only two Hebrew songs that she knew: *Oseh Shalom* and *Avinu Malkenu.*

It was at that moment, that Rosh Hashanah, when the *Hazzan* sang, that Genya knew, not just what the melody belonged to, but to what—to whom she belonged.

The FSU had tried to suppress the *Yiddisha Neshama* [Jewish spirit]—but the spirit could not be vanquished. It survived—a tenacious link—dor l'dor—generation to generation—the power of the *Avinu Malkenu.*

D.P.E.

Avinu Malkenu

Avinu Malkenu is perhaps the best known and loved prayer of the High Holiday liturgy, certainly one of the most evocative melodies of the season. The simple phrase "*avinu, malkenu*" describes the complexity of our relationship with God.

We relate to God, first of all, as *Avinu,* as our Parent. Just as our parents want the best for us, offering us unconditional love and forgiveness, so, too, do we experience God as being on our side and constantly rooting for us. Paralleling our relationship with God, we may question our parents' decisions, but we do cede to them ultimate authority. It is part of Judaism's uniqueness and greatness that the attempt to understand God's will has been raised to the level of a spiritual value, as our holy books recall the generations of teachers who have struggled to interpret God's word. Even when our response is less than enthusiastic, we firmly believe that God will hear our pleas for atonement and reconciliation.

However, at the High Holiday season, we see God more in the aspect of sovereign, as our Ruler, *Malkenu*. As a Ruler, God has the right to demand unquestioning obedience to the Divine will. It was Rabbi Akiva who first employed this phrase while officiating at a special service to intercede for rain during a period of drought. He was so successful in his mission that the people locked on to the formula "*Avinu, Malkenu*" as especially efficacious.

The rest, as they say, is history. In typical Jewish fashion, the prayer has taken on a life of its own. While Rabbi Akiva's version contained only five lines, the prayer has been expanded by numerous hazanim articulating the particular needs of their own communities. The Sefardic version has 29 lines, the Ashkenazi 38, and a Polish rite contains 44. The great 19th century liturgist Seligman Isaac Baer testifies to having seen as many as 53 variants in the texts he reviewed.

We include *Avinu Malkenu* in the prayer service following the *Amidah* on Ros Hashanah and Yom Kippur, and at the morning and evening services throughout the *Aseret Y'mei Teshuva*, the Ten Days of Repentance. Some scholars have suggested that we do not include it on Shabbat because of its correspondence to the weekday *Amidah,* while others suggest that it is excluded because of its petitionary nature. On Shabbat we feel especially close to God, secure in the knowledge that God is well aware of our needs without our having to articulate a "laundry list."

Indeed, we do ask for many things in this prayer. We pray for God's help as we seek repentance, we ask for a good year in general, for healing for all who are ill, for physical sustenance and for redemption, and we ask these things while acknowledging in the concluding verse that "*eyn banu ma-asim,*" we have an insufficient quantity of good deeds to override the verdict against us, therefore we rely on God's grace and lovingkindess to save us.

Rabbi Bonnie Koppell

ROOTS AND THEMES FROM THE TORAH

One of the most important and original terms of Jewish moral thought, *teshuvah* is quite inadequately rendered by the usual translation "repentance." To repent is to turn away from sin and seek forgiveness. *Teshuvah* is a broader concept, one that goes to the very root of human existence. It is no wonder that the Talmud lists the power of *teshuvah* as one of those seven things that existed before God created this world. Human life is inconceivable without *teshuvah*.

The first person to undertake *teshuvah* was the very first human. Adam realized the magnitude of his sin in the Garden, according to the Midrash, and sought to be reconciled with God. *Teshuvah* in this case would mean re-establishing the intimacy and trust that existed between God and God's beloved creatures before the expulsion from Eden. *Teshuvah,* in this key story, could not mean the re-creation of innocence. That childlike aspect of Eden was gone forever. But a new relationship, one more mature since it had faced and overcome the moment of doubt and betrayal, was Adam's goal. It is this deeper faith, one that emerges from struggle with the self, that is the goal of *teshuvah*.

RABBI ARTHUR GREEN, *THESE ARE THE WORDS*

Repentance as Halakhah

"And he shall make an atonement for the holy sanctuary, and he shall make an atonement for the Tent of Meeting, and for the altar, and he shall make an atonement for the priests, and for all the people of the congregation."

LEVITICUS 16:33

Rabbi Avraham Yitzhak HaKohen Kook (1865–1935), the Chief Rabbi of the Land of Israel after the First World War, was well known for his warm and heartfelt attitude to the settlers of the land of all parties and streams. From time to time he would meet with the members of non-religious *moshavim* and *kibbutzim* and he would also return enchanted and enthused at the pioneering enterprise of the young people of Israel in the new "Return to Zion" movement.

A delegation of rabbis once came to Rabbi Kook and wished to complain that the Chief Rabbi was seen in the company of young people who did not observe the Torah and the religious precepts.

Is it possible—one of the visiting rabbis challenged him—that the Land of Israel will be upbuilt and established by young men and women who deride the precepts of the Torah? Is this not literally tantamount to a desecration of what is sacred?

Certainly not, Rabbi Kook responded in his clear and enthusiastic voice. You can reach this conclusion yourselves! The holiest place in the Land of Israel is surely the Temple, and the holiest part of the Temple is without doubt the Holy of Holies. When the Temple was standing, nobody was allowed to enter the Holy of Holies except for the high priest who would go in there for ritual purposes just one single time a year—on the Day of Atonement. And even that he was allowed to do only after lengthy preparations and while wearing special clothes.

But when the Temple was being built, laborers and craftsmen from all strata of the people must surely have entered there, and they would not have been particularly outstanding in Torah and in the fear of Heaven. These many people came to the holy site at all times and at all hours, until the construction work was completed.

And so it is with these young pioneers. They are building our land and it is holy work that they are doing. We should, therefore, treat them with an extra portion of affection, and be both critical and friendly at the same time.

Rabbi Simcha Raz

Teshuvah and the Sacred Year

The holy days of the Jewish year are both commemoration and reenactment. Our words recall the creation of the world on Shabbat, the liberation from bondage on Pesach, Sinai on Shavuot, and so forth. But the inner meanings of these words is a drama of reenactment, in which these great events take place over and over again on an inner plane, allowing each Jew to feel him or herself to be a real participant, rather than a distant observer. The promise offered by our tradition that these ways actually work—that something of liberation's light may really be felt by the Jew sitting at the seder table—is attested by the faithfulness of Jews to these ancient forms.

But what is the root of the "Days of Awe" in the historical drama of ancient Israel? These festivals, at once more personal and more universal than any other in the calendar, are not ordinarily connected with sacred history. There is no apparent event in the biblical narrative that links up with this season. The rabbis attended to this lack, as they did in the case of Shavuot. A connection unmentioned in Scripture is offered in the *aggadah*. The rabbis claim that the New Moon of Elul was the date when Moses went up the mountain to receive the second tablets. He returned with them, having achieved the forgiveness of Israel, forty days later, on Yom Kippur.

The holiest day on our calendar is, then, the commemoration of an event nearly forgotten. It is a second holiday of revelation, the day of the giving of the second tablets. This is the occasion when Moses cries out to see God's glory and is hidden in the cleft of Sinai's rock as the glory passes by. In that moment, God's thirteen attributes of mercy are called out (again "in the voice of Moses"?). The recitation of these becomes a verbal talisman of atonement, and their frequent repetition froms the core of our penitential liturgy (*Selihot),* throughout this season, and especially on Yom Kippur. It is presumably a year later, and in commemoration of this event that the great atonement ritual of the tabernacle is enacted, the model for our Yom Kippur.

Rabbi Arthur Green

Inclusion in the Covenant

In the beginning of Parshat Nitzavim, Moses prepares the Israelites to enter the covenant with God. He declares that the whole community—elders, women, children, strangers—will be part of the covenant, "from your woodchoppers to your waterdrawers" (Deut. 29:10).

This is a typical biblical phrase. "From x to y," where x and y represent opposite extremes of a continuum, means "including everyone." Thus "from young to old" means "including everyone." Thus "from young to old" or "from the greatest to the smallest." Our problem is that woodchoppers and water-drawers are not opposite extremes. Both are menial laborers and neither was highly esteemed. What does the phrase mean?

Perhaps these jobs are meant symbolically rather than literally. Let's free associate. Woodchoppers are literally "choppers of your trees." The image of trees has echoes of the Tree of Life, the Torah. To "chop" such a Tree is to question, or reject Jewish tradition. On the other hand, the image of "waterdrawers" is reminiscent of the verse "*u-sh'avtem mayim b'sasson* ... ," the promise of Isaiah (12:3), "You shall draw water joyfully from salvation's wells." The image is of one who drinks deeply from the wellsprings of Torah. Understood this way, Moses is declaring the covenant to be inclusive of all, the pious and the rebellious, the faithful and the confused. The text warns us never to be so complacent about our commitment or devotion, or so sure of our faith, that we see the covenant of Israel as closed to those who are not convinced of its value or sure of its feasibility. Rather we must learn from the later verses of the *parshah* and approach such Jews with the assurance that the Torah, in its broadest sense, " ... is very close to you, in your mouth and in your heart" (Deut. 30:14).

Rabbi David W. Nelson

Fasting: Who Can and Who Has To?

" ... in the seventh month, on the tenth day of the
month, you shall afflict your souls."

LEVITICUS 16:29

The *tzaddik* Rabbi Abraham Joshua Heschel of Apta (1755–1825),
who was known for his work *Ohev Yisrael* (A Lover of Israel), used to
say: "If only I had the power, I would annul all the public fasts about
which we have been commanded because we are weak and exhausted
in this long and harsh exile with the exception of two: the fast of the
Ninth of Av and the fast of the Day of Atonement. Because, on the
Ninth of Av, when our temple and our glory was destroyed, who can
eat? And on the holy Day of Atonement, when we are purified of all sin
and wrongdoing before the Creator of the Universe, who has to eat?!"

Rabbi Simcha Raz

Yom Kippur and the "Scapegoat"—Seeking Meaning for the Strange Ritual of the Scapegoat

Yom Kippur, or "Day of Atonement," has been called "the climax and
crown of the Jewish religious year." Through twenty-four hours of
fasting and prayer, Jews are challenged to review the ethical and spiritual standards by which they live and to reaffirm their commitment to
carry out the mitzvot, or "commandments," of their faith. In defining
the message of Yom Kippur, Rabbi Bernard B. Bamberger writes that
"It speaks to each human being and seeks to bring each person into
harmony with others and with God."

The origins of Yom Kippur are shrouded in mystery. There are,
however, some fascinating traditions associated with the sacred day
that help us understand its popularity among the ancient Israelites.
One of the most significant and baffling of these is the ceremony of
the "scapegoat."

Defining "Scapegoat"

The term "scapegoat" was apparently coined by William Tyndale, the
first great English Bible translator. Thereafter, it came to be used for a

person, animal, or object to which the impurity or guilt of a community was formally transferred and then removed.... In common usage today, a scapegoat is someone whom people blame for their own misfortunes, and even for their faults and sins...." (Bernard J. Bamberger, *The Torah: A Modern Commentary*).

As described in the Torah, Aaron is to take two he-goats from the Israelite community as a sin offering. After he has slaughtered a bull as a sin offering for himself and his household, he is to bring the two he-goats to the entrance of the sanctuary. There he is to cast lots upon the two he-goats, designating one "for God" and the other "for Azazel." The one "for God" is to be slaughtered as a sin offering on the altar of the sanctuary. Aaron is then to place his hands upon the head of the other marked "for Azazel" and to confess all the transgressions of the Israelites upon it. Afterwards the goat is to be sent off to wander and die in the wilderness. (See Leviticus 16.)

According to the *Mishnah*, the ritual of taking the scapegoat from the Jerusalem Temple into the wilderness began as a very important ceremony, but later it became a cause for great commotion, even embarrassment. People would stand along the path and ridicule the ceremony. Some would point a finger at the goat marked "for Azazel," upon which the High Priest had confessed Israel's sins, and mockingly remark: "Such a tiny scapegoat for such a huge load of sins!" (*Yoma* 6:4).

Ibn Ezra

Commentator Ibn Ezra refers to the ritual of the scapegoat marked "for Azazel" as a "mystery." He suggests that it may be connected with a pagan religious practice of offerings to "goat-demons," which were prohibited by the Torah. Such sacrifices may have been gifts to a god many believed ruled the wilderness and was a power for bringing evil into the world. (See Leviticus 17:7.) The scapegoat was offered to protect people from evil influences.

If Ibn Ezra is correct, why would Jews have used a ritual that seems to mimic pagan practices forbidden by the laws of Torah? Modem interpreter Baruch A. Levine explains that the ritual of the he-goat "for Azazel" was not considered a gift to a pagan god. Nor was it seen as a pagan rite. Instead, the scapegoat marked "for Azazel" was a dramatic means through which the Jewish people rejected the influences and temptations of evil symbolized by Azazel.

Levine argues that the sanctuary ceremony was "based on the awareness that, even in a world ruled by God, evil forces were at work—forces that had to be destroyed if God's earthly home ... was not to be defiled."

In transferring all the sins of the people to the scapegoat and then sending it out into the wilderness marked "for Azazel," ancient Jews believed they were forcing "the iniquities of the people back on Azazel." In a way, Levine concludes, they created a "boomerang effect," returning evil influence "back to its point of departure, to the wilderness!" In doing so, they demonstrated that only God had power in their lives, and that they had defeated the symbol of evil—Azazel (JPS *Torah Commentary: Leviticus,* pp. 250–253).

Levine admits that "this entire complex of rituals seems to be predicated on magical perceptions" and that his interpretation is "unacceptable to many modern students of the Bible, as it was to certain traditional schools."

Rambam (Maimonides)

One of those commentators is Moses Maimonides, who rejects any identification with powers or angels of evil. He declares, "It is not a sacrifice to Azazel, God forbid." Instead of being a ritual with magical powers, says Maimonides, the scapegoat ceremony is an "active allegory" meant "to impress the mind of the sinner that his sins must lead him to a wasteland." When those who have broken the laws of Torah see that their sins are placed upon the he-goat and sent out into the wilderness, it is hoped that they will "break with their sins ... distance themselves from them, and turn back to God in sincere repentance" (*Guide for the Perplexed* 3:46).

Function of the Scapegoat

The function of the scapegoat ... serves as an expression of the educational message of Yom Kippur. Every year one is afforded the opportunity to determine one's own life for better, to purify the heart for service according to the will of God. This holy day teaches us our greatest gift: "Freedom of choice is given" (Avot 3:19; B.S. Jacobson, *Meditations on the Torah*, p. 173).

Abravanel

Abravanel also suggests a symbolic interpretation for the ritual of the scapegoat. He believe that the two he-goats, one marked "for God," the other marked "for Azazel, " are to remind Jews of Jacob and Esau. Esau, like the he-goat marked "for Azazel," wandered into the wilderness away from his people, its laws, and its traditions. Jacob, like the he-goat marked "for God," lived a life devoted to God's service. According to Abravanel, when Aaron, and the High Priests after him, cast lots to decide which of the two he-goats would be marked "for God" or "for Azazel," Jews were to be reminded that they had a significant free choice to make. They could live like Jacob or Esau, "for God," or "for Azazel." (See commentary on Leviticus 16.)

Hirsh: The Meaning of Casting Lots

Rabbi Samson Raphael Hirsh sees in the ceremony of deciding which goat will be "for God" and which "for Azazel" a symbol of the choice each Jew makes on Yom Kippur. "We can decide for God, gathering together all the powers of resistance we have been given to resist everything that would tear us away from our vocation to be near to God ... Or we can decide for Azazel and uphold, unmastered, our selfish life of desires, and ... give ourselves over to the uncontrolled might of sensuality ... " (Comment on Leviticus 16:10.)

Rabbi Hillel Silverman calls attention to the fact that, according to the Talmud, the two he-goats must be identical in size, appearance, and value. In this, he contends, is an important lesson. The two goats symbolize what we are willing to give for our own pleasure and enjoyment (for Azazel) and what we are willing to give for the welfare and security of others (for God).

The Talmud insists, says Silverman, that the two goats be identical in size, appearance, and value in order to teach the lesson that "all we devote to personal pleasure and self-aggrandizement (for Azazel) goes 'into the wilderness,' unless we also sacrifice for the Lord and 'make atonement.'" (*From Week to Week*, pp. 108–109.)

In other words, the ancient ritual is not just about the scapegoat, but it is about what is done to both he-goats. One of them ends up as a sacred sacrifice "for God," symbolizing our generosity to others and loyalty to God; the other, "for Azazel," is sent off to wander and die in the wilderness, a sign that serving only our selfish pleasures and pride is a waste of our precious potentials. It is like wasting them in the wilderness. The ritual for both he-goats on Yom Kippur is a reminder of the delicate balance, between caring about oneself and about others, that each person is challenged to achieve.

While its origins are clouded in mystery, the ceremony of the two he-goats continued until the destruction of the Temple in 70 C.E. Interest in uncovering its meaning and connection to Yom Kippur, however, has not ceased. Was it a magical way of ridding the people of Israel of its sins? Was the scapegoat, marked "for Azazel," actually sent out into the wilderness as a sacrifice to a demon or god of evil? Is the scapegoat ceremony a symbol of the various spiritual and ethical choices Jews must make on each Yom Kippur?

Perhaps, in the case of this ancient tradition of the scapegoat, we have an example where all the interpretations provided through the centuries may be correct!

Rabbi Harvey J. Fields

Azazel and Magic

One goat is "left standing alive before the Lord, to make expiation with it and to send it off to the wilderness to Azazel" (Leviticus 16:10). Who or what is Azazel? There have been three general approaches, from antiquity to our day.

First, some see "Azazel" as a description of the goat (so the Septuagint and the Vulgate and English since the 16th century, scapegoat, from "escape"). The Hebrew is understood as "the goat who went off," reflected by the Mishnah. Alternatively, Azazel is a place name, roughly, "tough" (e.g., Yoma 67b, the Sifra), describing a mountain. The root would be *azaz* (Saadia, Ibn Janach), the term reflected in the Mishnaic (not Biblical) ceremony where the goat is pushed off a high precipice.

Third, and most fascinating, is "Azazel" as the name of a demigod, power, demon or devil. Expected among modern Biblical critics, this view has roots in antiquity. In the Book of Enoch, Azazel is one of the demigods who mated with humans in Genesis 6 (and so too Midrash Pirkei of Rabbi Eliezer). Ibn Ezra saw fit only to hint at this interpretation, saying that "the truth in this matter is a mystery," one which could be understood "when one reaches 33." Nachmanides saw fit to explain—33 verses hence is a warning not to sacrifice to goats— Azazel is one of the desert pagan gods! Nachmanides calls them angels. "Azazel" is here read as a metathesis for *azz-el*, which is indeed the spelling in the Book of Enoch.

If this last interpretation is correct, our text's near syncretism of pagan and Jewish religions is indeed worthy of Ibn Ezra's "mysterious mist." However, apologists correctly point out several factors which limit and essentially empty the term's pagan origin of its content. This "force" is not independent. It is not a counter balance to the one God, nor does it remain one among many gods. Rather it represents some sort of evil realm. Nor is the goat a sacrifice. Indeed, its effective function is to carry sins away in a symbolic manner, similar to other nations' ceremonies transferring the "evil" or "plague" to some enemies' camp. This is not propitiation of another god. Even if the term's origin is pagan, the ceremony has been properly Judaized, placed in a monotheistic framework, a symbol more than an effective ceremony, an act whose essence has been transferred to the confession that precedes it.

Given this reconstruction, one must reexamine, not only historically but also in contemporary Jewish life, the roles played by ostensibly "semipagan" or magic customs: specifically, astrology (which can be traced from ancient synagogue floors all the way through modern newspapers), powers attributed to deceased rabbis and good luck charms. Instinctively, one wishes to categorically rule such practices out of the realm of normative Judaism. The example of Azazel may indicate that the picture is more complex. Yes, syncretism must be banned, but perhaps pagan practices might yet be Judaized if properly framed, limited and redirected. The readjustment of such beliefs and usage might be preferable to the idle attempt of totally uprooting them.

Rabbi Benjamin J. Segal

The Goat's Journey to the Desert

It seems odd that the goat which bore our sins would remain alive. Later interpretations, however, claimed that the goat for Azazel was sent away to die, and there are elaborate descriptions of the goat being pushed off a high craggy desert peak to its death. This interpretation has our sins being toted far away to die in impressive fashion. I have found it helpful to create my own image of what might have happened to that goat in the desert and what it does symbolically for us.

I imagine that the goat that is offered up to God represents the sins we have already worked through, and the goat sent to the desert are those deficiencies which continue to reverberate through us, repeating themselves in predictable yet destructive patterns. The desert is a good place to get clarity and vision to release us from the debilitating patterns. In the desert you can see the sky and the ground all at once. The light and shadow expose the structure of the landscape, each red, yellow, or gray rock taking its place. When I'm in the desert, I step out to the edge of a cliff, standing on strong thighs built from walking there, and begin to see myself in the same clear way that I can see the formation of the canyon in front of me.

So when Aaron confesses for the Community of Israel and leans his hands on the goat (the word for lean, *samakh,* also means "trust"), he's beginning a process that might lead to our "coming out" into the light of our true selves. By trusting that goat, Aaron is also sending us with the goat into the desert. He does this so that we can have the light of the desert shine on our souls while the goat carries our stuckness for us. By traversing the desert without the burden of our sins, we can begin to get an image of ourselves that can survive without our destructive behaviors. For in the corners of our civilized places, we have hidden successfully with our poorer selves and become dependant upon living with them. In the desert we are free from them.

Rabbi Shai Gluskin

Why Do We Fast?

Like all other animals, we eat to live. Like some other animals we eat because we enjoy the taste. Unlike any other animals, human societies vary in proclaiming what is fit to eat. On this Yom Kippur Day, Jews do not eat at all, to physically remind ourselves that:

"Humanity does not live by bread alone, but that mankind lives by everything that God says" (Deut. 8:3).

"This is the fast that I desire ... to share your bread with the hungry, to take the wretched poor into your home, and when you see the naked, to clothe them" (Isaiah 58:7).

"Better a dry crust of bread than a house full of feasting with strife" (Proverbs 17:1).

May we who constantly face the temptations to over consume learn the virtue of moderation and self-denial.

May we spend less on ourselves and our families, and give more to charity and education.

Oh God, may those who fast today realize the value of self-discipline throughout the next year.

And may those who still struggle to fast avoid the consequences of overindulgence in the year to come.

Rabbi Allen S. Maller

Judaism and Atonement

"For on this day, Atonement shall be made."

LEVITICUS 16:30

Just as Judaism emphasizes the closeness of God, so does it emphasize God's commandment and man's responsibility. It is in this dual emphasis that the Jewish idea of atonement finds its peculiar characteristic. Man is to return. In this concept, atonement is no mere act of grace, or miracle of salvation, which befalls the chosen. It demands the free ethical choice and deed of the human being. Even in man's atonement, "Thou shalt" confronts him; in it are spoken the commanding words: "I, the Lord, am thy God." Man is not granted something unconditionally. He has rather to decide for something unconditionally. In his deed is the beginning of his atonement. As the Talmud expresses it: "To us who sinned the commanding God speaks first, and only when we have listened to Him, does He speak to us as the God of love; therefore it is said in the psalm, 'The Lord is just in all his ways, and loving in all his doings,' first just and then full of love. The first step is the return of man, for atonement is the work of creative man.

Judaism is a religion of atonement. Two old rabbinic sayings express this thought: "The purpose and aim of all creation is atonement." It was evening and it was morning—one day, that is, the Day of Atonement. The customs of Judaism also give outward expression to this idea. Its most important holy day and sacred center of the year is the Day of Atonement. Joined with the New Year's Day, the "Day of Judgment," it speaks to man at the beginning of the year of his responsibility to God.

Rabbi Leo Baeck

Atonement in the Desert

When the children of Israel received the Ten Commandments on Shavuot, Moses ascended Mount Sinai and remained there for forty days to receive the two tablets of the Torah. On the seventeenth day of Tamuz, Moses descended, and, when he saw the people worshiping a golden calf, broke the tablets. Then, for forty days, Moses placed his tent beyond the camp: and the people mourned. On the first day of Elul, Moses went up the mountain again to receive the new, second set of tablets. During this period, the Israelites fasted daily from sunrise to sunset. However, on the fortieth day they fasted from sunset to sunset. This day was the tenth of Tishri. When Moses returned in the morning, the Israelites went out to meet him. He saw that they were weeping, and he cried as well as he became aware of their repentance. Then God said: "Your repentance is acceptable to me, and this day will remain the Day of Atonement throughout all generations."

Eliyahu Zuta 4

Celebrating Yom Kippur in the Past

In Israel, no days were happier or filled with more rejoicing than the fifteenth of Av and Yom Kippur, for on those days the unmarried women of Jerusalem would go out in white clothing (and these clothes were borrowed, so that no one would be ashamed because she did not have them).... And the women would go to dance in the vineyards. And what did they say? "Young man, lift up your eyes and see what you would choose for yourself; do not set your eyes on beauty, but on family; for favor is deceitful and beauty is vain, but a woman who fears God will be praised" (Proverbs 31:30).

Mishnah Taanit 4:8

Kohen Gadol Could Not Enter Holy of Holies Wearing Gold

Nowadays, a lot of people complain about how long and difficult synagogue services are on Yom Kippur. They should only know what things were like 2,200 years ago when the Yom Kippur rites were performed at the Holy Temple in Jerusalem. The Talmud relates how, even before sunrise on Yom Kippur day, the Temple courtyard was filled with tens of thousands of people who had come to observe the Kohen Gadol, the High Priest, offer the Yom Kippur sacrifices before God. Often standing in the blazing sun, they would remain in the courtyard all day long watching the Kohen at work. Tradition had it that if the High Priest was successful at his task of seeking forgiveness for Israel, all would know it, for a red woolen thread that had been attached to the Temple's hallway would turn white, indicating that Israel had been pardoned.... [The Kohen Gadol had to] be sensitive to the subtleties of his mission. During the Yom Kippur proceedings the Kohen Gadol had to keep changing his clothes, garments made in part of gold thread, to clothing that was all white. One could not enter the Holy of Holies to ask for forgiveness for the Jewish people's sins wearing gold; gold had been used in the making of the golden calf, the greatest sin the Jewish people ever committed.... An important part of the service revolved around an offering of incense brought into the Holy of Holies. The Kohen Gadol was only allowed in the Holy of Holies four times all year, all on Yom Kippur day. The first time was to place the incense spoon and pan before the ark and the last time was to retrieve them. The commentaries note from this that we should never underestimate the importance seemingly small matters can play in the scheme of things. A small incense spoon played a pivotal role in the year's most important holiday.

Rabbi Yehuda Appel

Where God Can't Enter

Wherever justice is perverted, there God is not. Wherever mercy is missing, there God is missing too.

I love the story about the poor man who tried to get into a rich *Shul,* and they were too polite to say to him that they didn't want to let him in. So they put him off with one excuse after another. "You need letters of reference," and then, "You need to wait until the committee meets," and so on. Until finally, the poor man began to get the idea.

One day he went to the *Shul* and got rebuffed with the same excuse, and as he was walking away, feeling downhearted and depressed, he chanced to meet God. And God said, "Why do you look so sad?" The man said, "Because I've been trying to get into that *Shul* for months and I can't get in."

And God says, "I know how you feel. I've been trying to get into that *Shul* for years, and I can't get in either."

It makes no difference how fancy the furniture, or how many times God's name is invoked in a place. Either justice and mercy are there, or else God is not there either. That is the message of [Isaiah] to humanity.

Rabbi Maurice Davis

A Sabbath of Sabbaths

Our sages asked why Yom Kippur is called "a Sabbath of Sabbaths." Indeed, they pointed out that the Bible declares that the regularly celebrated Sabbath is called "a Sabbath of Sabbaths unto the Lord" (Exodus 35:2). Yet the pious Rabbi Zevi ha-Kohen replied: "Indeed, of the Sabbath it is written, 'a Sabbath of Sabbaths unto the Lord,' but of Yom Kippur it is written, 'a Sabbath of Sabbaths unto you.' On Yom Kippur we draw the sanctity of the superior realm down nearer to us. The ten days of *Teshuvah*—'Repentance'—are a process of drawing upward from earth to heaven; on Yom Kippur the Holy One, Blessed be He, draws down from heaven nearer to Israel."

This Sabbath of Sabbaths, called by the Greeks "a seven of sevens," "a holier than the holy," carries its exalted title with reason and dignity. Yom Kippur teaches foremost the lesson of self-restraint. To one who has learned to disregard food and drink, which are absolutely necessary, are there any among the superfluities of life which a person can fail to despise, things which exist to promote not so much preservation and permanence of life as pleasure with all its powers of mischief? Second, the holy day is devoted in its entirety to prayers and supplications, as we look toward God's generous nature and hope He will set pardon before chastisement. Finally, we choose to fast at the time of the ingathering of the earth's fruits. This restraint evinces the perfect piety that teaches us not to put trust in what stands ready prepared before us as though it were the source of health and life. Those who abstain from food and drink in the midst of plenty have elevated themselves religiously, recognizing that humanity is preserved not through any material thing but through faithful reliance upon God, our Savior, Parent, and Creator, Who has the power and the right to nourish and sustain us according to His Divine will.

Author Unknown

Parshat Nitzavim: Choose Life

The Torah teaches that God is the source of life in the universe. On the High Holidays, which begin next week, we chant in each service "Remember us for life, King of life, and write us in the book of life for Your sake, O God of life." Life is mentioned four times in this little verse, which is chanted over and over on the holiest days of our year. God and life go together.

The Torah teaches that we humans can never know God's essence. All we can know is what God does in the universe. When we see life, we see the hand of God. And when we choose life, we are partners with God in creation.

There is something mysterious about the appearance of life on our planet. Life does not simply occur spontaneously. In nature, the laws of entropy teach that systems fall apart, become more random and less complex over time. And yet, we see life developing on earth, becoming more complex over time, more specialized. From random molecules emerge living cells, and from more and more complex organisms emerge consciousness. To the religious soul, the evolution of life on earth reflects the hand of God.

We humans have the ability to be God's partners in allowing life to flourish. Every time we use our medical resources to save a life, to extend life, to improve the quality of life, we are helping God. But we do not need to be medical professionals to choose life in our day to day actions. Whenever we enhance the soul of another human being, we are choosing life.

Something as simple as an act of kindness, a compliment, a helping hand to a fellow human being, becomes a way of choosing life. The Rabbis taught that visiting a sick person removes one sixtieth of their illness. When we stop someone from gossiping, we are adding to life. When we recognize the dignity of another, whether through acts of charity or kind words, we are choosing life.

On the other hand, whenever we act in a way that removes the dignity of any human being, we are choosing death. When we let our neighbor go hungry, when we refuse to honor our parents, when we gossip or cheat, we are acting against the God of life. The Rabbis taught that to publicly humiliate another human being is the equivalent of murder. Even ethnic jokes, or acts that denigrate another race or people, undermines life.

God gave us the ability to act as partners in creation. The High Holidays are the perfect time to think about our relationship with other human beings. It is a time to remember God's words Choose Life not simply on our license plates but in our day to day lives.

Rabbi Michael Gold

Deciding for God or for Azazel

We have a choice in deciding between God and Azazel, says Rabbi Samson Raphael Hirsch, leading neo-Orthodox rabbi of nineteenth century Germany (comment on Leviticus 16:10).

We can decide for God, mustering all our powers of resistance to everything that would remove us from our vocation, and thus become closer to God, belong to God, and become like God in our free-willed performance of God's will, in our free-willed realization of all that is good and pure.

Or we can decide for Azazel. Doing that, we turn our backs on God's demands. Choosing Azazel we refuse to give up our self-willed sensual life, with no controls. Such a sensuality belongs only in the wilderness, where free-willed human self-control does not act to elevate the terrestrial world into the sphere of Divine freedom.

D.P.E.

The Basis of Sin: Self-Deception

The Yom Kippur Torah reading is from "Aharei-Mot," and can be found in the Book of Leviticus 16. Most people assume that this part of the Torah is read on Yom Kippur because it speaks of expiation (cleansing) of sins and tells us that on the tenth day of the seventh month (Tishre) we are to practice self-denial (*inui-nefesh*).

Another possible explanation might be that in this section, the Torah again emphasizes the relationship between clothing and honesty. Clothing covers us up; clothing is the way that we keep ourselves warm and maintain our sense of modesty. It is the first thing that Adam and Eve miss when "discovered" by God. Clothing, however, serves another function. It is the way that we mask who we are. The golden calf in Hebrew is called "*egel masekhah*" meaning "the molten or covered calf." This *parashah* may be indicating that the basis of sin lies in the act of self-deception. Aaron could not purify himself until he faced himself; Joseph had to be stripped of his robe before he could lose his arrogance, and this section seems to tell us that we can never develop ourselves as long as we hide our faults from ourselves. This week's Torah portion then may be teaching us that it is bad to lie to others and commit wrongs, but when we lie to ourselves it is not only worse, but our self-deceptions prevent us from ever seeking expiation or cleansing ourselves from our sins.

Rabbi Peter Tarlow

Celebrating and Revealing the Invisible— Yom Kippur Torah Reading

It's fascinating that two of the
most elaborate rituals of the year,
Yom Kippur and the Passover Seder,
are among the most popular
observances remaining in Jewish life.

In an age when ritual is unpopular
there's something about these two occasions which attract us
    and
bring us back to our heritage each year.
Services on Yom Kippur are long and arduous.
They are based on
the ancient rite of atonement
which took place in the temple
over two thousand years ago.
We not only read the passage
in the Torah which
describes the original rite of atonement
but we also tell the story
and re-enact portions of this ceremony
in the *Avodah,*
a portion of the *Musaf* service.
And Passover, of course, demands hours of preparation and
    hard labor.
We clean our homes, and change our dishes.
We cover our counters,
we buy food, cook elaborate meals
and invite guests to our homes.
And though we complain
what a pain it is to prepare for this holiday
we would never think of forgoing this annual ritual of remem-
    brance and freedom.
Maybe part of the appeal of Passover
and Yom Kippur
is that they only occur once a year.
They do not make daily demands on us
As other rituals might,
such as putting on *Tefillin,*
the daily *Minyan* or reciting *Berachot.*
Still, they are rituals that we embrace
despite our doubts and questions.
They are symbolic actions based more
In the heart and in emotions
Than reason and the mind.

So what is the point of these rites?
In an age that is decidedly anti-ritual why are we still willing
    to suspend our reason,
and celebrate these arcane and ancient rites?
Rabbi Alan Lew
of Congregation Beth Shalom in San Francisco
writes that the purpose of all ritual
"is to render the invisible visible."
He writes, "In the visible world,
we live out our routine
and sometimes messy lives.
We have jobs, families, and houses.
Our lives seem quite ordinary and un-dramatic.
It is beneath the surface of this world
That the real and unseen drama
of our lives is unfolding…"
This morning as we recall
the ancient rite of atonement,
as we speak of immersions and sacrifices and bullocks and
    goats;
as we recall the *Seir L'azazel*
which was sent off to die in the wilderness carrying the sins of
    the people
on its head;
as we recall the books of life and death,
the throne of judgment,
the angels of mercy
and the closing of the gates,
we might consider that we are here
to render the invisible, visible.
That is what draws back each year.
We want to believe that …
there are realities deeper than the ones we can see or measure
    or count;
there is a world that gives meaning
to the one we inhabit;
there is a Power greater than us
that we cannot see.

Ritual uncovers the things that really count,
that motivate and inspire us,
that shape our being
not because they are "real" but because they reveal the
    invisible.

Rabbi Mark B. Greenspan

Torah Reading—Yom Kippur

If Rosh Hashanah is about awareness of God, a proclamation of divine sovereignty and transcendence, then Yom Kippur is about getting close to God. The ritual is a "dance" to help establish the connection, reveal our personality and demonstrate by our behavior that we want such a relationship to exist.

Our tradition teaches that the final set of the Covenantal Tablets, the *luḥot haberit*, were brought to the people on Yom Kippur. The ritual of Yom Kippur as described in the Torah is an elaborate ceremony designed to recreate that experience of Sinai, when the divine Presence was felt among the people.

Prior to ascending the mountain, Moshe removed his shoes and purified himself to be prepared to come closer to the Presence. The people also engaged in elaborate purification rituals. To recreate such an experience through ritual required the purification of the sanctuary and those who serve in it. The word for such ritual purification is *toharah* and we will find it repeated many times in the Yom Kippur liturgy.

Just as the core of the Sinai event was limited to Moshe, the ritual reenactment limits entry to the inner sanctuary, the *kadosh kodoshim*, to the *kohen gadol*, the chief priest, and permits such entry only on Yom Kippur.

The Torah tells us that when the Sinai event took place, there was thunder and lightening and the mountain was full of fire. The people were frightened. Closeness to God and closeness to another person creates vulnerability. The Presence of God is desired, yet awesome. All the prophets that speak about such an encounter are afraid. In his award-winning book, *The God of Old*, James Kugel of Harvard discusses ritual as a way of taming the encounter with a being that transcends our human experiences and control.

In its ritual reenactment for Yom Kippur, the purification was intended to protect that holy space and those priestly attendants when the Presence of God would be perceived in the *mikdash*, the sacred sanctuary. The word for such protection is *kapparah*, a term that will also recur many times in our liturgy. Originally, *kapparah* meant to place a protective covering over something. Later it came to be understood as the covering of sin to enable a person to go forward in the process of *teshuvah*/repentance and turning to God.

While this ritual seems arcane, ancient and alien to us, it helps if we try to understand it as a type of courtship with rules about how the two lovers might get close. There is a "dance" that we go through as we see or hear about someone, Google the person, check them on J-match or j-date, or talk to a friend to find out a bit more about him or her. Eventually we call or e-mail, set up a coffee date—a limited encounter—to protect ourselves, slowly reveal something of our personal life, and gradually deepen the relationship.

Perhaps Yom Kippur might be seen as a variation on the play, *I Love You. You're Perfect. Now Change*. The haftarah we read later will try to tell us how to change in our relationship as we try to move to greater and greater intimacy. As we read the Torah, think about people and think about God, for all of Yom Kippur is about trying to get close.

Rabbi Baruch Frydman-Kohl

Aaron's God—and Ours

Consider God's instructions to Aaron about preparing to enter the Shrine: "He shall be dressed in a sacral linen tunic, with linen breeches next to his flesh, and be girt with a linen sash, and he shall wear a linen turban. They are sacral vestments; he shall bathe his body in water and then put them on." Let us imagine these garments gathering up his fear and grief and anger, and allowing him to feel clothed—which is to say, safe—before God, rather than raw and naked in his loss. Dressed in God's compassion, but still angry and fearful, Aaron enters God's dwelling place, where he reenacts the same ritual of animal sacrifice during which, the last time it was performed, he watched his sons die. But the ritual of slaughter is familiar to Aaron, and God is careful explicitly to ensure that this encounter will be safe for Aaron, twice spelling out ways in which Aaron can protect himself from getting closer to God than a human can handle. Aaron performs this ritual with practiced hands but a new mindfulness.

What strikes me about this passage is its unrelenting physicality. Put yourself in Aaron's shoes. Still blaming God for the death of your sons, you are to bathe, dress, and enter God's dwelling place, alone. You are to perform a ritual in which you get so much blood on your hands that it drips from your fingers, and then splash the curtains and the altar and the Ark with it. You are to burn so much incense that you can barely see for the sweet-smelling smoke. It probably makes you cough; it probably makes your eyes water and your throat burn. Standing amid the blood and dung and carcasses of the bull and the goat you've slaughtered, you are to confess your sins while resting your hands on the head of a live goat. You are to send this goat—a witness to the entire ritual—running into the wilderness with all your sins heaped on his head. And then you are to emerge from the Shrine, strip off your bloody clothes, bathe again, put on full priestly regalia, and rejoin your people.

What happens here that restores Aaron's and Aaron's household's right relationship with God? What happens is that God reminds Aaron who God really is. To understand this we must put aside our knee-jerk repugnance for ritual sacrifice, which had a very different meaning for Aaron than it does for us today. The equivalent for us, I think, would be to take a week's paycheck and set it on fire. It is about giving up to God some basic element of our sustenance, without which we could not live. But even as we are repelled by the image of animal sacrifice, I think we can nonetheless appreciate the power in such a ritual, a ritual that was Aaron's familiar way to approach God. In performing this ritual, Aaron finds himself once again intensely in the presence of the true God—a God who guides him into doing what will release him, and makes the process safe.

Then, there is the innovation for Aaron in this ritual: his confession of sin—never before today has this been part of the ceremony. And the final way in which God reminds Aaron who he is: God makes no comment upon his confession. He simply invites Aaron to speak his sins aloud and then offers him a way to let them go. It is Aaron's letting go of sin, not God's judgment of sin, that sets Aaron free and returns him and his people to joyful participation in a covenantal relationship—which is to say, a two-way relationship—with God. This is the sort of relationship into which God is inviting us on this holy day—not one in which we are judged, but one in which we are released. Yom Kippur offers us the opportunity to let go of the attitudes and behaviors that create estrangements of all kinds—including estrangement from God—and enter into renewed contact and renewed possibility.

Sarah Polster

Peace between People

May God's holy name be praised! For in God's love of Israel, He ordained the Ten Days of Repentance for them, so that if even only one of the House of Israel actually repents, that person's repentance is accepted as though it were that of the entire congregation. Therefore, all Israel should be sure to repent. Let them make peace with one another and forgive each other on the evening of Yom Kippur in order that the Holy One, blessed be God, in God's own presence, accept their repentance and prayer with special love. Indeed, we find the power of peace among people to be so great that for its sake God revises words a person has already said. For example, in the passage "And Sarah laughed within herself, saying ... 'Shall I have pleasure, my lord being so old?' [Genesis 18:12], but unto Abraham the Lord said, 'Why did Sarah laugh, saying: Shall I of a surety bear a child, old as I am?'" (ibid. 13). Note that Sarah had said, "My lord being so old," but God revised her words, repeating to Abraham "Old as I am," in order that Abraham not be angry at Sarah for calling him old.

Pesikta Rabbati 50:6

When God Is High Above, Awe Comes; When God Is Close, Love Comes—Peace to the Far, Peace to the Close (Isaiah 57:19)

> "Shalom to the one who is far away;
> Shalom to the one who is very near." (Isaiah 57:19)

When a person's soul is in balance, she realizes that she is far
    from God.
At the very same moment, however, she knows that she is
    close to God.
We all tremble with incffable reverence when we think of the
    Almighty as
way, way above and beyond.
But, when we feel in our deepest being that God is close to
    us, right next to us,
our profound love of God comes into our hearts.
Both awe and love are the polarities that keep our soul in
    balance.

Adapted from Rabbi Levi Yitzhak of Berditchev

Is Not This the Fast I Have Chosen ... to Feed the Hungry, Clothe the Naked....

The book of Psalms, in a famous passage, declares: "Open the Gates
of Righteousness." Whereupon the Midrash comments (Midrash
Tehillim 118:17):

> On judgment day in the next world, everyone will be asked:
>   "What was your occupation?"
>   If one answers: "I fed the hungry," they will say: "This is
> God's Gate. You, who fed the hungry, may enter."
>   If one answers: "I gave drink to the thirsty," they will say:
> "This is God's Gate. You, who gave water to the thirsty, may
> enter."
>   If one answers: "I clothed the naked," they will say: "This is
> God's Gate. You, who clothed the naked, may enter."
>   Similarly, those who raised orphans, performed acts of
> *Tzedakah* and *Gemilut Hasadim* (acts of lovingkindness), may
> enter...."

D.P.E.

What Does God Ask of Women?

What does God really want of women? Docs God want something different or special from us? This question is also at the core of Jewish feminism and must be addressed, like Isaiah's question, as one of morality. For generations, women looked on, as study and most ritual practice was reserved for men. Powerful mourning rituals were established, yet women were prevented from saying *Kaddish* for loved ones. The doors to leadership—leadership that could have lifted the people— were closed. Like the prophet Isaiah, contemporary women raise their voices and ask: "Is this the fast that God has chosen?" A fast of the spirit of half of the Jewish people? Does God want to have a glorious and scrupulously maintained tradition that excludes half its members?

Isaiah's question "Is this the fast that God has chosen?" seemed to reject practices like fasting altogether. It called into question, and discredited, much of the religious enterprise. Likewise, feminist critiques of Judaism have led some people to replace religious observance with social activism. This haftarah calls on us to reach a balance.

After Isaiah criticizes the people, he offers hope that if Jews act justly, God will answer their prayers with redemption (58:7–12). Isaiah then abruptly shifts his focus from his original critique of "empty rituals" to stress the importance of keeping the Sabbath (58:13–14). This juxtaposition is striking to commentators. As Plaut writes: "Seeing the prophet's disdain for spurious fasting and praying, the mention of strict Sabbath observance comes as a surprise. Isaiah's focus on the Sabbath sheds new light on his earlier message. The prophet is arguing in favor of powerful ritual, coupled with equally compelling moral action. Isaiah maintains that ethical conduct is the essence of what fasting represents. Actions create "the fast that God has chosen."

This is what God requires of women as well—a Jewish feminism ready for action but steeped in the traditions of Judaism itself. Women should not give up their Jewish ritual practices in the pursuit of social action, no matter how exclusionary those rituals may have been in the past. Isaiah's message is not to repudiate ritual but to prompt everyone to fulfill those principles upon which Jewish customs are built. One of those principles is that both male and female were created in God's image, as we learn from Genesis 1:27 when God brought people into existence: "God created humanity in God's image ... male and female existence God created them." As feminists, we have sometimes undermined our own position by losing touch with its religious core. But it takes a long time to learn what God wants.

When we hear the *haftarah* on Yom Kippur, we can see ourselves as bearers of Isaiah's legacy, asking tough questions and calling for moral actions. Recognizing injustice, we can take upon ourselves the work of repair, *tikkun*. Then, indeed, we can embark upon the "fast that God has chosen."

Rabbi Ilana Berenbaum-Grinblat

The High Priest: An Eager Servant Awaiting Rebirth

The narrative of Jonah's journey thus provides us with a poetic and intuitive model for the *teshuvah* process, in all of its subconscious drama and weightiness. Although we pray with full hearts on Yom Kippur, Jonah's story reminds us that we are more often reluctant and flawed. We are in some respects like the Jonah who resists being awake and alert and who must be led by God's hand into the very belly of God's creative center in order for the dark mysteries of the transformative powers of this day to take effect and cleanse. God's power to assist the human being in this process is humbling. The *teshuvah* process is represented by the potent raging and dark, mysterious, oceanic, womblike, primal forces of God's nature. It is in these waters that our antihero journeys to his own transformation and growth.

But unlike Jonah, who ran from God when God began calling to him, the high priest is the model of one whose being is oriented fully and authentically toward serving the Divine. There is no sleeping nor floating for the high priest. Rather, in preparation for his Yom Kippur journey, he has been purifying himself actively for seven days, and is not permitted to sleep at all the night before, lest his lapse in consciousness cause him to inadvertently become impure in any way. While Jonah's mystical encounter of God happens in the dark, in the waters, in dreamlike liminality, the high priest is on dry land, known terrain, and the high priest's journey is undertaken with the watchful eye of someone for whom the dream world is, at this time, off limits.

In the Holy Temple, the high priest emerges to perform a most holy action, in the innard of innards, the Holy of Holies. He performs a series of actions, including uttering the Divine name—which is done only on this day, at this time—and which enables the Israelites to experience cleansing and rebirth. This place, this innermost point of holiness and intimate connection with the Divine, says Bonna Haberman, represents none other than the sacred female enclosure. She argues that the priest's entering and performing holy actions, which include the appearance of blood as well as words, represents a heterosexual, mystical coupling of the male and female on a cosmic, life-giving level.

Jonah and the high priest stand in sharp contrast to one another in terms of their readiness, their understanding of the nature of their missions, and the ways in which they enact their entrance and time spent in the innermost realms of the female enclosure spaces. Yet both indeed do so, and the coupling of these two very different narratives on this most holy day gives us a particular insight into the complexity of the *teshuvah* process.

The high priest serves as a model for total concentration and devotion to a practice of serving God; a willingness to risk even one's life in order to "get it right" on behalf of self and others. There is an expectation that, when we seek to reach God in such a clearly explicit manner, we will in some way make that connection point that provides for us the seeds of our regeneration.

Rabbi Myriam Klotz

Just When…. An Introduction in Poetry, to the Haftarah of Yom Kippur Morning

If you put yourself out for the hungry and relieve the
    wretched
then shall your light shine in the darkness and your gloom at
    noonday.
Isaiah
Just when your stomach
reminds you that
you're hungry,
and just when you scale

the walls of piety,
certain that your fast will make
you, oh so holy,
and just when the quiet hours
spent in prayer
begin to lull you into lethargy
and your eyes begin to close
no matter who the Rabbi is,
Isaiah enters the room
and preaches holy terror.
Standing there as he stood
on the steps leading
to the Temple Mount,
railing at the fat cats
and the pampered mamas,
screaming obscenities that
no one understands
or wants to hear,
trying to teach
what can't be taught.
"What's it all about,"
he says, somewhat impatiently,
"This fast of yours?"
"These pious flagellations?"
"Do you think that's
what God really wants?"
And then he tells them
what he needs to tell them:
"To feed the hungry,
to house the homeless,
to free those in bondage,
to clothe the naked,
to embrace the despised
to reject the obscene
and to destroy complacency.
That's what God wants—
nothing more and nothing less."
And I,

listening plaintively,
wonder where he has gone,
this strange man
with the gleam in his eye,
whose words shout determination.
Did I see him
standing on a street corner
screaming certain destruction?
Did I hear him on the radio
telling us the truth?
Did I stand by him
in the soup kitchen,
at the shelter,
in the clinic?
Did I read him
on the editorial page
indignant and insightful?
No, its here that I see him
in my hands as they repair
In my words which speak
comfort to the depressed
In my heart that is determined
to right every wrong
In my eyes that can't look away
from the suffering.
In my soul that is broken
and in pain.
Just when it seems so dark
I hear his call, and know
I must answer his challenge.

Rabbi Mark B. Greenspan

Shalom Shalom La-rahok Ve-la-karov

Judaism as a religion preaches as one of its ultimate ideals the idea of religious responsibility. Individuals are not supposed to avoid responsibility for their actions. There must be a realization that actions bear consequences. This being said, since human beings are not perfect, there must be a religious mechanism for dealing with this frailty. This dilemma and the requisite solution seem to be found in the opening verses of the haftarah for the morning of Yom Kippur: "For I will not always contend, I will not be angry forever; Nay, I who make spirits flag also create the breath of life. For their sinful greed I [God] was angry; I struck them and turned away in My wrath. Though stubborn, they follow the way of their hearts, I note how they fare and will heal them: I will guide them and mete out solace to them and to the mourners among them heartening, comforting words: It shall be well, well with the far and the near—said the Lord—and I will heal them" (Isaiah 57:16–19).

This obscure passage contains a crucial message. While initially God is intent on punishing evildoers, He realizes that the world cannot withstand absolute justice, as Rashi points out: "If I [God] bring afflictions upon man, he [man] will not exist for long." God's main thrust is rather to heal people and to bring them comfort. What is the significance of God's healing? Rashi explains: "When a person's spirit comes before God and becomes enveloped by God's spirit, that person will have the strength to admit to his or her wrong-doings and set these wrongs aside. Then there will be no reason for God to contend with him or her" (Adapted from Rashi).

The results of this process can be seen in the following midrash: "And so Isaiah prophesied: 'Peace. Peace be to the one who is far and to the one who is near,' said the Lord, 'And I will heal him.' (Isaiah 57:19). And who is the one who is far? The person who has distanced himself [from God]. But [if that is the meaning of the one who is far] what healing does the one who is close need? But rather who are we talking about in this passage? It is the wicked person who has repented and consequentially becomes close to God. The verse talks about just such a person and should be read to mean: 'Peace, peace to the one who was far and became close to God ... [God will heal him]'" (adapted from Pesikta Rabati Parshah 44).

God has created the opportunity for people to draw closer to Him, whether they are already close to God or whether they are far away from God because of their waywardness. The message of Yom Kippur is that if a person yearns to be closer to God, then God will be available to assist him.

Rabbi Mordechai Silverstein

The Ritual of the Goats

Our Torah reading deals with a strange ritual, the casting of lots to choose the goat sent out to the wilderness symbolically bearing our sins; the so-called scapegoat. This is a ritual we no longer observe because that aspect of Judaism has changed significantly. But the concept and importance of rituals remains a constant. Jews today want to adopt more rituals.

Our Torah reading refers to this day, Yom Kippur, as Shabbat Shabbaton, a Sabbath of Sabbaths. The Shabbat is itself one of the most significant rituals in our tradition. In our Haftarah, the prophet Isaiah again deals with the issue of rituals, making the point that they must be understood for what they mean, not be simply rote behaviors. In his book, *Why Be Jewish?*, Rabbi David Wolpe deals with this subject most eloquently. I want to share a passage with you dealing with Shabbat and the subject of rituals in general.

"Jewish ritual is the discipline of pause and focus. Perhaps the premier Jewish ritual, the Sabbath, forces one to pause, put down the distractions of life, and pay attention anew to the sounds of the soul and to God's place in our lives.

"The Sabbath is often called a day of rest, but it is equally a day of refocus. During the week we hear the sounds of the world changing and moving. The predominant rule of the Sabbath is to live in harmony with what is, not to seek change; this day is for renewal, not transformation. The Sabbath asks us not to be creative but restorative; not to give out but to take in; to sanctify time and recall our souls to their Source.

"That is why so many of the seemingly restrictive rules of the Sabbath, such as a prohibition on spending money, are truly liberating. There is an Eastern poem that speaks about a violin string. Lying untouched on a table, the poet writes, the string is free. But it is not free to do what a violin string is supposed to do: to produce music. Only when it is strung and taut on the bow can it truly be free to be a violin string and offer its beautiful sounds. Discipline is critical for freedom. At certain times, ritual pares our lives to the core, so that we can hear and produce our true music."

Rabbi Richard Plavin

T'SHUVAH, T'FILLAH, T'ZEDAKKAH
(REPENTANCE, PRAYER AND ACTS OF RIGHTEOUNESS)

Tefillah or "prayer" is the living heart of Jewish faith, the daily out-pouring of the soul before God. This flow of human emotion may come in the form of joyous exultation or desperate plea. Both are part of the complex and universal phenomenon of prayer. Prayer expresses itself directly in the language the heart knows best. Sometimes it is given expression in words spoken aloud, while at other times prayer is beyond words, the speechless call of the innermost self.

RABBI ARTHUR GREEN, *THESE ARE THE WORDS*

Maimonides' Eight Degrees of Charity

There are eight degrees in the giving of charity, one higher than the other:

One who gives grudgingly, reluctantly, or with regret.

One who gives less than he should, but gives graciously.

One who gives what he should, but only after he is asked.

One who gives before he is asked.

One who gives without knowing to whom he gives, although the recipient knows the identity of the donor.

One who gives without making his identity known.

One who gives without knowing to whom he gives, neither does the recipient know from whom he receives.

He who helps a fellowman to support himself by a gift, or a loan, or by finding employment for him, thus helping him to become self-supporting.

Maimonides

I Am Canceling My Word and Fulfilling Yours— The Thirteen Divine Attributes

The version of the Thirteen Divine Attributes (*Shlosh Esray Midot*) in the *mahzor* is radically different than the biblical version. The rabbis cut the verse in half when quoting it in the High Holiday liturgy, and totally reverse its meaning. In the Torah it states that God will punish the children for the sins of their parents. Obviously feeling uncomfortable with this outdated theology, the rabbis cut off the biblical verse just before the word "no" when it says that God will not forgive the next generation.

The following *midrash* clarifies why the rabbis chose to do this, and justify it by putting the change in the mouth of God instead of their own voice:

When the Blessed Holy One said to Moshe:

"… visiting the iniquity of the parents upon the children" (Exodus 20:5), Moshe said:

Many are the wicked who have begotten righteous children; shall they take the consequences of their parents' iniquities?

Terah served images, and Abraham's son was righteous, the same with Hezekiah who was righteous, and Ahaz his father wicked, the same with Josiah who was righteous, and Amon his father wicked. Is it right then that the righteous be struck down for the iniquity of the parents?

The Blessed Holy One said:

"By your life, I am voiding my words and fulfilling yours. As it is said: 'The parents shall not be put to death for the children, neither shall the children be put to death for the parents' (Deut. 24:16). And, by your life, I am writing them down in your name, as it is said: 'According to that which is written in the Book of the Law of Moshe' (II Kings 14: 6)."

Midrash, Bemidbar Rabbah 19:33

U-Teshuvah ...

The Baal Shem Tov taught that in the heavenly court there is no one who can judge you for what you have done in your life on earth. So this is what they do: They show you someone's life—all the achievements and all the failures, all the right decisions and all the wrongdoings—and then they ask you, "So what should we do with this somebody?" And you give your verdict. Which they accept. And then they tell you that this somebody was you. Of course, those who tend to judge others favorably have a decided advantage.

Better get in the habit now.

Rabbi Tzvi Freeman

Fund-Raising Story

Tzedakah (righteousness, the moral obligation to help the poor) has always been the hallmark of the Jewish People. To illustrate this ancient, noble ideal, the late Rabbi Pinchas Peli of Jerusalem tells the following story. In an army morning roll call, each recruit was to answer to the shout of his name. The corporal called out "Kelly," and "Here" was the response. "Armstrong." "Here." Next came Private Cohen's turn. "Cohen." Being habituated to charity appeals so often in his life, Private Cohen yelled out "Twenty-five dollars."

The Rabbis in the Talmud (Bava Metzia 71a) teach that there are priorities in giving *tzedakah*. A Jew must give to those of his/her own community before those of another. In other words, in a series of concentric circles, givers of *tzedakah* must contribute to those closest to them (immediate family, kin, other Jews, the community), and only after these primary obligations are met do we give to those farther away in relationship and in place.

According to the Talmud, those of us who give generously to many causes must consider their own synagogue before giving to broader and more universal causes.

Rabbi Dov Peretz Elkins

Kedoshim Tih'yu—Be Holy!

(For those who read Leviticus 19 as Mincha Torah reading):

"It is striking that [Rudolph] Otto, a pious Lutheran, made no mention of this chapter of Leviticus in his book [*The Idea of the Holy*]. He spoke only of holiness as an emotional experience, not of *kedushah* as aspiration and task to be approached through a disciplined life. In his zeal to give religion a unique character, Otto reduced the ethical component of holiness to a mere 'extra.' This is not the Jewish view of the subject, as is plain from the text before us, and also from the recurrent declarations in our prayers and benedictions that God 'sanctifies us through His commandments.' In Judaism, religion and ethics, though not identical, are inseparable....

"The idea of holiness implies that what we do and what we make of our lives matters not only to us as individuals, not only to society, but to the entire cosmos. A divine purpose runs through all existence. We can ally ourselves to it or oppose it—or, perhaps, worse, we can ignore it."

Rabbi Bernard J. Bamberger

Atonement and Repentance

Rabbi Eleazar Mattiah ben Heresh went to call upon Rabbi Eleazar Hakkappar at Laodicea, to ask him about the four categories of atonement. And he asked him: "Have you heard what Rabbi Ishmael used to teach in regard to the four categories of atonement?"

"I have heard," Rabbi Eleazar replied, "but they are three, and along with each of these there must be repentance.

"Now how is all this to be understood?

"If a man transgressed a positive commandment and repented, he is forgiven on the spot, before he has so much as much as stirred from his place. Of such it is said, 'Return, ye backsliding children (Jeremiah 3:22).'"

"If a man transgressed a negative commandment and repented, repentance suspends the sentence and Yom Kippur atones. Of such it is said, 'For on this day shall atonement be made for you (Leviticus 16.30).'"

"If a man transgressed commandments punishable by extirpation or by death from the courts and repented, repentance and the Day of Atonement suspend the sentence, and his sufferings during the remaining days of the year atone. And of such is said, 'Then will I visit their transgression with the rod (Psalms 89.33).'"

"But when one profanes the name of heaven, there is no power either in repentance to suspend his sentence or in sufferings to cleanse him of his sins or in the Day of Atonement to atone. Rather, repentance and sufferings suspend the sentence, and death, along with these, cleanses him of his sins. And of such it is said, 'Surely this iniquity shall not be expiated by you until you die (Isaiah 22.14).'"

Avot d'Rabbi Natan 29

Like a Fading Flower, a Passing Shadow, a Fugitive Cloud and a Vanishing Dream

[In] the PBS retrospective on the life and work of Leonard Bernstein, I found it fascinating, particularly when he confronts members of the Vienna Philharmonic Orchestra as they rehearse a symphony by Gustav Mahler. Mahler had converted to Christianity so he could be appointed conductor of the Vienna Opera. But in the eyes of musical Vienna, he remained an outsider; his music was too "Semitic." The orchestra's hostility emerged in their playing of his score.

Abruptly, Bernstein stops the rehearsal and speaks to the players, in German: "You've got all of the notes. But what's missing is Mahler. Mahler is nowhere to be found in your playing."

Much of what we do over Rosh Hashanah is playing the notes: going to the synagogue, reciting the prayers, dipping an apple in honey, joining with our families. Notes are important; without the notes, there is no symphony. But just as the symphony is more than the notes, Rosh Hashanah is more than the synagogue, the prayers and the honey. It is a reminder that our lives are fragile. We are like a fading flower, a passing shadow, a fugitive cloud and a vanishing dream, the prayer says. It is a reminder that we are responsible for the lives we lead, and that the power to shape our lives is in our own hands.

Dr. Neil Gillman

U-teshuvah—How to Cleanse Ourselves

A Hasidic tale tells of a conversation between a Rabbi and a Soap Maker.

The Soap Maker was troubled by a theological conundrum.

"Rabbi," he asked, puzzled, "why is it that we have been studying our sacred Torah for thousands of years? It teaches us values of truth, kindness, compassion and love. Yet, if we look at the world, all we see is lies, meanness, apathy and violence. Why has not the Torah succeeded in helping us do *teshuvah*—changing our lives for the better?"

As the two were strolling along the street they came upon a young boy, dirty and grimy from head to foot.

Said the Rabbi to the Soap Maker: "What good is the soap you make? It has been around for years and years, and yet look at this dirty little boy. Why hasn't your soap helped to make little boys more clean and neat?"

The Soap Maker replied: "Well, soap is no good unless you use it!"

"Aha!" replied the Rabbi. "So it is with the Torah. Unless we apply its teaching to our daily lives, and cleanse our immoral souls with its moral values, it is of no use."

The *U-Netaneh Tokef* prayer teaches us that three things will help us change and purify our lives: *Teshuvah, Tefillah, u-Tzedakah*. However, they are useless unless we take them seriously, and put them into practice in our daily lives.

Hasidic tale

U-Tefilah ... Can Prayer Heal?

I'm pleased to see that this growing body of research has captured the attention of the medical community. In the mid-1990s, only three US medical schools taught courses on religious and spiritual issues; today, more than 60 (about half of medical schools) offer such courses. Duke University has its own Center for the Study of Religion/Spirituality and Health, and the University of Minnesota's Center for Spirituality and Healing just opened a Mind Body Spirit Clinic.

Here at the University of Arizona's Program in Integrative Medicine, we encourage the physicians in our fellowship program to explore spiritual practices in their own lives and train them to take a spiritual inventory of patients seen at our clinic. An inventory typically begins with an open-ended question such as, "What are the sources of strength in your life?' When patients express strong religious beliefs, we might ask if they would be interested in talking with a clergy member or pastoral counselor about any issues arising from their medical condition. For nonreligious patients, we might ask if they would be open to trying spiritual practices such as breathwork or meditation.

Some physicians may be hesitant to discuss spiritual issues with patients, because of a lack of training or because they consider it inappropriate to their role as a physician. If you feel comfortable broaching the subject with your doctor, you might start with a general question such as, "Do you think that spiritual practice could influence my health?" As more medical schools cover the topic of spirituality and health, I expect that physicians may become increasingly open to discussing these issues, and that the result will be more satisfying partnerships between patients and doctors.

Dr. Andrew Weil

How Prayer Leads to Morality

Does prayer produce any practical moral results? I believe that it does. It is one of the consequences of our involvement with God in prayer that we come to hunger and thirst after righteousness. How else can we return the love with which we are loved? How else can we understand the meaning of the divine concern that makes us human, except by joyously translating our responding love not into merely sentimental declarations, but into specific acts of justice, decency and kindness? How else can we deal with the whole truth about ourselves, including the nasty part, except by struggling to overcome everything in ourselves and in our environment that attacks our precious God-given humanity?

In prayer, if nowhere else, we express our loyalty to the Utmost and thus achieve a clearer knowledge of our duty. When God's love becomes God's commandment, moral consequences *do* follow—not easily, not without struggle and not without the constant need for revision and rethinking, *but they follow*. And they follow not merely as *knowledge,* as the technical ability to make ethical judgments about theoretical situations and to say what is right and wrong. They follow as the courage to be and to *do* what our human nature with its divine dimension requires. The creative effort of prayer moves us from the *knowledge* of the good to the deed which is good.

Rabbi Dudley Weinberg

Teshuvah: A New Factor in the Divine Relationship

A new factor enters into the complex God-human relationship—namely, the power of *teshuvah,* or repentance, specifically what may be called preemptive repentance, repentance that preempts punishment. That kind of repentance is unknown in the Torah. There, repentance can emerge only after punishment; only then is God prepared to be reconciled with the people who have sinned. Deuteronomy 30:1–6 reflects that stage in the development of the doctrine of repentance. In prophetic literature, repentance has the power to cancel out the punishment before it takes place.

Take the case of Jonah. Jonah is the only successful prophet in the Bible. After many adventures, he eventually does go to Nineveh and preaches a brief sermon, and the entire land, from the king down to the beasts, fasts and mourns. The king orders that everyone should turn back from their evil ways: "Who knows but that God may turn and relent ... so that we do not perish" (3:8–9). Whereupon, "God saw ... how they were turning back from their evil ways and God renounced the punishment He had planned to bring upon them and did not carry it out" (3:10).

We have now gone well beyond Moses' arguments with God. God's power is not automatic or unbridled; it is, rather, an expression of God's will. God can choose how and when to use that power. *Teshuvah* is God's gift to us, a singular opportunity to reverse God's power from anger to compassion. It also teaches that, ultimately, it is human beings who have the power to determine how God will use that power. That theme is also invoked throughout the liturgy of the High Holidays. We pray that God's compassion should "conquer" God's anger. Note the militaristic term "conquer"; it indicates a power struggle within God. This dynamic interaction between God's power and human power is the core of the prophetic reading of history. Sometimes, God's power to punish bows before the human power to effect a change in God's plan.

Dr. Neil Gillman

Homecoming and *Teshuvah*

Coming home is *teshuvah*, but in the fullest sense of that rich term. This word for "turning" or "returning" means much more than "repentance," as it is often translated. *Teshuvah* is the universal process of return. All things turn toward their center, as fully and as naturally as plants grow in the direction of light, as roots reach toward their source of water. The same universal will that is manifest in the evolution of life, ever striving toward "higher" forms of consciousness, is present in the desire of all things to turn inward and to show that they are tied to their single source. The world that flows forth from the One seeks to return to the One. Y-H-W-H is manifest throughout being, we recall, only to attest anew in each moment to the oneness of all that is. Each individual being contains within it the presence of all being, the fullness of Y-H-W-H. From the moment that "separate" reality exists, its heart is filled with a longing to re-create the primal state of oneness, to be reunited with the source of all life.

This universal longing is marked in human consciousness by the desire to "return" to God. The human act of contrition that we call *teshuvah* shows this universal tendency as it is manifest in our own lives. We seek to overcome barriers that keep us from the One, to break down the walls, however thin or even illusory, from one point of view, that separate us from our own truest self. Our desire to return home is the manifestation in the human spirit of the most universal and basic longing, one far more ancient than the individual who feels its pull or the various cultural forms in which it is seen.

All *teshuvah*, according to the kabbalists, is ultimately *teshuvah* to *binah*, to the first *heh* of the divine name. This aspect of the Divine represents God as cosmic womb, as great mother of the universe. It is our distance from that ever-nourishing and sustaining root that defines our exile. But it is not only we who are in exile. *Shekhinah* herself, the second *heh* of Y-H-W-H and mother of the lower worlds, has gone into exile with her children. The one who returns is seen both as Israel, the king's lost son, and as exiled *Shekhinah*, the second *heh* that is cut off in exile from the other three letters of God's name. She is the lost princess, whose return to the palace is the final redemption. Thus, our dream language of redemption is that of mother and daughter, as well as that of father and son. In *teshuvah* we are wayward sons, returning to our royal father; we are also sparks of *Shekhinah*-light, restored to our mother's bosom.

Rabbi Arthur Green

U'netaneh Tokef

On Rosh Hashanah it is written, and on Yom Kippur it is sealed. How many will die and how many will be born? Who at a ripe old age and who before their time? Who by fire and who by water? Who by sword and who by beast?

It hurts so much to live in the face of death that even on Yom Kippur, even when we rehearse our own death by fasting and wearing shrouds and non-leather shoes, we want "*u-netaneh tokef*" to be a metaphor. We want the inevitable question of who was here last year that isn't here now and who is here this year that won't be here next year to be a poem, or a parable. It's not. It's a wake-up call, it's a shofar blast of warning. No one knows when the gates will close forever so while we are inside them we had better love passionately, fight passionately, learn passionately, live passionately. "*U-netaneh tokef kedushat hayom, ki hu norah v'ayom*: Let us declare the holiness of this day, because it contains an awful truth."

Awe-full. I'm filled with awe every day now. Every sunrise, every sunset. I say *"shehecheyanu"* a lot now: who has kept us alive, and sustained us, and helped us to reach this day. This day. *"U-netaneh tokef kedushat hayom,"* let us declare the holiness of this day, because it is the only day we have for sure. I love with urgency now. I fight with urgency now. I live with urgency now. I'm not waiting to have that anniversary party, I'm taking the kids to Disneyland when they are too young, I'm going to that family Bar Mitzvah in New York, I'm eating another chocolate.

Rabbi Elyse Goldstein

Teshuvah Is Not Repentance, *Tefillah* Is Not Prayer, and *Tzedakah* Is Not Charity

"Repentance" in Hebrew is not *teshuvah* but *haratah*. Not only are these two terms not synonymous—they are opposites.

Haratah implies remorse or a feeling of guilt about the past and an intention to behave in a completely new way in the future. The person decides to become "a new man." But *teshuvah* means "returning" to the old, to one's original nature. Underlying the concept of *teshuvah* is the fact that the Jew is, in essence, good. Desires or temptations may deflect him temporarily from being himself, being true to his essence. But the bad that he does is not part of, nor does it affect, his real nature. *Teshuvah* is a return to the self. While repentance involves dismissing the past and starting anew, *teshuvah* means going back to one's roots in God and exposing them as one's true character.

For this reason, while the righteous have no need to repent, and the wicked may be unable to, both may do *teshuvah*. The righteous, though they have never sinned, have constantly to strive to return to their innermost. And the wicked, however distant they are from God, can always return, for *teshuvah* does not involve creating anything new, only rediscovering the good that was always within them.

"Prayer" in Hebrew is not *tefillah* but *bakashah*. And again these terms are opposite. *Bakashah* means to pray, request, beseech. But *tefillah* means, to attach oneself.

In *bakashah* the person asks God to provide him, from above, with what he lacks. Therefore when he is not in need of anything, or feels no desire for a gift from above, *bakashah* becomes redundant. But in *tefillah* the person seeks to attach himself to God. It is a movement from below, from man, reaching towards God. And this is something appropriate to everyone and at every time.

The Jewish soul has a bond with God. But it also inhabits a body, whose preoccupation with the material world may attenuate that bond. So it has constantly to be strengthened and renewed. This is the function of *Tefillah*. And it is necessary for every Jew. For while there may be those who do not lack anything and thus have nothing to request of God, there is no one who does not need to attach himself to the source of all life.

The Hebrew for "charity" is not *tzedakah* but *hesed*. And again these two words have opposite meanings. *Hesed,* charity, implies that the recipient has no right to the gift and that the donor is under no obligation to give it. He gives it gratuitously, from the heart. His act is a virtue rather than a duty.

On the other hand, *tzedakah* means righteousness or justice. The implication is that the donor gives because it is his duty. For, firstly, everything in the world belongs ultimately to God. A man's possessions are not his by right. Rather, they are entrusted to him by God, and one of the conditions of that trust is that he should give to those who are in need. Secondly, a man has a duty to act toward others as he asks God to act toward him. And as we ask God for His blessings, though He owes us nothing and is under no obligation, so we are bound in justice to give to those who ask us, even though we are in no way in their debt. In this way, we are rewarded: measure for measure. Because we give freely, God gives freely to us.

This applies in particular to the *tzedakah* which is given to support the institutions of Torah learning. For everyone who is educated in these institutions is a future foundation of a house in Israel, and a future guide to the coming generation. This will be the product of his *Tzedakah*—and his act is the measure of his reward.

These are the three paths which lead to a year "written and sealed" for good. By returning to one's innermost self *(teshuvah)*, by attaching oneself to God *(tefillah)*, and by distributing one's possessions with righteousness *(tzedakah)*, one turns the promise of Rosh Hashanah into the abundant fulfillment of Yom Kippur: a year of sweetness and plenty.

Based on talks from *Torah Studies* by the Lubavitcher Rebbe, adapted by Rabbi Jonathan Sacks

Teshuvah, Tefilah and *Zedakah*—Judaism Is a Religion of Action More Than Thought

While philosophy and theology are not alien to Judaism, our religion is more oriented toward action and deeds than to abstract speculation. Of the two major works by Moses Maimonides, the legal text of the *Mishneh Torah* had greater status than his philosophical collection, *Guide to the Perplexed*.

Rabbi David Wolpe highlights this difference with a story about the great Catholic theologian Thomas Aquinas, who spent a good part of his life writing his *Summa Theologica*. When asked why he abandoned the work in old age, he related the following dream:

An angel was emptying the ocean with a teaspoon. Aquinas asked what he was doing. The angel replied: Theology.

As Jews we often spend time trying to empty the ocean of theology with a spoon, but in the *U'Netaneh Tokef* we focus on Judaism's main task: the achievements of *Tefila, Teshuvah* and *Tzedakah*—prayer, changing our behavior, and doing acts of kindness.

D.P.E.

... U-tzedakah—Make Your Home a Wellspring of Charity

The late Lubavitcher Rebbe, Menachem Schneerson, wrote:

"A container is defined by its contents. A pitcher of water is water. A crate of apples is apples. A house, too, is defined by what it contains.

"Fill your house with books of Torah, and your house becomes a Torah. Affix charity boxes to its walls, and your house becomes a wellspring of charity. Bring those who need a warm home to your table, and your house becomes a lamp in the darkness."

Rabbi Tzvi Freeman

Tzedakah: How Important a Value for Us?

There is no word for chemist or physicist in the Talmud, yet why are we so impressed by them? If, at a get-together, a guest in our house says he is doing critical research in sub-atomic particles, or cracking through the far reaches of DNA behavior, why is there such admiration for this person?

(I am speaking, of course, of good Jewish men and women.)

But let us suppose this Jew says, "I am a celebrator of mitzvahs" or "my occupation is *ziesskeit,* human sweetness, and I study the way it plays itself out among Jews ... " What would the reaction be?

Surprise, of course.

A little, "A *meshuggener*—must be an artist."

Or, unable to suppress our urge to think, we blurt out, *"Fun dos macht men a leben?*—This you call a living?"

We ask our children about their grades in history and literature, though rarely do we enquire about "excellence in *Tzedakah* and *rach moniss,*" generosity and uniquely Jewish loving and giving.

Danny Siegel

Tzedakah Lines in Our Personal Budgets

Several people were asked the question: "What is the most important thing we can do to ensure Jewish survival in America?" by *Hadassah Magazine.* The following answer was given by Rabbi Richard J. Israel, Director of the Rabbinic Program for the College Campus of the Reconstructionist Rabbinical College: "I would give priority to personal change over institutional change and five things, not one. There are foods we should and should not eat. We must organize our lives so they are in touch with the Jewish calendar, Shabbat and holidays. We must actively attach ourselves to Jewish community here and in Israel. We must have *tzedakah* lines in our personal budgets. We must engage in continuing Jewish learning. Without individual change, structural change won't help. With it structural change becomes possible...." These suggestions by Rabbi Israel, as he points out, are personal rather than institutional changes. The High Holy Day period is about personal change. The three things demanded of us in the *U'Ne-taneh Tokef* prayer are all *personal* changes—*Teshuva, Tefilah, Tzedakah.*

Rabbi Dov Peretz Elkins

Zedakah: **Money, Money, Money**

Rabbi Marc Angel tells a story about Satan who came before God one Yom Kippur and accused the Jews of uttering meaningless prayers.

The angel suggested to God that the Almighty take all the prayers of the Jews and dump them into a machine and grind them out. When you do that, said Satan, you will see what their prayers really consist of. God complied and ground all the Jews' prayers from all over the world into a giant machine. Out of the machine came the words: "Money, money, money."

See, said Satan, I was right!, with a big smile on his face.

A kind angel then approached God and suggested that the Almighty put the prayers through the same machine a second time, asking for more detailed clarification.

God agreed and this time the prayers came out in these words: Money for schools, money for synagogues, money for the poor and oppressed, money for hospitals, money for medical research, money for arts and culture, money for university endowment funds, money for Israel, money for a just society, etc., etc., etc.

The kind angel sat quietly, and rested his case.

D.P.E.

Penitence

Where penitents stand, the wholly righteous cannot stand.
—BABYLONIAN TALMUD, BERACHOT 34B

The Jewish tradition has always accorded the highest of status to those who have turned their lives around through *teshuvah*, repentance. They are considered even more pious than the ones who had never sinned. As the noted Talmudist Rabbi Adin Steinsaltz puts it, "The penitent has at his disposal not only the forces of good in his soul and in his world, but also those of evil, which he transforms into essences of holiness." Beyond the person, *teshuvah* is seen as an act of cosmic significance. This is perhaps the essential message of *Shabbat Shuvah*, the Sabbath of Return, between Rosh Hashanah and Yom Kippur. You can always return; the power to do so is in your hands.

Recovery gives us a chance to transform bad into good, suffering into love. It may be much more difficult to get back on track than to have been rolling smoothly all along, but it is certainly is a more memorable ride. Sometimes you have to walk down into the valley to get to the mountaintop. Perhaps, for us, there was no other way.

For Growth and Renewal: Is there something that you have been meaning to fix for a while, but you just haven't gotten around to it? Fix something that is broken. Remember, it's possible to repair.

Rabbi Kerry M. Olitzky

The Chance to Repent

If a person says, "I will sin and repent, and sin again and repent," then that person will be given no chance to repent. If he or she says, "I will sin and Yom Kippur will effect atonement," then the Day of Atonement effects no atonement. For transgressions that are between humans and God, Yom Kippur effects atonement, but for transgressions that are between fellow people, the Day of Atonement effects atonement only if a person has appeased the one wronged. Thus did R. Eleazar b. Azariah teach: "*From all your sins shall ye be clean before God* (Leviticus 16:30). This means for transgressions that are between people and God, Yom Kippur effects atonement; but for transgressions that are between fellow people, the Day of Atonement effects atonement only if a person has appeased the one wronged." R. Akibah said: "Blessed are you, O Israel! Before whom are you made clean and who makes you clean? Your Parent in heaven; as it is written, And I will sprinkle clean water upon you and you shall be clean (Ezekiel 36:25)."

Mishnah Yoma 8:9

Remaking Yourself

The Holy One, blessed be God, said to Israel: "Remake yourselves by repentance during the ten days between New Year's Day and Yom Kippur, and on the Day of Atonement I will hold you guiltless, regarding you as a newly made creature."

Pesikta Rabbati 40:5

... *U-tzedakah*—There Is a Healing Power in Doing Good

Many years ago, when I was visiting my grandmother in her nursing home, I encountered a very elderly, gaunt woman putting pennies in a *pushke* [box for charity] she kept on the table by her bed. She told me that the *pushke* contained the coins she found between sofa cushions or on the floor, and that she considered them to be God's way of enabling her to "make her life count by helping others." Saving this money and making modest gifts to various charities bolstered her sense of personal esteem and purpose. Her life had worth, *she* still had worth, so long as she could contribute to improving the lives of others.

I also remember a man I met one autumn night when we were both delivering food and clothing to homeless people scattered around New York City. Though his body appeared frail, there was a fire burning in his eyes. In the midst of our early-morning deliveries, I learned that my companion had been diagnosed with a particularly malevolent form of cancer. Rather than stay at home where it was warm and dry, he kept his appointment with his homeless friends each month because "as long as I can get out to help somebody else, I can't be that sick." As well, he confided, it simply made him "feel good" to express kindness this way. There is a healing power in doing good.

Rabbi Steven M. Rosman

U'*Tzedakah*—God Makes Opportunities for Redemption

My colleague Rabbi Jeremy Kalmanofsky tells the story of sitting in a New York subway, with the holy mystical book of the Zohar in his hand, studying away until his stop arrived. As the subway rolled along, he reached the following passage:

"This is the way of the Blessed Holy One: Why does God give wealth to a person? Only to feed the poor and to do mitzvot" (Midrash HaNe'elam 1.121d).

Rabbi Kalmanofsky continues: "At *that very moment* a poor person asked me for *tzedakah. Emes,* my hand to God, it happened exactly like that. Blessed is the One who gave me merit to fulfill that mitzvah."

Maybe God provides such opportunities to help us pass the big test at Yom Kippur time.

D.P.E.

Acts of Lovingkindness

Once, as Rabbi Yochanan ben Zakkai was leaving Jerusalem with Rabbi Joshua, they beheld the ruins of the Temple. "Woe unto us!" Rabbi Joshua cried, "that this, the place where Israel atoned for its sins, is destroyed!" "My son," Rabbi Yochanan said to him, "do not be upset; we have another atonement as effective as this. And what is it? It is acts of loving-kindness, as it is written, 'For I desire mercy and not sacrifice'" (Hosea 6:6).

For thus we find concerning Daniel, that he was engaged in acts of lovingkindness. Now, what were the acts of lovingkindness in which Daniel was engaged? Can one say that he offered animal sacrifices in Babylon? What then were the acts of lovingkindness that he did? He used to outfit the bride and rejoice with her, accompany the dead, give money to the poor and pray three times a day, and his prayer was received with favor.

Avot d'Rabbi Natan 4

U'Tzedakah

A cartman's horse suddenly stumbled and fell dead. To the cartman, this was a catastrophe. He depended on his horse for his livelihood. A crowd gathered, observed the poor man's predicament, shook their heads sympathetically, mumbling, "Too bad, too bad."

A rabbi amongst the observers took out a paper bag, placed ten dollars in it, and said, "Friends, I'm sorry for this man, ten dollars worth. How sorry are you?"

When the crowd followed suit, they moved from observers to doers, from people with feelings to givers of *Tzedakah*.

Adapted from Rabbi Geoffrey J. Haber

Ve-tiftah et Sefer Ha-Zikhronot—You Record and Seal, Count and Measure....

An elderly carpenter was ready to retire. He told his employer/contractor of his plans to leave the house-building business and live a more leisurely life with his wife, enjoying his extended family. He would miss the paycheck, but he needed to retire. They could get by.

The contractor was sorry to see his good worker go and asked if he could build just one more house as a personal favor. The carpenter said yes, but in time it was easy to see that his heart was not in his work. He resorted to shoddy workmanship and used inferior materials. It was an unfortunate way to end his career. When the carpenter finished his work and the builder came to inspect the house, the contractor handed the front-door key to the carpenter. "This is your house," he said, "my gift to you."

What a shock! What a shame! If he had only known he was building his own house, he would have done it all so differently. Now he had to live in the home he had built none too well.

So it is with us. We build our lives in a distracted way, reacting rather than acting, willing to put up less than the best. At important points we do not give the job our best effort. Then with a shock we look at the situation we have created and find that we are now living in the house we have built. If we had only realized, we would have done it differently.

Think of yourself as the carpenter. Think about your house. Each day you hammer a nail, place a board, or erect a wall. Build wisely. It is the only life you will ever build. Even if you live it for only one day more, that day deserves to be lived graciously and with dignity. The plaque on the wall says, "Life is a do-it-yourself project."

Who could say it more clearly? Your life today is the result of your attitudes and choices in the past. Your life tomorrow will be the result of your attitudes and the choices you make today.

Author Unknown

Repentance, Prayer and *Tzedakah*

The sainted Reb Levi Yitzhak was very upset a few days prior to Rosh Hashanah because he had received word from the revered Reb Boruch'l of Mezritch that things were in a bad way. That a terrible calamity was about to strike the people of Israel, and that the only one who could avert the evil decree was Reb Levi Yitzhak himself. What a terrible burden for him to bear on his shoulders!

Reb Levi Yitzhak had to appear before the Heavenly Tribunal and argue against Satan so that a year of pain and evil would not be decreed against the household of Israel.

During *Selihot* time the great *Zaddik* prepared his heart and soul in the most diligent way. He did repentance, he prayed, he studied. But when the Saturday night before Rosh Hashanah arrived, and it was time to chant the *Selihot* prayers, he could not capture the proper spirit and mood of the Penitential Season. The words of his prayers were without the breath of life, a body without a soul. The syllables fell off of his lips as cold as bitter winter. The words flew about in the air, but did not have the vigor and zest to ascend to Heaven and intercede before the Eternal Judge.

Reb Levi Yitzhak was plagued by fear and trembling. The fate of all the Children of the Covenant, even women and little children, was placed in his hands—and he was failing his mission! What to do?!

At this crucial juncture in the history of Israel, Reb Levi Yitzhak employed his three trusted, tried and true methods to avert the impending doom.

First, he spoke *Sanegoria*—he argued with God, defending Israel, and demanding justice in Abraham-like fashion, from the Judge of the whole earth. He called God to task, as it were, for permitting pain and suffering and destruction to descend upon his people.

These were his words at that *Selihot* service: *Ribono shel olam*: Lord of the Universe: Act at least as any ordinary Jew would act! A plain, simple, untutored Jew, if his *tefillin* would fall on the ground, what would he do? Well, of course, he would bend over, with fear and trembling, pick up the sack of holy *tefillin,* dust them off carefully, and lovingly plant a kiss upon them. But you, dear God, you have cast down to the earth your *tefillin,* your chosen people Israel. For two thousand years you have seen them grovel in the dust and mire of *Galut,* of Exile, and you haven't yet bent down to pick them up.

Tatenyu, Guttenyu—is it too much to ask that you act like a plain, ordinary Jew?

Then Reb Levi Yitzhak saw the words climb toward the sky to the very gates of Heaven. But, alas, the gates of Heaven remained locked.

So the Saint of Berditchev turned to his second tried and true technique in averting such crises. This time, *Tefilah,* Prayer! Perhaps the heart-felt words from the mouth of a *Baal Teshuvah*—one who repented in all sincerity—would sway the Mighty Judge to grant mercy. So he began again to chant the *Selihot* with the fervor and feeling of a contrite and sorrowful heart. And when he came to the *Ashamnu,* he even wept.

"Oh, dear God, what an upside down world we live in! In olden days the squares and market places were filled with truth. Only in the Synagogue did we hear falsehood. But now, falsehood rules in the marketplace, and words of truth are heard in the Synagogue.

"It used to be that men were honest in their business, and when they arrived at Synagogue they spoke lies—*Ashamnu, bagadnu, gazalnu*—we dealt treacherously, we robbed, we blasphemed. Their words were false, they were honest, God-fearing people. But now? Heaven help us!

"Today, we speak falsehood in the squares and in the marketplace, and what they say in the synagogue is true: *Ashamnu, bagadnu, gazalnu, dibarnu dofi.*"

At that point, when Reb Levi Yitzhak reached a high moment of contrition and sorrow and repentance, a bitter cry of remorse was heard in the Synagogue—a cry that beat upon the very gates of Heaven— but to no avail.

Only one thing was left to do. *La-asot milhamah!* To wage war against Satan! But *you* know, a Saint, one of God's *Zadikim,* does not wage war as does a *melekh basar vadam*—a king of flesh and blood. The soldiers in Reb Levi Yitzhak's Army are the children of Israel, and the *Hasiday Umot Ha-olam*, the pious people of the nations of the world. The weapons in this great battle are deeds—acts of compassion, tenderness, love, piety and honesty.

Armed with such weapons, the *Zaddik* of Berditchev and his army prepared to face the enemy. And on that *Selihot* night, when *Sanegoria*, pleading with God for Israel, and *Tefilah*—sincere prayer of a repentant congregation—were of no avail before the Heavenly Judge, Reb Levi Yitzhak waged war!

Before the Heavenly Tribunal he brought his weapons of war: acts of charity, sacrifice and mercy. Then he stood up to the Court and said: "Let these good deeds speak, and not I."

> Two rubles that the widow Sara paid her son's Rebbe, denying herself the Shabbas dress she always longed for.
>
> A bowl of soup that a Berditchever Yeshivah Bochur gave his even hungrier *chaver,* and so had to go without a meal that day.
>
> A strip of forest that Reb Chaim Mekler the broker lost, because he wouldn't go back on his word.

And there were many, many more weapons that his army supplied him. Simple, kindly acts of charity and goodness by good men and good women. Poor, but kind; simple, but good!

When Satan saw Reb Levi Yitzhak's army and their weapons, he turned his head in confusion and defeat. The Almighty Himself descended from the Throne of Judgment, and mounted the Throne of Mercy. The gates of Heaven opened wide and the prayers of Israel ascended to the Heavenly Throne, and fashioned themselves into a crown for the King of Mercy.

That year, so the story goes, was a year of happiness and blessedness for Israel and for the world.

Retold by Rabbi Abraham J. Karp

Memory and *Teshuvah*

Teshuvah does not happen all at once. It happens in increments, and maybe something will stir for you this day that will percolate during Yom Kippur and long after.

Perhaps the projections we place on others may not withdraw back into our own souls until the first notes of Yom Kippur, when *Kol Nidre* and the confessionals spark a place of blocked grief or anger, withheld love or apology, and struggle for meaning and purpose in life. Maybe not even then! Maybe your time will be after the Days of Awe. Our sages wisely offer that *teshuvah* between us and God is the explicit work of Yom Kippur, but for *teshuvah* between human beings, the gates of heaven on earth are open until Hoshannah Rabbah, the end of Sukkoth, when we traditionally take willow branches and go to the river side and hit the ground with them until all the leaves come off as if to try and shake the last vestiges of sin and spiritual blindness still clinging to us. It is in the journey that we can find hope amidst the challenging world around us, and the struggles within our own hearts.

This Day of Awe, we return and turn again to face the dreams we yearned for, comforting the broken hopes that lie aching on the ground of a lifetime. We turn to face the dreams we buried, that with some watering are lying, waiting for nurturance to blossom into heaven in our lifetime. We return to seek forgiveness with those who share our lives that we have forgotten under the weight of making ends meet or habitual ways of relating, or taking for granted. We remember that "I'm sorry" is not a defeat, but freedom from our own prison of closed-heartedness. We remember the world outside our little narratives, a world that longs for us to accompany it in discovery, compassion and healing.

We return to the world in our own neighborhoods and communities, which need our hands and hearts to avoid declining into environmental, social and economic hardship. We return to those who have come before us, family and friends, inspirational people of many ages ago, and those we knew fleetingly that gave us an angel's touch and changed our lives. And we return to those who left our world this past year, whether through death's door, or through relationships severed or lost. It is painful to return. It is joyful to return. It is this day of actively returning that reminds us to claim what we hold dear, and reclaim what we have forgotten or repressed.

Rabbi Shawn Israel Zevit

Man and Beast Will Be Saved by God

It is written, "God is my light and my salvation." The righteous are written and sealed in the Book of Life on Rosh Hashanah, and on Yom Kippur they already see the light. But the mediocre people, those who are neither good enough nor very evil, need lots of help until Yom Kippur to be written in the Book of Life. As it is written, "Your righteousness is like mighty mountains—Your judgment is like the vast deep waters. Man and beast will be saved by God" (Psalms 36:7). The words "your righteousness" mean the righteous who can be as sure of their fate as the mighty mountains that stand firmly. The words "your judgment" speak of the wicked who are judged to the very depths. But the mediocre ones, who have both human and beastly parts and repent by Yom Kippur, will be saved by God.

Who is that arrogant to think of himself as a complete *tzaddik* without sin or blemish? Let us then not consider ourselves more than the mediocre ones and quickly repent and be saved by God.

Moshe Braun

Repenting for Those Who Cannot

There is something very positive you can do for someone who has been unable to change or repent or for someone who has died before she was able to do so. The Talmud cites a teaching about Rabbi Meir, who had prayed for highway robbers in the neighborhood to be struck down. His wife, Beruria, corrected him, saying, "Rather, pray for them to repent" (Berakhot 10a). So, too, we can pray for those who have hurt us to lose that compulsion in this life, or, if they have died, on the next plane of being. If their souls do return to life on this planet, we can pray for them to be free of such terrible compulsions, that they might have a new experience of life and that no more people might be hurt by them. This is a new kind of *teshuvah* for many of us. To turn anger, once we've had sufficient time to vent and process it over the years, into prayer.

This is a way not to forgive but rather to turn a new face to an old wound so that the scar can be resurfaced and healing can tentatively begin.

And what if you have wronged someone who will not accept your *teshuvah*? Maimonides suggests bringing three character witnesses with you to entreat forgiveness, and to do this up to three times. If after that the person you have wronged still does not accept your *teshuvah*, the burden of guilt transfers to the one who will not forgive. And what if the person wronged dies before you are able to confess your culpability? Again, Maimonides has the answer. At the grave of the person you have wronged, assemble ten people who recognize the depth of your *teshuvah* and express it out loud as if the deceased could hear. If the situation also involves money you owe the deceased, give it to the heirs, and if there are no heirs, to a bona fide charity.

Rabbi Goldie Milgram

FAITH AND BELIEFS

God's seal of truth commands us to be honest and to live with integrity. This has to do with every aspect of our lives, from our business dealings to the way we express our faith in God. What we do and say should be out in the open, accessible to all who want to see it, and capable of passing common human tests of truth.

In the Bible *emet* refers to a deeply held and unshakable belief; it is closely related to the word *emunah* or "faith." The truth of one's position is shown by how firmly it is held. Ultimately that which we are willing to live for and die for becomes our personal truth. It is in this spirit that our liturgy adds the word *emet* to the conclusion of the *shema'*, affirming our personal witness to God's truth.

RABBI ARTHUR GREEN, *THESE ARE THE WORDS*

Ve-khol Ma-aminim—Emulating God's Attributes

The prayer/poem known as "*Ve-khol Ma-a-minim*" describes many of God's attributes. Perhaps the most important of these is that God is a faithful God. We can trust God.

As humans we try to emulate God's attributes, and hope that in the course of our lifetimes we will be able to encourage others to trust us.

The story is told of the late Rabbi Daniel Leifer, who served for some 30 years as Hillel Director at the University of Chicago until his premature death in 1996. When Rabbi Leifer was a rabbinical student he had the occasion to meet Prof. Martin Buber of Jerusalem's Hebrew University. Buber asked him what was his goal as a rabbi. Rabbi Leifer reports that his answer was that he wanted to teach Torah and encourage mitzvot.

Buber's reply touched him deeply, and it was one he tried to implement his entire life as a rabbi to his university community. Buber said: "No, the purpose of a rabbi is to establish trust."

Like God, as described in the prayer "*Ve-khol Ma-aminim,*" we pray that we become more faithful and trustworthy in the eyes of all who know us.

Rabbi Henry B. Balser

Where Is God?

Where is God? Is that what we say when we learn that 22% of all households in Israel are living below the poverty line? That one out of six children in Westchester County will go to bed hungry tonight? Where is God?

God is here, friends, hiding.

Jewish tradition has a name for God's hiddenness; it is called *hester (panim)*. *Hester*. [whirr] It is the Jewish response to the mystery of the story of Purim. Where is God in the story of Purim? Absent, you thought. No, no. Not absent—just hidden. And in a time of God's hiddenness, in a time of *hester,* we must each step forward and be like Esther. "Do not imagine that you, of all of the Jews, will escape with your life by being in the king's palace. On the contrary, if you keep silent in the face of this crisis, relief and deliverance will come to the Jews from another place, while you and your father's house will perish. And who knows, perhaps you have attained to royal position for just such a crisis." Who knows, perhaps you are in this place, at this time, for a reason.

Where is God? I used to take some comfort from the image of cable cars in San Francisco. What enables those cable cars to move up and down the steep hills of San Francisco? There are powerful cables that run underneath these ups and downs. When the cable car wants to move, it latches on to the cable, which pulls it up or down the hills. If you look down into the opening that runs down the middle of all these streets, you will see that, underneath, the cable is always running.

God is the force of life that runs through our lives, day in and day out—in the inexplicable force that gives a person the simple, heroic courage to open the door. To hide a child. To shelter a family. To move against our self-interest, against our own survival instincts—and reach out to help.

Where is God? To paraphrase today's Torah reading, "not in the heavens, that you should say, who can possibly go up to the heavens to find it there? Neither is it beyond the sea, that you should say, who among us can cross over to the other side of the sea to find it there. No, it is very close to you, in your mouth and in your heart." Not out there. In your very being. Running through your life.

"God" is when you care enough that every day, nearly 30,000 children die in the developing countries for lack of food and basic medicine. "Where is God?" is what you say when you don't care enough—when you'd rather have someone else take care of it. "God" is when it really bothers you that a person working full-time with minimum wages cannot make it in America. It is simply not enough to live on. "God" is the outrage when our government continues to cut public services for the poor and provides tax cuts for the rich.

"God" is the irrational courage to love in the face of inevitable loss—in the face of separation, in the face of disappointment, in the face of death. "God" is the knowledge that life matters. In a real, ultimate and forever way.

Yom Kippur. Yom Kippurim. A day like Purim. God has been hidden and disguised. It is a day to take off the mask and know that God has been there all along, masquerading as you.

Rabbi Shira Milgrom

The Glory of Life

The realm of mystery tells us, You live in a world full of light and life.

Know the great reality, the richness of existence that you always encounter. Contemplate its grandeur, its beauty, its precision and its harmony.

Be attached to the legions of living beings who are constantly bringing forth everything beautiful. In every corner where you turn, you are dealing with realities that have life; you always perform consequential acts, abounding with meaning and with the preciousness of vibrant life. In everything you do you encounter sparks full of life and lights, aspiring to rise toward the heights. You help them and they help you.

The glorious wisdom that you comprehend is not a faint shadow of some spiritual mirage that is devoid of meaning, to be displaced by research and science. These phenomena are the children of a real world, introducing themselves to you, sending you good news from afar, news about their well-being and their state of health. Their well-being also contributes to your well-being.

When you ascend to greater heights you raise yourselves to a more noble fellowship, to surroundings of greater splendor.

And everything aspires, longs, yearns, according to a pattern that is adorned with holiness and girded with beauty. For this life of yours is not a meaningless phenomenon. The light of your own expression, O Lord, our God, is imprinted on the law that governs life.

Rabbi Abraham Isaac Kook

Ve-khol Ma-aminim—We All Hope ... We Trust

As we [approach the end of] [enter the beginning of] the 2nd millennium, many fears arise in our minds. The world is filled with pitfalls and dangers, atrocities and dehumanization.

Can we survive in this confused and hate-filled planet? An ancient *midrash* offers us hope—as is expressed in the High Holiday prayer, "*Ve-khol Ma-aminim*"—that we can and should hope, trust, and have faith.

The *midrash* talks of the first time humans experienced darkness. When Adam and Eve approached their first evening, they too were frightened, even terrified. Would the sun shine again? They had no experience to justify such hope.

At God's behest, they took two stone flints and rubbed them together to make a spark and produce light. The fire gave them both warmth and light. These two stones are called by the *midrash* "*afelah*"— darkness, and "*mavet*"—death. The light they produced drove away the darkness, fear, violence and death that might have engulfed them.

The definition of an optimist is one who tries again in the face of bad experience. We pray that our High Holiday prayers will enable us to transform the new millennium into a time when we can all confidently and joyously say, with the medieval Hebrew poet, "*Ve-khol ma-aminim ...* "—we all believe, hope, and trust—in the basic goodness of God's world.

Rabbi Dov Peretz Elkins

Saving God's Life

A sage once wrote that whenever we reach out to help someone who is suffering, God speaks words of gratitude to us. God says, "Thank you for saving My life." What does this mean? Why would God say these words? Isn't God immortal? How can any person save God's life? I'll explain:

When a poor mother lives on the streets with her children, she cries out day after day, "Help me, God. Save me. Lift me and my children out of hunger and homelessness." And when no help comes, when she watches people walk by her without even glancing her way, she lowers her head to the ground and says to herself, "There is no God. God is dead."

But when someone draws near and provides solace and support, she turns her face up to the heavens and whispers, "Thank You, God."

Whenever we rise above our indifference and complacency, whenever we refuse to ignore cries of suffering, whenever we make the choice to help any human being in need, we become God's partners. And a sacred voice echoes across the world speaking softly, "Bless you, thank you, for saving My life."

Rabbi Naomi Levy

Ve-khol Ma-aminim—All Believe

In the refrain of the very popular prayer, "*Ve-khol ma-aminim*," we remind ourselves again and again of our belief in God and in God's just ways.

But do all of us truly believe? We are told that even during the Shoah people walked to the gas chambers chanting "*Ani Ma-amin*," "I believe."

In Maimonides' famous statement of the Principles of the Faith, one was "I believe with perfect faith (*Be-emunah sh'laymah*) in the coming of the Messiah."

Is there such a thing as "perfect faith"? In the Hasidic tradition we learn that no one has perfect faith. Doubt is the annoying intruder in all true religion. So why did Maimonides, and why can we say, now, or during the Shoah, that anyone has "*Emunah Sh'layma*—perfect faith"?

The Hasidic tradition teaches that even though no one really has perfect faith, we are constantly moving from doubt to faith, each day a little closer to full faith.... Each day an inch closer and closer....

Dr. Avram Davis

Ve-khol Ma-aminim—Defining Faith, the Jewish Way

The faith which is limned in the beautiful *piyyut*, "*Ve-khol Ma-aminim*," is the traditional Jewish faith, which is faith that is trust in a relationship with God. This is the "*emunah*" [faith] of the biblical and talmudic tradition.

Martin Buber, in his book *Two Types of Faith—A Study in the Interpenetration of Judaism and Christianity*, distinguishes this type of faith from the classical Christian faith which is different from faith in a relationship (*emunah*). In Buber's analysis, Christian faith is faith in the truth of a *proposition*, or *pistis* in Greek. Buber described "*emunah*," Jewish faith, as "that unconditional trust in the grace which makes a person no longer afraid even of death because death is also of grace." Paul and John, in the New Testament, in contrast, made faith in Jesus (*pistis*) the one door to salvation. According to Maurice Friedman, Buber's student and leading interpreter, "This meant the abolition of the immediacy between God and man that had been the essence of the biblical Covenant and the kingship of God. To Paul and his followers, one cannot step into the door of *emunah* unless he believes in the door. To the Hebrew Bible, the relationship to God was essential, not any entrance ticket of acceptance of the belief in Jesus" (Maurice Friedman, *A Heart of Wisdom,* p. 115).

Rabbi Dov Peretz Elkins

Ve-khol Ma-aminim—Trying to Believe

When the great psychoanalyst Carl Gustav Jung was asked: "Do you believe in God?" he replied, "I know. I don't need to believe. I know." How can anyone reply with such certainty and conviction? How can anyone be so sure?

Perhaps the answer lies in the way we understand what faith really means. There is something beautiful about the origin of the Hebrew word for faith, *Emunah.* Most of us are familiar with a slightly different form of it—the response, Amen. Both of these words come from the root *a-m-n,* which is related to the concept of "nursemaid" or "nurturer." Hidden within that root is the word for "mother" *(em).*

When we seek faith, we are actually searching for an inner mother, someone or something to nurture us, particularly during the hard times.

Often before a young couple marries, one of them gets cold feet. Some actually cancel or postpone their weddings. Some just need reassurance from a dear friend or parent. "Get me my Mama," one bride-to-be cried out to those around her an hour before her wedding. "I need to talk to Mama now."

Similarly, at the end of life, many people seek the same sort of comfort. Dying patients, even when they are surrounded by other loved ones and friends, cry out one word more than any other: "Mama."

Regardless of your actual relationship with your mother, the word "Mama" symbolizes the person who gave birth to you and nurtured you. So as you reach your final moments, you may once again call out, "Mama," as you give birth to a new part of yourself.

Rabbi Levi Meier

On Eagles' Wings

The words of the *mahzor* are meant to mirror our lives. They teach us that life is fragile, that we can be here today and gone tomorrow. They teach that our lives are full of tremendous opportunities for praise but also for questioning and fear. As my friend and teacher, Rabbi Richard Hirsh, teaches in the *Kol Haneshamah Mahzor*, our task is to live our lives fully, directed to godliness, reflecting who we are and where we are going, and acknowledging our deep connection with others.

So there I was at St. Vincent's Comprehensive Cancer Center on Yom Kippur—which also coincided with my 35th birthday. I was saving my own life while feeling the warm companionship of the rabbis of old, who were also confronted by their mortality in a more dangerous time. This was only my third chemo treatment out of a total of eight, but I already had a ritual life to go along with the treatment. My dear friend, Sarah Fenner, who had been diagnosed with breast cancer the previous year, had created a *siddur* to take with her to treatment and had sent me a copy. It was filled with prayers, psalms, and empty pages to which I could add readings, family pictures, anything that would bring me comfort in a most uncomfortable experience.

When the first chemotherapy drug, Adriamycin, began to flow, I recited Sarah's *berakha* [blessing]: *Brikh Rahamana Malka d'alma marei d'hai tipa*—Blessed are You Compassionate One, Master of this drop. I associated these droplets with the "saving dew" and "saving rain" that we pray for on *Pesah* and *Sukkot* (*Shemini Atzeret*). The connection was obvious between the waters that quench, nourish, and literally save the earth and the fluids that were available literally to save my life. As afraid as I might have been, each time chemo began, I felt protectively held in suspension above the void of the unknown.

On Yom Kippur I began my prayers with the words *hadesh yameinu kekedem*—"renew our days as in the beginning." Never before had those words meant so much. I was praying to be able to return to myself, to look back on this experience simply as a blip on the glorious horizon of my life. While the diagnosis of breast cancer wasn't something to be grateful for, I was also praying to be renewed by this challenge and to rededicate myself to living a full and vibrant life.

We don't usually take the opportunity to do this kind of deep work until we are staring our deepest fears in the face.

There is no question that upon learning that you have cancer or any other illness, or when confronted by any number of crises in life, the natural tendency is to ask "Why?"—as if God, or the universe, or even the Power that makes for Salvation, could ever answer such a question. The texts and liturgy of our tradition were comforting to me because I found that they transform the question "why" into "what" and "how" and "when."

> What is there to learn and experience from the challenges
>   each of us must face in our lives?
> How might we garner all the strength and determination to
>   face what might lie ahead?
> When will we know that this experience is yet just one more
>   fold in the fabric of our life?

I deeply believe that these questions emerge from the "circumcised" or open heart that is described as part of our covenant with God in the book of Deuteronomy, as read in the weeks just before Rosh Hashanah. The open heart might be challenged or even broken, but it is still open to receive.

In one of my favorite *parshiot, Parashat Nitzavim*, in chapter 30 of Deuteronomy, the last verse reads: *"u'vaharta bahaim l'ma-an tihye"*—choose life that you might live. One commentator, Abraham Ibn Ezra, a Jewish scholar and scientist of the 12th century, comments that *"hahayim khem l'ahava"*—life is for love—and immediately following, *"ki hu hayekha"*—for God is life. Ibn Ezra teaches that the experience of God, love, and life are tightly woven together and are critical to our conception of the covenant between God and the Jewish people that we affirm on these days. The Israelites didn't know what they would encounter in the Promised Land any more than you or I know what tomorrow will bring. But their connection to something bigger than themselves is what often sustained them as they made their way through uncharted territory—even if they had to be reminded of it later by the prophets.

The experience of being diagnosed with a life-threatening illness brings out just about every emotion, including fear—and each has the potential to teach us something important about life. Yet even without the challenges of breast cancer and other hardships, our holiday cycle, liturgy and ritual life offer the opportunity for theological confrontation and reconnection to the covenant. But the opportunity for covenantmaking, which is so embedded in our Jewish tradition, doesn't only come our way on the holy days or festivals. We read in the daily liturgy, *"hamehadesh b'tuvo bekhol yom tamid ma'aseh bereishit"*—each day the acts of creation are renewed for the good. We cannot choose all the things that will happen in our life, its beginning or its end. But every day we are responsible for the quality of love and commitment that defines our life. That is our part in the covenant.

Although the memories of chemotherapy are thankfully beginning to fade in my mind, my experience last Yom Kippur is one that will remain as one of the greatest opportunities I have had to embrace our tradition in an untraditional way. More importantly, it was, for me, one of the most profound expressions of the famous teaching of the first Chief Rabbi of Palestine, Rabbi Abraham Isaac Kook: "The old has become new, and the new has become holy." As every day my recovery and healing are more and more secured, I feel blessed by my physical and spiritual resilience. God didn't have anything to do with my diagnosis, and being a rabbi didn't save me from this encounter, either. But my faith, my spiritual life, and my deep connection to community are those things which carried me on eagle's wings through this passage.

Rabbi Yael Ridberg

YIZKOR—
IN MEMORIAM

Yizkor or memorial services are conducted four times a year according to widespread Ashkenazic custom. These occasions are Yom Kippur, the final days of *Pesah* and *Shavu'ot*, and *Shemini Atseret*.

The word *yizkor* means "May He remember," the opening word of the memorial prayer. Traditionally one recites *yizkor* (referred to as *maskir* in German-Jewish tradition) in memory of close relatives, including parents, siblings, spouse, and children. Many *siddurim (siddur)* published in recent years have added prayers for the martyrs of the Holocaust, for Israeli soldiers killed in battle, and for victims of terror attacks against Jews.

The text of the traditional *yizkor* prayer mentions that charity (*tsedakah*) has been given in memory of the deceased. In Jewish folk belief this gift and the recitation of *yizkor* prayers were a way of adding merit to the dead, helping them rise to a higher level of heavenly reward, or at least to be saved from punishment for sins. The belief in *yizkor* was especially strong among Jews of the immigrant generation, many of whom bore great guilt for having forsaken the religious norms of the "old country" and feared their fate in the "other world," in which they still very much continued to believe.

The *yizkor* service traditionally follows directly after the Torah and

haftarah readings on the days mentioned. Some liberal synagogues
have moved the Yom Kippur *yizkor* service to the afternoon, in order
to increase attendance at the concluding services of that day.

RABBI ARTHUR GREEN, *THESE ARE THE WORDS*

Yom Kippur and Memory

Yom Kippur brings us back to memory. We let ourselves sit amidst the powerful memories of those with whom we have lived our lives—those who gave us life, or perhaps those with whose legacy we still wrestle, or those whose love continues to nurture us. Sometimes, it is possible for us to see aspects of their lives we never saw when we shared life with them. Sometimes, the eye of memory sees things more clearly than can be seen in life itself. The gift of *Yizkor,* the gift of remembering, is that sometimes things are seen more accurately in their reflection than in looking at them directly.

There's something about a funeral that brings us close to what really matters, the real sense that some things die, but that some things don't. The way we live this life has impact on what lives after us. Ask a child: would you rather be hurt in your arm or in your love? The child who understands this question will probably say, "I'd rather be hurt in my arm." It is much more difficult to sustain a hurt where we love. But when you bury someone you love, you say good-bye to the arm, to the body; you don't say good-bye to the love. Life is precious; we must not defer to tomorrow the love we can give or receive today. All the love that has been given to you is yours, yours to keep, yours to grow, yours to share fully with others, so that it lives forever. Energy does not die in this universe. Neither does love.

This is the gift of Yom Kippur. To stand for twenty-four hours where life and death meet. And to look back at life with the eyes of memory. What, in the end, does really matter to me? How do I want to be remembered? Can I see now, in those I love, what I will remember about them later? Can we be blessed with moments of vision to glimpse the core of eternity embedded within all of life?

> Blessed are You, our God, who has created us to reflect
> your infinite splendor
> for You have put eternity into our hearts,
> the gift to see with the eye of memory,
> and implanted within us a vision of life everlasting.

Rabbi Shira Milgrom

Time Out—Life Is Temporary

I don't wear a watch. I haven't worn one in years; not since I read a book on how overly time-conscious people drive themselves to an early grave. But lately I've been reconsidering. The watch is designed by David Kendrick of Berkshire, New York.

A little over a year ago, Mr. Kendrick received a patent for a "Life Expectancy Timepiece." The watch contains a tiny computer into which you feed your age, medical history, life-style, eating habits and exercise regimens. The watch then uses actuarial data to compute your life expectancy and begins counting to zero.

Imagine walking down the street and someone asks you the time. You glance at your watch and say: "Oh, about 37 years, 110 days, 21 hours, 4 minutes and 42 seconds until I die." Isn't that more interesting than saying "3:45"?

I don't need to wear the hour on my wrist. There are clocks everywhere; but being able to glance down and watch my life ticking away before my eyes, now that's something!

Some of you may be thinking: "God, how depressing!" On the contrary, being reminded that my life is temporary is incredibly liberating: "You mean I won't have to stand in line at the Post Office forever? Fantastic!"

Let me tell you five ways Mr. Kendrick's watch would effect my life.

First, it would shock me. "Whoa! You mean I've only got this much time left?" Knowing I'm going to die in 37 years, 110 days, 21 hours, 4 minutes and 42 seconds (41 seconds, 40 seconds, 39 seconds …) In the face of death life becomes awesomely simple: acts of love and kindness, justice, and compassion are what count rather than the acts of revenge and one-upmanship that occupy most of our lives. In the face of this awesome simplicity I would love more and lie less.

Second, Mr. Kendrick's timepiece would focus my attention on doing rather than feeling. Feelings are fleeting, uncontrollable and unstable. Anger, love, sadness, joy trip over each other as they flit into and out of consciousness. Seeing the transience of my life would make the transience of my feelings even clearer. When we try to lock certain feelings in and other feelings out we live in constant frustration. By focusing attention on doing rather than feeling, I can make my life constructive, productive, effortful. Effort often leads to success, and success often brings positive feelings. Waiting to feel before we do is waiting to fail. Doing alone brings success. The old adage: Those who can do, do is backward. The truth is: Those who can do, can.

Third, Mr. Kendrick's watch would focus my attention on the present. So much of our time is spent dwelling on the past or dreaming about the future. Both past and future are figments of the imagination distracting us from now. All there is is now and here and the work of the moment. Which brings me back to the fourth impact of this timepiece: ordinariness.

I'm nothing special: just a temporary animation of cells. I am simply God's way of getting things done. Do you want to know why you were born? To pick up the trash, to do the laundry, to parent a child, to feed the hungry, to visit the sick, to care for an aged parent, to brush your teeth. You were born to do whatever life gives you to do right now.

The illusion of specialness is at the root of so many adult problems. We are wrong. As Hillel taught: "If I am not for myself who will be for me? But if I am only for myself what am I? And if not now when?" Taking care of me requires taking care of you. What is a person who is only for the self? An aging adolescent perpetually seeking the inner child.

Lastly, Mr. Kendrick's watch would help me relax. Rather than feeling I've got to cram my years with meaningful experience, I would experience the years as they come. So many of us are convinced that the way our lives should have turned out is somehow other than the way they did turn out. Why? Why do we deserve other than what we got? Why think we deserve anything?

Here I've got 37 years, 21 hours, 4 minutes and 42 seconds to go and life is what it is for the moment. And if I don't like what I've got I can do something to change it; do something other than whine and dream and dwell on why I deserve better. Most of us are unhappy that we didn't get what we imagine we "deserve." Maybe we did. Scary thought, isn't it?

I think Mr. Kendrick's watch would be a life saver for me, and many others like me. Unfortunately, the watch is not yet on the market. Too bad. I'd buy one. Better still, I'd wear it. And the next time someone asked me "What time is it?" I'd say "Thanks!"

Rabbi Rami M. Shapiro

Death Does Not Exist

Death is non-existent. According to the Biblical legend, Adam was punished for his sin of disobedience by becoming mortal. His sin brought death as well as man's fear of death into being. But the return of the world to its source will conquer death. Every improvement of the individual or the world; every act leading toward the achievement of perfection constitutes a step toward the conquest of death by the return of the world to its original state of union with God. Death is a lie; it is an illusion. The very fact that Jewish tradition associates death with ritual uncleanliness is a symbol of its falsehood. What men call death is in reality the intensification or reinvigoration of life. The liberation from the fetters of corporeality is the indispensable means of mankind's self-renewal and the instrument of its progress. Fear of death is the universal disease of mankind, but death is terrifying and inexorable only where man is alienated from the source of his being. If sin brought death into being, *teshuvah,* man's return to the source of his being will conquer it. The soul is not a mere appendage to the body which perishes together with the body; it is part of that undying current of vitality which returns to its source at death.

Samuel Hugo Bergman

Together We Can Stand Anything

Maybe some of you have seen California's magnificent Sequoias. Did you know that these trees, some of which are as tall as a skyscraper, have roots practically at surface level? A lone sequoia's roots are so shallow that it can hardly stand up to a strong breeze. So how do they grow so tall? They spring up in groves, and their roots intertwine. In other words, they hold each other up—they give each other the strength necessary to withstand the angriest winds. And it is the same with us. Alone we can *kvetch* and *hok me a chynick* … alone we will know pain. But when we are together … we can stand anything.

Rabbi Dannel I. Schwartz

Driving Sorrow Out of Your Life

There is an old Chinese tale about the woman whose only son died. In her grief she sent to the holy man (her rabbi) and asked, "What prayers, what magical incantations do you have to bring my son back to life?" Instead of sending her away, he said, "Fetch me a mustard seed from a home that has never known sorrow. We will use it to drive the sorrow out of your life."

The woman set off at once in search of the magical mustard seed. She came first to a splendid mansion, knocked at the door, and said, "I am looking for a home that has never known sorrow. Is this such a place?" They told her, "You've certainly come to the wrong house," and began describing all the tragic things that had recently befallen them. The woman said to herself, "Who is better able to help these poor unfortunate people than I, who have had misfortune of my own?"

She stayed to comfort them for a while, then went on in her search for a home that had never known sorrow. But wherever she turned, in hovels and in palaces, she found one tale after another of sadness or misfortune.

Ultimately, she became so involved in ministering to other people's grief that she forgot about her quest for the magical mustard seed, never realizing that it had in fact already driven the sorrow out of her life.

Rabbi Steven Carr Reuben

A Special Prayer for Those Not Saying *Yizkor* for Parents

The following prayer may be recited by worshippers who are blessed by having their parents still living while others are reciting *Yizkor:*

Almighty God, while those who have lost their parents and their dear ones call to mind those who have gone to their eternal rest, I at this solemn moment raise my eyes unto You, the Giver of Life, and from a grateful heart thank You for Your mercies in having preserved the life of my beloved father and mother.

May it be Your will, *Adonai* my God and the God of my ancestors, to bless them with health and strength, so that they may be with me for many years to come. Bless them even as they have blessed me, and guard them even as they have guarded me.

In return for all their affection and the sacrifices which they have made for me, may I bring them joy and lighten their cares. May it be my privilege to help them in every way that lies within my power; may I learn to understand and recognize the duty I owe unto them, that I may never have cause to reproach myself when it is too late.

Shield my home from all sorrow. May peace and harmony and Your spirit ever reign within its walls. Keep me true to You and to all with whom I come in contact so that I may do Your will with a perfect heart, my Creator in Heaven.

Amen.

Adapted from the South African *Mahzor*

The Plan of the Master Weaver

Our lives are but fine weavings,
That God and we prepare,
Each life becomes a fabric planned,
And fashioned in God's care.
We may not always see just how
The weavings intertwine,
But we must trust the Master's hand,
And follow God's design.
For God can view the pattern
Upon the upper side,
While we must look from underneath,
And trust in God to guide.
Sometimes a strand of sorrow
Is added to the plan,
And though it is difficult for us,
We still must understand
That it's God who moves the shuttle,
Who knows what's best,
So we must weave in patience,
And leave to God the rest …
Not till the loom is silent,

And the shuttles cease to fly,
Shall God unroll the canvas
And explain the reason why
The dark threads are as needed
In the Weaver's skillful hand,
As the threads of gold and silver,
In the pattern God has planned.

Author Unknown

Still Warm from an Old Jacket

The late master of Jewish storytelling, Reb Shlomo Carlebach, tells the following tale, which will help us put the *Yizkor* Memorial Prayers in their proper context.

It seems that many years ago a little seven-year-old boy and his family were about to leave their native Poland. The day before their departure the father took the little boy to the town where the Rebbe lived so he could receive the Rebbe's blessing. They remained overnight in the home of the Rebbe, and the little boy slept in the Rebbe's study.

Staring at all the holy books, the little boy could not sleep. In the middle of the night he saw the Rebbe enter the room, and he pretended that he was asleep. The Rebbe whispered "Such a sweet child!" Thinking the child might be cold, the Rebbe took off his coat and placed it lovingly on the sleeping child.

Many years later, when the little boy became an old man of eighty years, when asked what the source of his kindness and comfort was, he said that seventy-three years ago the Rebbe showed him love and comfort, and placed his coat on him to keep him warm. "I am still warm from that coat," said the eighty-year-old man.

The *Yizkor* prayers that we recite remind us that at many occasions in our lives, many people put their warm coats on us, touched us, loved us, comforted us. Their coats still provide warmth for us today—whether they are living or not—and will continue to do so.

From these coats we are still warm, and we thank them for their love and warmth. May their memory be for a blessing.

D.P.E.

So Too Does the Soul Evolve....

The process of dying is painful,
Especially if it is prolonged.
But death itself is a transition,
A transfer from here to there,
A recycling of the body and the soul.
Matter is never destroyed, only transformed.
So too does the soul evolve, higher and higher.
From instinct to inspiration, from haughtiness to holiness,
From selfishness to service, from individualism to union,
Until it returns home to the Soul of Souls—
the Ein Sof—the Infinite One.
Thus is the Divine Source of Life Magnified and Sanctified.

Rabbi Allen S. Maller

Yizkor

It's almost midnight
and I'm sitting here in the living room
keeping your *yahrzeit* candle company.
It's so many years now
I closed my eyes to remember
something real about you
and you know what I thought of?
I saw you ironing—
it was his underwear!
When I was a girl I wondered if someday
I'd love someone enough to iron his underwear.
Well, I've been married twenty years
and I love him very much but I don't iron his underwear.
I don't even turn it right side out
I don't even fold it
I sort of stuff it in the drawer.
Truly I love him very much
but I still think what I thought when I was 11—
no one sees your underwear.
I'm all grown up now

Completely grown up now
and still I don't get it—
no one sees your underwear.
I'm not being critical
I'm not making fun
It's just that we both have to face it–
I'm a different kind of wife.
You're gone
and he's gone
the foyer is gone
the ironing board is gone
and the underwear is gone.
All that remains is me
sitting in this chair
looking at the *yahrzeit* candle
remembering.

Merle Feld

From Beyond the Grave Our Loved Ones Reach Out and Touch Us

Rabbi Eli Schochet, of California, tells a story of his childhood. He grew up in Chicago, where his father and his grandfather were both rabbis. One Sabbath afternoon when he was a young boy at his grandfather's home, a big Cadillac pulled up. Three burly guards stepped out with a well-known Jewish gangster. The man walked in and laid an envelope on the rabbi's table filled with cash. "This is for my mother's *yahrzeit*." [*Yahrzeit* is the anniversary of one's death. It is a special Jewish religious obligation to give charity on a *Yahrzeit* in memory of a beloved parent or others.] Then he left.

Eli was angry at his grandfather. "How can you accept money from that man, on the Sabbath of all times?" [Religious Jews may not touch money on the Sabbath.] His grandfather softly answered, "Don't you understand what happened? This man is a criminal who lives an ugly life. But for one brief moment he looked on a calendar and saw that it was his mother's *yahrzeit*. He remembered his mother's dreams for him, that he grow up to be a Jew, that he grow up to be a *mentsch*.

For one brief moment, he wants her memory to live within. That was a sacred moment, and I do not want to take away from it."

That story says it all. Even from beyond the grave, our loved ones can reach out and touch us, and change us.

Rabbi Michael Gold

A *Yizkor* Guided Imagery Exercise

Yizkor is brief. Following a few prayers, we are left with moments of silence to think about those who were closest to us. What should we do during those moments? How should we best remember those who no longer walk this earth?

During these silent moments let's take a journey into the hearts of our loved ones. Close your eyes, and imagine walking into a room, perhaps a room in the home in which you grew up. Now shut the door and envision your beloved father or mother, husband or wife, sister or brother, son or daughter, other relative or friend. Look into their eyes, touch their hands and feel their skin. Listen to their voices.

Let's speak with our loved ones. What do we want to say that we didn't when they were alive? Perhaps we will say "I am a new mother" or "new father" and then introduce them to the child they never met. Or, show them how their little grandchild has grown since they left. We may share professional news. Maybe we will say "Thank you for all you did." We might apologize for hurting them or grant *them* forgiveness. Or we might simply say "I love you and miss you so very, very deeply." During these moments see them, hear them, touch them. And make peace with yourself, your beloved and with God. Then you will have transformed these ordinary moments into sacred moments.

A man who lost his mother this year told me that he would give anything just to have a few more minutes with her. *Yizkor* provides those minutes.

Adapted from a *Yizkor* sermon by Rabbi David Woznica,
based on the teaching of Rabbi Elie Spitz

Good Grief

We often hear people speak of birth as a miracle. Seldom do we hear of death spoken of in the same way. But if there is something miraculous about life coming into existence, certainly the same holds true for death. To watch an active person reduced into inorganic nothingness before our very eyes is also a miracle, albeit a terrible one.

But if death is the other side of the coin which we call life, then grief is the other side of love. Bereavement is love not wanting to let go. Each tear we shed is a midwife which helps bring us into a new world. We mourn our loss. Then we face a new day. We turn a new page. We start a new chapter. We begin our own new life.

We are all terminal. From the moment we are born, we are destined to die. Our happiness is bound up in our ability to accept death as a fact of life. Acceptance of our mortal end is not something which comes easily. Such growth takes work. None of us has time to lose in accepting this reality.

How do we die? Each death, like each life, is unique. Some deaths are noble. Some are petty. Some are loving. Some are angry. Most are a combination of these things. But just as our lives are, to a great extent, at our command, so too are our deaths. Although we cannot determine precisely the day and hour of our passing or its ultimate cause, we can often orchestrate how we want our last days to be. We can live until we die.

Death is not entirely tragic. Our loved ones can bask in the afterglow of something that was once wonderful and be grateful that they once shared something beautiful with us.

As a rabbi, you might expect me to tell you that everything in the Bible is true. But I would be lying if I told you I believe that. We are taught "the Lord gives and the Lord takes away." But, in truth, not everything is taken from us. Memory is ours as long as we live.

Every person is like a snowflake. Every person, like every snowflake is unique. Both people and snowflakes have intricate patterns which have never been replicated and never will. Yet both people and snowflakes melt away before our eyes. Each is frail. Each is, in its own way, something beautiful. Each is so very delicate and vulnerable. Each is precious beyond words.

Literature is full of "famous last words" by celebrated individuals. (It is simply amazing how loquacious some of these people were considering the state they were in.) Nowadays, due to improvements in palliative care, it is highly unlikely that we will be conscious enough to have that kind of lucidity. In all likelihood we will be tethered to all kinds of devices which are intended to ease our passing. While these improvements will make our deaths more comfortable, it will be at the expense of mental clarity.

The time to express one's thoughts and wishes is now.

When my mother died I inherited her needle point tapestries. When I was a little boy I used to sit at her feet as she worked on them. Have you ever seen needle point from underneath? All I could see was chaos, strands of thread all over with no seeming purpose. As I grew, I was able to view her work from above. I came to appreciate the intricate patterns. What is more, I learned that the dark patterns were every bit as essential to the success of the work as the bright and gaily colored ones. Sometimes I think that life is like that. From our human perspective, we cannot see the whole picture. We have a limited view of reality. Nevertheless, we should not despair that there is an explanation, meaning and purpose.

The Welsh poet Dylan Thomas wrote a poem reflecting on the death of his father: "Do not go gentle into that good night/ Old age should burn and rage at close of day/ Rage, rage against the dying of the light." But in the end all rage and anger will pass. We will enter a realm of peace where nothing can hurt us, ever.

We are the people of the book. Each of us is an author writing the book of his or her life. Authors dream of their work becoming a classic, but few ever do. Whether or not the book of our lives becomes a classic depends on us, but not only on us. To an even greater extent it depends on those who remain behind. For what is a classic but a work to which others make reference after it is finished? It is not for us to finish the task.

Franz Rosenzweig concluded his classic, *The Star of Redemption*, with these words: "To walk humbly with thy God—the words are written over the gate, which leads out of the mysterious-miraculous light of the divine sanctuary in which no person can remain alive. Whither, then, do the wings of the gate open? Thou knowest it not? INTO LIFE."

Rabbi Kenneth L. Cohen

Lesson from the *Titanic*—Love Flows Continuously

A grocery buyer from Macy's, John A. Badenoch, had been traveling to Europe and was on the rescue ship, the *Carpathia*. He knew that the Strauses were on the *Titanic* and he gathered stories from survivors, trying to piece together what happened to the couple. He wrote to the Straus children that their parents showed courage and composure to the end. The following is the account relayed in his letter:

> "Mr. and Mrs. Straus were in bed at the time of the accident.... Shortly thereafter, they appeared on the deck, fully clothed, mingled with the other passengers and discussed the danger in a perfectly calm and collected manner.
>
> "They evidently did not believe that there was any great danger of the ship sinking. On the advice of the captain, they put on a life preserver over their fur coats and assisted other passengers in doing the same. By that time, the boats were being filled with women and children, and your mother was asked by the officer in charge and urged by your father to get into one of the lifeboats. She refused to do so and insisted that the maid take her place in boat number 8....
>
> "Finally, when it became apparent that there was no hope of the *Titanic* staying afloat, your father insisted that your mother enter the second from the last boat that was being launched from the side they were on. She still refused, saying she would not go without him ... an officer in charge again urged her to enter and, in fact, attempted force, aided by the urging of your father. She placed her foot in the boat, thinking at the time that your father would accompany her.
>
> "Mr. Isidor, thinking that your mother was safe in the lifeboat, stepped back with the other men. Your mother, looking around and seeing your father was not with her, got out of the boat, went to where your father was standing and put her arms around him. The officer in charge, seeing that it was no use in trying to get your mother to leave your father, ordered the boat lowered away.
>
> "She was quoted as saying 'We have been living together for many years, and wherever you go, I do.'"

A Straus family mausoleum was erected in Woodlawn Cemetery in the Bronx. The stone contains Isidor's and Ida's date of birth and death. An inscription from the Song of Songs reads: "Many waters cannot quench love—neither can the floods destroy."

The Strauses understood the love that flows continuously from bonds nurtured by their faith; in death, they affirmed that faith.

D.P.E.

Judaism's Advice for a Meaningful Life

Some of the great religions of the East propose to teach their members how to avoid pain and heartbreak and their secret is really a very simple one; they can teach you, in two words, how to avoid ever being hurt by life. Would you like to know their secret? Don't care!

Don't care about people, and you'll never be hurt if you lose them.

Don't trust anybody, and nobody will ever disappoint you or break your heart. Don't cherish anything, and you'll never be saddened at its being taken from you. Don't love, don't trust, don't cherish, and I guarantee that you will never weep. There are religions, great and venerable ones, that teach that. But Judaism teaches us just the opposite: Care deeply and be prepared to pay the price that loving entails.

Love your parents, though it means someday seeing them grow old and weak, and your hands will be powerless to help them. Love them, though it means that someday you will lose them and feel that a part of you has died with them.

Love your children, though it will cause you so many sleepless nights. Love them, though it means feeling the pain of the scraped knees and their hurt feelings. Love them, though that will only make it harder for you one day to see them grow up and go out on their own. But do it the hard way; love them and trust them enough to let them do that.

It says, love your fellow humans, even though it would be so much easier to be callously indifferent to them. But love them, because to do anything else is to abdicate your humanity. To avoid the pain of being alive. To live means to be sensitive to pain and hurt, in the same way that the living raw flesh is so sensitive to every touch, while the dead cells can be cut and scraped and never feel a thing.

Judaism doesn't teach us how to avoid pain and sorrow; it teaches us how to stand up to it without being broken by it. How to live in a world where painful tragic things happen, and still affirm it to be God's world.

And then there is one more thing that Judaism would offer to do for us, to help us live as people were meant to live. There is a dream each of us has secretly in our heart—unless some of us have already given it up as untenable or unattainable—the ambition to be somebody significant, to matter, to make a difference in the world. None of us wants to feel that, at the end of his days, he will have passed through the world and left no trace behind, that he has had no real impact on the world. We would like to justify our existence, to stake our claim to some sort of immortality, on some remarkable achievement that will leave the world different for our having been part of it. And yet, what can we do? Very few, if any, of us will write a book that will be read twenty years from now. It's not likely that any of us in this room today will come up with a medical discovery that will save lives, or an invention that will enrich lives. Who of us will have a bridge, a street, a building named after him?

But Judaism speaks to this secret yearning of ours, and says that it is possible. It is within the power of everyone of us to be a memorable person, to live a significant and impressive life. Judaism offers us not only the secrets of life, but the secret of immortality, of living beyond our appointed years—how to be the kind of parent who will be remembered with words of blessing, how to be a friend who won't easily be forgotten, how to be the kind of neighbor whose impact on a community will remain even after he is gone from the scene.

Anyone's life can be fashioned into a spiritual masterpiece. The equivalent of sainthood is not reserved for a small group of unusual souls who are separated from the rest of society. Sainthood, that is, a life of spiritual excellence, is the prerogative of every normal husband or wife, parent, working person, anyone who takes life seriously. You don't have to have a particular talent for religion to be a spiritual remarkable person.

Rabbi Steven Saltzman

The Rest Is Up to Me....

In his popular book, *Kaddish*, Leon Wieseltier, writer for *The New Republic*, reflects on the role that the synagogue plays in his spiritual life, especially during recitation of the mourner's *kaddish* ("*Kaddish Yatom*"). He writes:

> It occurred to me today that I might spend a whole year in *shul,* morning prayers, afternoon prayers, evening prayers and never have a religious experience. A discouraging notion. Yet I must not ask for what cannot be given. *Shul* was not invented for a religious experience. In *shul,* a religious experience is an experience of religion. The rest is up to me.

Too often we expect the synagogue to do for us what we should be doing for ourselves. The aura of the recitation of the *Kaddish Yatom* in the synagogue setting is a powerful one, but we must open our hearts to let it in.

D.P.E.

A Short Visit—For a Divine Purpose

Strange is our situation here on earth. Each of us comes for a short visit, not knowing why, yet sometimes seeming to a divine purpose. There is one thing we do know definitively: that we are here for the sake of each other.

Many times a day I realize how much my own outer and inner life is built upon the labor of others, and how earnestly I must exert myself in order to give in return as much as I have received and am still receiving.

Albert Einstein

The Common Lot of All of Us

How many of us perform our small acts of charity and goodness for the wrong reasons. We expect a kind deed to be rewarded by a kind fate, to preserve us from trouble and misfortune. More than once have I heard this melancholy verdict: "When my mother died, I stopped believing in God. She was such a good person, how could God let this happen to her?"

Goodness does not confer immunity to disease, disaster, or death. It does not guarantee a life without trouble or tragedy. These are the common lot of all of us.

Is there then no reward for living a life of rectitude and uprightness? There is, indeed. We are rewarded not for our good deeds but by our good deeds. The reward for doing good is becoming a better human being. The greatest compensation for any good deed is simply to have done it. It is inherent in the act itself. Moses Maimonides, the twelfth-century Jewish philosopher, gave us the right reason for doing the right deed: "It is not enough to serve God in the hope of future reward. One must do right and avoid wrong because one is a human and owes it to one's humanity to seek perfection."

Rabbi Sidney Greenberg

Yizkor

We thank You, O God of life and love,
For the resurrecting gift of memory
Which endows Your children,
Fashioned in Your image,
With the Godlike sovereign power
To give immortality through love.
Blessed are You, God,
Who enables Your children to remember.

Rabbi Morris Adler

MARTYROLOGY

Yissurim is "suffering." In a religious context it may refer to several sorts of suffering, some physical and some existential. The figure of the righteous one (*tsaddik*) who suffers is well known in Judaism, not only as a theological conundrum but as a symbol of Jewish existence through history. This image of Israel as the righteous suffering servant of God, first created by the second prophet who wrote under the name of Isaiah, has been central to the way Jews have seen their fate for more than two millennia. Of course there have been significant periods when the picture was largely an accurate one, thanks to the nations in whose midst and at whose whim we lived. But recent history also shows that even when this is by no means our situation, it is hard for us to break loose from the ancient and deeply rooted pattern.

RABBI ARTHUR GREEN, *THESE ARE THE WORDS*

Punished for Being Jewish

Nathan the Babylonian gives the following account of the martyrs of the Hadrianic Persecutions:

"Of them that love Me and keep My commandments" [Exodus 20:6] refers to those who dwell in the land of Israel and risk their lives for the sake of the commandments.

"Why are you being led out to be decapitated?"

"Because I circumcised my son to be an Israelite."

"Why are you being led out to be burned?"

"Because I read the Torah."

"Why are you being led out to be crucified?"

"Because I ate the unleavened bread."

"Why are you getting a hundred lashes?"

"Because I performed the ceremony of the *lulav*."

Mekhilta of Rabbi Ishmael Tractate Bahodesh, chap. 7

A Martyr's Prayer for the New Year

Dear Friends:

It is the hallowed custom of Jewish women, at the time of candle-lighting, which in our tradition is a moment of divine good-will, to pray—and the prayer is always a very personal one; an outpouring of the heart, a sacred moment between woman and God

My late mother, *aleha hashalom,* used to pray with greater fervor on Rosh Hashanah than on the eve of other holidays. Please find below her candle-lighting prayer for the New Year.

> In honor of God and His Torah, in honor of the solemn Festival which the Lord has given us together with this beloved *Mitzvah*, I have kindled the *Yomtev* lights, praying that this act may be weighed by the Heavenly Tribunal and accepted as the symbol of my loyalty and the loyalty of my household to the Lord, our God. Because of the Covenant between God and the Jewish people, my loyalty must be reciprocated. So help me, *Riboyno shel Oylom* (Creator of the World), to bring up my children in Thy ways. And do Thou give them excellent health. *Du weisst doch zisser Tate, az kranke kinder kennen Dich nisht dienen.* (You know, sweet Father,

that sick children are not able to serve You.) And hear and heed this my prayer for a real *Yontev*, and forgive us all our iniquities, and give us a good and prosperous year. And I wish You too, dear God, a good year, a year in which even the goyim will sit and study your holy Torah … Amen.

My mother was taken away from her home in April, 1944, by the German Nazis who later killed her. She has no grave. May her simple prayer be a memorial for her, and may her piety inspire you to walk in the ways of reverence, and follow the spiritual paths of our forebears.

May God bless you and grant you a very good, a happy new Year.

Rabbi Martin Kessler

A *Kaddish* for the Children

On our melancholy journey through Hungary, Poland, and Czecho-slovakia we visited several of the concentration camps, death factories that did their grisly work during the black night of Nazi rule. As we walked through the haunted grounds and barracks of Terezin, our non-Jewish guide mentioned rather casually the macabre statistic that 15,000 children passed through this camp. Of these, 100 came back.

And to get the true dimensions of the unspeakable bestiality, we have to multiply that number by 100—1,500,000 children among the Six Million. Some 1,500,000 Dovidlach and Ruchelach and Yankalach and Chanalach and Moishalach and and and and …

To the sacred memory of these murdered children, I dedicate these heavy lines by way of remembering them, weeping for them. This is my *Kaddish,* as I randomly list some of the places where they perished, the depth of their suffering and the futile attempts to capture in broken words the anguish that is their legacy …

Yit-gadal v'yit-kadash sh'mey raba

Yiddish poet Abraham Sutzkever was the father of a little girl who was one of the 1,500,000. In a poem addressed to her, he wrote: "I remember a day—Bitter and wild—Seven streets and everywhere dolls, And in the whole town no child."

B'alma di v'ra chirutey, v'yamlich malchutey

When the SS physicians at Auschwitz were determining which chil-dren would live and which would die, they hung a bar at a certain height. The children who were too short to reach the bar were considered unfit to work and were immediately sent to the crematory. Realizing this, the small children tried to stand as tall as possible in order to be in the group that was to live—for a while longer.

B'cha-yey-chon uv-yomey-chon uv-cha-yey d'chol beyt yisrael

In his *Notes from the Warsaw Ghetto*, Emmanuel Ringelblum wrote in 1941: "People cover the dead bodies of frozen children with handsome posters designed for Children's Month, bearing the legend, 'Our Children, Our Children Must Live—A Child Is the Holiest Thing.'"

Ba-agala u-vizman kariv, v'imru amen.

In another entry, Ringelblum tells us about a child who tried to collect an extra lunch at a public "soup" kitchen. "When discovered, the child begged with tears in his eyes to be allowed to have two lunches, because he did not want to die like his little sister."

Y'hey sh'mey raba m'varach l'alam ul-almey alma-ya.

Ringelblum further informs us that they have received news that the Jews in the Lodz Ghetto have been forbidden to marry and to have children. Women pregnant up to three months had to have an abortion. Exceeding even the malice of Pharaoh, the Nazi decree was aimed at Jewish baby girls and baby boys alike.

Yit-barach v'yish-tabach v'yit-pa-ar v'yit-romam v'yit-na-seh'.

One of the survivors later recalled: "When I woke up in the mornings, I used to come out and gaze at the crematoria chimneys and the barracks and the barbed wire. I used to smell the filth and disease, and see what a fine lot of skeletons we all were—and I was still alive, they hadn't got me yet, it was wonderful. Wonderful! To see the dawn coming up, to know one was alive for one more day. One more beautiful day."

V'yit-hadar v'yit-aleh v'yit-halal sh'mey d'kud-sha

Gisella Perl was a Hungarian physician incarcerated in Auschwitz. Dr. Mengele gave Dr. Perl instructions that all pregnancies must be reported to him. He said that pregnant women would be sent to another camp for better nutrition. But Dr. Perl discovered that they were being taken to be used as guinea pigs in Dr. Mengele's sadistic medical experiments. She says, "I decided that never again would there be a pregnant woman in Auschwitz." So night after night she performed abortions on a dirty floor using her hands. "Hundreds of times I did this. No one can ever know what it means to destroy these babies.

But I must do it or both mother and child will be so cruelly treated by Mengele."

B'rich hu, l'eyla ul-eyla mi-kol bir-chata v'shi-rata

Adam Cherniakow, who served for nearly three years as chairman of the Warsaw Judenrat in the ghetto, left us the most important diary of the Holocaust. In an entry dated June 14, 1942, he writes about hungry children, street children, beggars, naked and barefoot skeletons.

Tush-b'chata v'ne-chemata da-amiran b'alma, v'imru amen.

Another entry—July 22, 1941:

> In front of 16 Krochmalna Street I was stopped by a commander of a military sanitary column and shown the corpse of a child in an advanced state of decay … On the basis of subsequent investigation it was established that the body had been left behind by its own mother … and that the child's name was Moszek, age 6.… It was ascertained that the child had indeed died of hunger.… "

Y'hey sh 'lama raba min sh'ma-ya

Adam Cherniakow committed suicide on July 23, 1942. He left a note explaining that the SS had wanted him to kill the children with his own hands. Death was his only way out.

V'ha-yim aleynu v'al kol yisrael, v'imru amen.

What do these black memories do for us? What do they speak to us? Alan Dershowitz, in his book *Chutzpah,* says: "Every time I attend a gathering of Jewish children … I imagine SS guards lining up these children for the gas chambers."

Eliezer Berkovitz, the Israeli theologian, takes a more belligerent stance. He is especially furious that after the Christian silence during the Holocaust and their centuries old anti-Jewish poison that prepared the ground for it, some Christians still seek to convert Jews to their faith. "All we want of Christians," he cries, "is that they keep their hands off us and our children."

For myself, I think that there are more positive responses that we can make to the wanton murders. There are two things, it seems to me, that we can do. In the first place, we need more Jews. We need larger Jewish families. To all young people still planning their families, I say: Every Jewish child that is born constitutes our most dramatic frustration of the enemies of our people. Our answer to death is life. *La amut kee echeyeh*, "I shall not die but live."

In addition to needing more Jews, we need better Jews—that means us, you and I. With more than one-third of our people destroyed, we must each take upon ourselves an added measure of responsibility. The prayers they might have offered, we must offer. The books they might have created and read, we must create and read. The Shabbat candles they would have kindled, we must kindle. The *tzedakah* they would have given, we must give. Every day, we must be more devout, more devoted, more dedicated.

Our beloved children could not save their own lives, but if we used their wasted lives and their brutal deaths to enhance our own lives, and to strengthen our commitment to our common faith, we may thereby add to their memories an undying glory.

Oseh shalom bi-m'romav, hu ya-aseh shalom aleynu v'al kol yisrael, v'imru amen.

Rabbi Sidney Greenberg

There Is One Synagogue Left in Kiev

They do not talk of loss at Babi Yar. These aged men who blink into the sun on benches in the courtyard of the *shul* have no more words or tears. *What's done is done.*

Their faces speak, each furrow slaughter-etched. They sense the stranger's grief, yet know the cost of grief is small to him who merely sees, then journeys on his way. *What's lost stays lost.*

Their ninth of Av came clearly and stayed on. There were forty temples once. Now one is all that stands in Kiev, their Jerusalem, a crumbling, wordless, tearless Western Wall.

So long ago their Queen of Sabbath fled, all that's left is *kaddish* for the dead.

Yaacov Luria

The United States Holocaust Memorial Museum: Opening Ceremonies

In the *New York Times* article describing the opening of the new U.S. Holocaust Memorial Museum, we find the following description:

"... The television journalist Ted Koppel, whose parents were refugees from the Holocaust, read Edward R. Murrow's famous 1945 broadcast from Buchenwald: 'There surged around me an evil-smelling horde. Men and boys reached out to touch me; they were in rags and the remnants of uniform. Death had already marked many of them, but they were smiling with their eyes.'

"Some wept as they heard Elie Wiesel describe a Jewish woman somewhere in the Carpathian mountains, who read a short newspaper article about the Warsaw Ghetto uprising. She wondered aloud: 'Why are our Jews in Warsaw behaving like this? Why are they fighting? Couldn't they have waited quietly until the end of the war?'

"{Wiesel continued}: 'Treblinka, Ponar, Belzec, Chelmno, Birkenau; she had never heard of these places. One year later, together with her entire family, she was in a cattle-car traveling to the black hole of history named Auschwitz.' At the end of his speech, the writer said: 'She was my mother.'"

D.P.E.

Remembering, Not Forgetting

When Pharaoh restored the chief butler to his position as foretold by Joseph in his interpretation of the butler's dream, he forgot Joseph. "Yet did not the chief butler remember Joseph, but forgot him" (Genesis 40:23). Why does the Bible use this repetitive language? It is obvious that if the butler forgot Joseph, he did not remember him. Yet, both verbs are used, remembering and forgetting. "The Bible, in using this language, is teaching us a very important lesson," said the Rabbi of Bluzhov, Rabbi Israel Sira, to his Hasidim.

Said the Rabbi of Bluzhov, "There are events of such overbearing magnitude that one ought not to remember them all the time, but one must not forget them either. Such an event is the Holocaust."

Hasidic teaching

We Will Outlive You, Globochnik!

In his book *Sparks of Glory*, the Holocaust writer Moshe Prager tells how Lublin, one of the centers of Jewish life and learning, was taken over by a German Obersturmfuhrer named Otto Globochnik. Herding all the Jews into the city square, he shot into the air and screamed:

"Sing, Jews, sing!" But no one felt like singing. He ordered his troops to push all the Jews up against the barbed-wire fence. As many of them bled, again he screamed: "Sing, Jews, sing!"

One hasidic Jew began a Yiddish song, *Lomir zoch ibber betten*—"Let us make up, God. Let us become friends again"—a plaintive song sung by Eastern European Jews during the High Holy Days as a plea to God to return them to their homeland. Only, spontaneously he changed the lyrics.

After a few minutes, everyone in the square began to sing new words to an old tune—*mir velen dir ibber leben!*—"We will outlive you, Globochnik!" They sang with faith and joy, and they sang with ecstasy. They sang until they could sing no longer.

Every Jew in the world today is a living testament that we have outlived the Pharaohs, Antiochuses, Hamans and Globochniks. What we have to do is make sure that our descendants will land on their feet too. Most of all—we must believe in ourselves, in the truth of our Torah and in our right to our homeland.

Rabbi Shlomo Riskin

Martyrology—The 614th Commandment

There emerges what I will boldly term a 614th commandment: *the authentic Jew of today is forbidden to hand Hitler yet another posthumous victory.* If the 614th commandment is binding upon the authentic Jew then we are first commanded to survive as Jews, lest the Jewish people perish. We are commanded, second, to remember in our very guts and bones the martyrs of the Holocaust, lest their memory perish. We are forbidden, thirdly, to deny or despair of God, however much we may have to contend with Him, or with belief in Him, lest Judaism perish. We are forbidden, finally, to despair of the world as the place which is to become the kingdom of God, lest we help make it a meaningless place in which God is dead or irrelevant and everything is permitted. To abandon any of these imperatives, in response to Hitler's victory at Auschwitz, would be to hand him yet other, posthumous victories.

Rabbi Emil Fackenheim

A Jew Cannot Be Without God

Elie Wiesel, who endured the horrors of the Holocaust and witnessed the death of his father in a camp, at first refused to say *Kaddish,* the prayer expressing praise of God in death as in life. Ultimately Wiesel recited the *Kaddish,* which (in an autobiographical novel) he calls "that solemn affirmation filled with grandeur and serenity by which man returns to God his crown and his scepter." Wiesel's confession of doubt and struggle and his refusal to abandon God have empowered him to help us remain sons and daughters of the covenant in a post-Holocaust world. Wiesel has said: "A Jew can be for God and with God and against God but not without God."

Rabbi Samuel E. Karff

An Elegy for the Six Million

One day they will assemble in the valley of bones—
Ashes sifted out of furnaces, vapors from Auschwitz,
Parchments from some fiend's books, cakes of soap,
Half-formed embryos, screams still heard in nightmares.
God will breathe upon them. He will say: Be men.
But they will defy Him: We do not hear you. Did you
    hear us?
There is no resurrection for us. In life it was a wondrous thing
For each of us to be himself, to guide his limbs to do his will.
But the many are now one. Our blood has flowed together,
Our ashes are inseparable, our marrow commingled,
Our voices poured together like water of the sea.
We shall not surrender this greater self.
We the Abrahams, Isaacs, Jacobs, Sarahs, Leahs, Rachels
Are now forever Israel.

Almighty God, raise up a man who will go peddling through
    the world.
Let him gather us up and go through the world selling us as
    trinkets.
Let the peddler sell us cheaply. Let him hawk his wares
    and say:
"Who will buy my souvenirs? Little children done in soap,
A rare Germanic parchment of the greatest Jew from Lodz."
Men will buy us and display us and point to us in pride:
"A thousand Jews went into this and here is a rare piece
That came all the way from Cracow in a box car."
A great statesman will place a candle at his bedside.
It will burn but never be consumed.
The tallow will drip with the tears we shed
And it will glow with the souls of our children.
They will put it in the bathrooms of the United Nations
Where diplomats will wash and wash their hands
With Polish Jews and German Jews and Russian Jews.
Let the peddler sell the box of soap that once was buried
With *Kaddish* and Psalms by our brothers.
Some night the statesman will blow upon the candle
And it will not go out.
The souls of little children will flicker and flicker
But not expire.
Some day the diplomats will wash their hands and find them
    stained with blood.
Some day citizens of the German town
Will awake to find their houses reeking
With all the vapors from all the concentration camps,
From Hell itself, and the stench will come from the soap box.
Then they will rise up, statesmen, diplomats, citizens
And go hunting for the peddler: "You who disturb our rest
And our ablutions, you who haunt us with your souvenirs,
You who prick our conscience, death upon you!"
But the peddlers shall never cease from the earth
Until the candles die out and the soap melts away.

                          Rabbi David Polish

Remember Us unto Life

On a day filled to overflowing with prayers that God "remember us to life," it is especially significant that we recite *yizkor* prayers, the *avodah* service, and the martyrology. In the first we ask God to remember those without whom we could not have been, or been as worthy of remembrance as we are. It is as if, through our remembrance of them, God remembers, just as many of God's mercies are given to us to give to each other, and revealed by God only through us. The lesson of the *avodah* service, I think, is that our lives would possess only the barest of meanings if we had to invent such meanings as we went along. How fortunate that our acts are not of our own authorship, that we can remember them. "Happy was the eye that saw these things"—that is, the person who learned the art of begging forgiveness up close—from the high priest in the temple. "May the memory of these things be our pardon"—for we rest secure in the knowledge that the acts of atonement we perform are not of our own devising.

In the martyrology, however, we remember that some acts should never have occurred, and so remind God, as it were, that God has often failed to remember God's own mercies. We recall this precisely at the moment when God's memory is of the utmost importance to us; and, emboldened by this recollection, we ask God to forgive all our failures to remember, reminding God of ancestors who *did* remember, even when *God* did not. "Remember us," therefore, "unto life."

Dr. Arnold Eisen

A Memoir of the Yom Kippur War

From that first peek into the room at Tel Hashomer I had eased myself into looking at what I was doing. When working on the tank I had slowly steeled up the courage to look at the burned remains of what had been human. But there still had been no confrontation with a dead body, a recognizable human form. Until now all my contact had been with objects, and my feelings of anguish arose from the thought of who these objects had been, what they had done and what they stood for. I had not yet been challenged to associate these thoughts with the recognizable body which shortly before had been a living Jew. Slowly

I had been working up to it. I had looked under the blankets bit by bit to see if I could stand it. But the confrontation with such great numbers of dead was shocking despite all my preparation. I had always imagined that nothing Jewish could be foreign to me. I had always identified with the Jewish plight, even the Holocaust. If all of us were present at Mount Sinai, all of us were present at Auschwitz.

The burden of Jewish being is to live all of Jewish history. I see no difference between the victims of Auschwitz and the victims of the war I dealt with; they are all casualties of Jewishness and Jewish history. What difference could there be? Did they die less painfully, did the burns affect them less, are little pieces of men less horrible scattered around a tank than burned in an oven? Is their Kiddush HaShem less?

Maybe the statistics of the wars of Israel should be added to the statistics of Jewish martyrdom of the Holocaust, the pogroms and the Crusades. Perhaps we should make up a grand total of Jewish martyrdom and proclaim that the world owes us that many lives. Each and every war casualty lives for me in his death, whether he be a stump burned beyond recognition or a clean body marred only by a small hole through the head; whether his uniform be burned and ragged with arms and legs missing, or whether it be whole and pressed with shining boots and the insignia of a colonel adorning his epaulettes; whether he be from a wealthy family of industrialists living in a villa in a Tel Aviv suburb, or the son of a poor family of thirteen children barely existing in a two room hovel in a Tel Aviv slum.

Each and every one of them is a victim of the Holocaust. No matter that their fathers and mothers escaped the Holocaust and brought forth this child as a rebuttal to the brutality and Jew-hatred they had experienced. Out of the ashes of European Jewry they wanted to create a new, independent Jewry; out of the mouth of death they created life. Their offspring jumped back into the mouth of death, running willingly back to the Holocaust of their parents.

And so the horror of that night I find impossible to express. The faces of the soldiers young and old, dark and fair, recognizable and unrecognizable. The torture that modern weaponry can inflict on the human body is almost infinite in its possibilities. The burns and tearing of flesh, the mangling of limbs and faces—these images could be written down, but no one who was not there can know this particular hell. Faces swollen with death, lips puffed out and red as with lipstick but it is blood, the whooshing sound of a body being turned over or lifted as the air leaves collapsing lungs or rushes through the holes of the body, those made by God and those made by war. The constant flow of blood, the emptying of souls onto the concrete floor of the installation or onto the sandy wastes of the desert. All this I can describe. And the pain, oh the pain deep inside, the desire to flee and the strange ineffable push to continue, the mystical drive that sends you back to work, the coming of the almost unbearable pain and the mysterious passing of pain, allowing you to work again. Early in the evening I learn a lesson of the trade. Looking at papers found on a soldier whose identity we are trying to establish, I read part of a postcard written by the soldier " … Be good kids and pray that Daddy will return safely. Help Ima out in the house and listen to what she says. I will bring you back some candies and good things from the army … I love you most of all."

I could have written that to my own kids. I did write it to them. I feel dizzy, I want to cry. Outside into the night of beautiful stars. A moment of sorrow and tears for that man. It is too much for me. And so I learn: never read the letters, never pry too much, keep it on an impersonal level. It's the only way you can survive. In the midst of this holocaust, in the midst of this great sorrow, I adopt a rule of self-preservation: mourn for them collectively, not individually. No one has enough strength, enough emotional depth to mourn for so many martyrs one by one. If we cry, let us cry for our people, all of them together. The enormity of what is happening is almost too much for us. We take a few steps into the desert away from the installation, sigh or cry, stand up straight and return to unloading.

Everything is automatic. No one thinks about what he is doing. We just do it. We pray *minhah,* then *maariv,* eat, all automatic. At last it is night, the festival is over and it is time to start our work.

Rabbi Michael Graetz

My People Are Being Consumed

Together with a number of families, my wife and children and I are cowering under a storm of bullets over our heads. We remain power-less, useless, paralyzed.

On the seventeenth we were "presented" with the constitution for which our brothers spilled their blood like water. On the same day a rumor was spread abroad that orders had been given to attack the Jews—and the attack began from all sides. Simultaneously, an order was issued that we should not shoot from the windows, and not throw stones. If we should do that, the soldiers would fire back and destroy our houses. Seeing soldiers on the street—and Cossacks—we felt reas-sured; and they did help, but not us. They helped to rob, to beat, to ravish, to despoil. Before our eyes and in the eyes of the whole world, they helped to smash windows, break down doors, break locks and to put booty in their pockets. Before our eyes and in the eyes of our chil-dren, they beat Jews grievously—men, women and children—and they shouted, "Money, give us your money." Before our eyes women were hurled from windows and children thrown to the cobblestones.

The local newspapers publish only one hundredth part of the frightful details of the happenings in Kiev. Now, imagine what is hap-pening in hundreds of Jewish towns and villages. Too dear will our freedom cost, and God only knows whether we will live to enjoy it. The tyrant will not surrender his rod, the swords are being sharpened ... In God's name, brethren, help. To act, to help, to resist, that we are not permitted. For the life of one drunken brute that we take when he attacks our wives and our children we pay with hundreds of innocent lives.

What shall we do? No place to hide. Gentiles will not give shelter to Jews.

Brother, do something. Publish this in English as well as in the Jewish press.

Well then, if I cannot be saved, if I must die, I am ready. Perhaps it is better that I shall fall a sacrifice with the rest. My people are being consumed. The whole of Russian Jewry is in danger.

Sholom Aleichem (Shalom Rabinovitz, 1859–1916)

Golden Silence

We know that Judaism exalts the power of words, and the power of speech. We are a tradition devoted to capturing the world in words. Yet, perhaps because we are so attuned to the word, Judaism is also keenly aware of the strength found in silence.

The midrash *Aleh Ezkerah* [These I will remember—the theme words of the Martyrology Service] describes the final moments of the great sage Rabbi Ishmael. During the second century CE, those who remained faithful to Judaism were persecuted and killed by the Romans. Sages and scholars who had continued to teach Torah in defiance of imperial decrees met their death as retribution for their devotion.

Rabbi Ishmael was captured by the Romans and sentenced to death. He endured the tortures inflicted upon him in silence. Finally, unable to contain his suffering any longer, a cry escaped his lips. Taking note of the anguish of this pious man, the Rabbis tell us that God declared: "If one more word comes from Rabbi Ishmael, I shall overturn the world."

Hearing that, Rabbi Ishmael would not speak. He refused to cry out. Dying in silence, he saved the world.

Rabbi David Wolpe

What Did We Lose?

What did we lose in the Holocaust?

In the simplest, most basic terms, we lost 6,000,000 human souls. In 1939, two-thirds of the world's Jews lived in Europe: and three-quarters of those, half of the world's Jews, were concentrated in Eastern Europe.

We lost one eye, one arm, one leg, one ear, one half of every living Jew.

The Holocaust brought the thousand-year-old culture of Ashkenazic Jewry to an end. The Jewish people lost the skilled bearers of a culture whose religious teachings and traditions molded its character and values, its intellect and spirit.

We lost the stronghold of our Yiddish language, the language in which Jewish men studied Talmud, in which mothers sang their babies to sleep and in which little children played their games, in which merchants conducted their business, in which rabbis delivered their sermons, in which young men courted their sweethearts.

Gone are the pious, the righteous, the good, who filled their days with ancient books and yearning chant. The mothers who faithfully kindled the *shabbas likht,* wept at prayer, prepared for Passover, mourned at graves. Gone are the thick-necked burly ones who ruled the streets: the porters and drivers, the beggars, peddlers, merchants, and those remarkably shrewd lords and ladies of the stalls and stands that filled the Jewish marketplaces.

Gone are the grandmothers and grandfathers with snowy heads and hands like trembling branches. The ones who had earned their right to sink peacefully into quiet graves, but who saw instead the destruction of their offspring, the devastation of all they had built.

Gone are the giants who, with honor, carried the precious store of three hundred generations of painstaking study and exquisite talents—doctors and pharmacists, teachers and scholars, poets and musicians, artists and architects.

Gone, too, the craftsmen, all those golden-fingered Jewish tailors, watchmakers, shoemakers, printers and bakers, who labored in sweat and swore together to free all mankind.

A culture unique in Jewish history, it was East-European Jewry that fashioned it. It was the wellspring of Jewish creativity for Jewish communities all over the world.

And the children ... there lies the worst of the Holocaust. The children who might have passed all that on in love and learning to their children, and their children's children, all cut off, gone forever, no more.

If only that million children had survived. In our memories only their names remain—Blimele, Rivcle, Perele, Hatzkele, Muttele, Kivele, Hershele, Shaiele, Goidele, Mendele, Rohele, Hayele, Dvoyrele, Sorele, Shimele, Shiyele, Blumele, Leybele. How they ring in beauty. The *nigun* of their names persists like a *Shabbes zemirah,* soft and sweet, and more than a little sad, much more.

Hazzan Samuel Rosenbaum

Looking into Our Own Hearts

After the close of the Eichmann trial, the *New York Times* asked editorially:

"What was the object and justification of the trial?" The answer it gave to this question is worth pondering. "It was and it is to do all that can be done to eradicate an evil thing out of our civilization ... a thing so incredibly wicked that it would not have been believable of modern man if it had not actually occurred. This evil, this wickedness began with intolerance and hate in a few men's hearts. It spread until it almost wrecked the world. Now the obligation is to remember, not in hate, not in the spirit of revenge, but so that this spirit cannot ever flourish again so long as man remains on earth. And to this end, let us begin, each of us, by looking into our own hearts."

D.P.E.

Zakhor—Never Forget

Death Toll in All United States Wars

Civil War—600,000
World War I—116,700
World War II—408,000
Korea—55,000
Vietnam—58,000
Total killed in action: 1,237,700

In World War II, in Poland alone, the Nazis murdered 2,800,000 Jews. More than twice the number killed in action in all our wars— *just because they were Jews!!*

And then the Nazis murdered 3,200,000 more Jews.

Zakhor—Never forget!!

D.P.E.

Why We Stay in Israel

It feels crazy to live in Israel right now. A few people are leaving. I understand them. It's horrible to live with the violence, and the attendant stress and anxiety. We Israelis are so vulnerable: traveling in a car or bus, going to a cafe, even staying home. All have been woven with terror. Every time of day and night, we know we are targets.

One recent Friday night, we were awakened at 1 in the morning by the loudspeaker in our community. The announcement said: "There is a warning that there is a terrorist in Tekoa. Lock your windows and doors, sleep with a gun, guard your children. Turn out all of the lights."

We quickly turned off the lights even though we are Sabbath observers. We locked the doors and windows. We put a chair in front of the front door. Then the phone rang. Our neighbor was calling to make sure that we had heard the warning.

The kids were scared, shaking. I told them that we would protect them, take care of them. That they should try to go to sleep.

The kids fell to sleep, all of them in our bed. I prayed and then slept fitfully, hoping that morning would soon be on its way. Around 3:00 the loudspeaker came on again. The warning was over. For now. But as I told my children, it's rare that terrorists warn you.

They certainly didn't warn my son, Koby, 13, before they stoned him and his friend Yosef to death, crushing their skulls so they were unrecognizable. Koby and Yosef were hiking near our home in Tekoa. The two boys wanted to know the canyon beyond our house like the backs of their hands.

They were killed for their love of the land. They were killed for being Jews.

My friend was at a movie in Jerusalem on Saturday night, the night of the massacre at the Moment Café when a terrorist killed 11 people. The manager stopped the movie and told the patrons what had happened and asked if they wanted the movie to continue. They didn't. They all went home.

Why do people continue to stay here even though we are being slaughtered by terrorists? Because many of us feel a deep sense of connection here, to our country, our heritage, and to each other.

The sense of connection manifests itself in surprising ways. Today I go to the *makollet,* the grocery store, and there is a man filling a cardboard box with goodies to send to his son in the army. The man picks out a bar of chocolate, plain milk chocolate. And the *makollet* lady, Rena, says: "Your son doesn't like that kind of chocolate. Noam likes crunchy chocolate."

Another story: My friend Ruth is at a kiosk buying a drink. A little girl says shyly to the proprietor: "What can I get for 2 shekels?" He says, "Nothing." Then he hands her a shekel. "But now you have three. You can buy gum or a candy." Ruth fishes into her pocket. "Now you have four."

Here there is a feeling of family. Here in the face of pain and suffering, we don't feel alone. We feel that we are a net that is woven together and though it is full of holes, it is strong enough to lift us up.

If we make a hole in the net, the net is weakened. Of course it can be mended. But it will never be quite the same.

We don't want to make a hole in the net. We don't want to leave the place where our son is buried. We don't want to leave the only place in the world where time is measured by a Jewish calendar, where the celebrations center on the Jewish holidays, where the language is the language of the Bible. We don't want to leave the center of Jewish history. Now we are part of that long, hard history. We are part of the struggle of the Jewish people trying to live in their land.

My son died for being a Jew. I want to live as one.

Sherri Mandell

Martyrology—9/11 and Lamentations

[*Rabbi Irwin Kula had an interview on PBS.org about 9/11. In it, he applied* Eikhah trop *to the final phone messages of people dying on 9/11. Here is a small piece of the interview.*]

These are final conversations that were recorded on cell phones, recorded on voice mail. They seem to me to be incredible texts, because they were at the moment of confronting life or death. They're so pure about the expression of love between husband and wife, between mother and child.... When I read them, I just felt they were texts as sacred as the text that we end up having recorded, that we transmit from generation to generation.

I read these every single morning now, or most mornings, because they remind me that whatever my tradition is about, it's about this. It's about being able to express love. It's about being able to understand, taking care of our children. It's about being in real, genuine friendships. They just seem so real to me....

I know all these chants, because my father is a cantor. He transmitted all these ancient Jewish chants to me, so they almost naturally came out in chant. I realized, "My God, the chant that we use to read one of the Scriptures that tells the story of the destruction of the temple in Jerusalem and the burning down of that temple, those chants fit this perfectly," although that's not how I thought about it. The chant came and then I said the chant worked, which, of course, is the way a good tradition works. The chant has made them even more alive to me and then links these new texts to my traditional text, even though I don't know these people. But the fact is, we all knew these people in our own way....

[*Singing*]:

"Honey. Something terrible is happening. I don't think I'm going to make it. I love you. Take care of the children."

"Hey, Jules. It's Brian. I'm on the plane and it's hijacked and it doesn't look good. I just wanted to let you know that I love you, and I hope to see you again. If I don't, please have fun in life, and live life the best you can. Know that I love you, and no matter what, I'll see you again."

"Mommy. The building is on fire. There's smoke coming through the walls. I can't breathe. I love you, Mommy. Good-bye."

"I love you a thousand times over and over. I love and need you. Whatever decisions you make in your life, I need you to be happy, and I will respect any decisions you make."

It's incredibly life-affirming, because it's knowledge from Ground Zero. It's knowledge from real experience, and that's what religion always was about to me, [and] I think I got away from that. That was from the head; 9/11 is about being from the heart.

                                                      Rabbi Irwin Kula

Before the *Kaddish:* At the Funeral of Those Who Were Killed in the Land of Israel

When a king of flesh and blood goes forth to war against his enemies, he leads out his soldiers to slay and to be slain. It is hard to say, does he love his soldiers, doesn't he love his soldiers, do they matter to him, don't they matter to him. But even if they do matter to him, they are as good as dead, for the Angel of Death is close upon the heels of everyone who goes off to war, and accompanies him only to slay him. When the soldier is hit, by arrow or sword or saber or any of the other kinds of destructive weapons, and slain, they put another man in his place, and the king hardly knows that some one is missing—for the population of the nations of the world is big and their troops are many. If one person is slain, the king has many others to make up for him.

But our Sovereign, the Ruler of rulers of rulers, the Blessed Holy One, is a Ruler who delights in life, who loves peace and pursues peace, and loves the people Israel, and chose us from among all the nations: not because we are a numerous folk did God set divine love upon us, for we are the fewest of all people. But because of the love God loves us with and we are so few, each and every one of us matters as much before God as a whole legion, for God hasn't many to put in our place. When from Israel one is missing, God forbid, a diminishing takes place in God's legions, and in God's kingdom, be it blessed, there is a decline of strength, as it were, for God's kingdom now lacks one of its legions and God's grandeur, be it blessed, has been diminished, God forbid.

That is why for each dead person in Israel we recite the prayer "Magnified and sanctified be God's great Name." Magnified be the power of the Name so that before God, blessed be God's name, there be no decline of strength; and sanctified be God in all the worlds which God created according to God's will, and not for ourselves let us have fear but for the superlative splendor of God's exalted holiness. May God establish God's sovereignty so that God's sovereignty be perfectly revealed and visible, and may it suffer no diminishing, God forbid. In our lifetime and in your days and in the lifetime of the whole house of Israel speedily and soon—for if God's sovereignty is manifest in the world, there is peace in the world and blessing in the world and song in the world and a multitude of praises in the world and great consolation in the world, and the holy ones, Israel, are beloved in the world and God's grandeur continues to grow and increase and never diminishes.

If this is what we recite in prayer over any who die, how much the more over our beloved and sweet brothers and sisters, the dear children of Zion, those killed in the Land of Israel, whose blood was shed for the glory of God's blessed Name and for God's people and God's land and God's heritage And what is more, everyone who dwells in the Land of Israel belongs to the legion of the Ruler of rulers of rulers, the Blessed Holy One, whom the Ruler appointed watchman of God's palace. When one of God's legion is slain, God has no others as it were to put in his place.

Therefore, members of the whole house of Israel, all you who mourn in this mourning, let us fix our hearts on our Father in heaven, Israel's Sovereign and Redeemer, and let us pray for ourselves and for God too, as it were: Magnified and sanctified be God's Great Name in the world which God created as God willed. May God establish God's kingdom, may God make God's deliverance to sprout forth, may God bring nigh the messiah, and so to the end of the whole prayer. May we be found worthy still to be in life when with our own eyes we may behold God who makes peace in God's high places, in God's compassion making peace for us and for all Israel, Amen.

S. Y. Agnon, translated and adapted by Judah Goldin

Musaf—V'ye-e-tayhu

There have been many things written in the aftermath of 9/11 and there will be much more coming out [in the future]. One of the pieces that I found most meaningful was an article published on the editorial page of the *New York Times*, the week after the attack. It was written by the evolutionary biologist from Harvard, Stephen Jay Gould. Although he died this past May, the contribution that he made to how we think about the world will long be remembered.

He was in New York with his family when the airplanes hit the World Trade Center Towers. He was acutely aware of people lamenting the evil that exists in the world that could lead one to the conclusion that there is somehow an equal balance between decent and depraved people in the world that explains the good and evil experienced in human history. Drawing on his experience as a scientist of human and animal development he wrote:

> We need to expose and celebrate the fallacy of this conclusion so that, in this moment of crisis, we may affirm an essential truth too easily forgotten, and regain some crucial comfort too readily forgone. Good and kind people outnumber all others by thousands to one. The tragedy of human history lies in the enormous potential for destruction in rare acts of evil, not in the high frequency of evil people. Complex systems can only be built step by step, whereas destruction requires but an instant. Thus, in what I like to call the Great Asymmetry, every spectacular incident of evil will be balanced by 10,000 acts of kindness, too often unnoted and invisible as the "ordinary" efforts of a vast majority.

He observes that in the week after the attack "ground zero" became "the focal point for a vast web of bustling goodness, channeling uncountable deeds of kindness from an entire planet—the acts must be recorded to reaffirm the overwhelming weight of human decency."

He goes on to write about several acts of kindness that prove his point. It is human nature to focus on the evil that we experience. At this time of year let us not forget the far greater number of acts of kindness that sustain our world.

Rabbi Harold J. Kravitz

THE SERVICE OF THE HIGH PRIEST: IN TEMPLE TIMES AND TODAY

Yom Kippur is also one of the most ancient Jewish festivals. Its ritual, probably as practiced in First Temple times, is fully elaborated in Leviticus 16. The purpose of that ritual was to atone for Israel, its priests, and its Temple, to "cover" their sins and allow for a new purity. This was accomplished by sacrifice, the sprinkling of blood, and the unique expulsion of the scapegoat, who carried the sins of Israel off into the wilderness.

An account of that Temple rite, called the *'avodah,* is still read in the traditional synagogue during the Yom Kippur *mussaf* service. But Yom Kippur has been transformed in the rabbinic tradition to a day of intense prayer and soul-searching, encouraged by the atmosphere of the fast.

RABBI ARTHUR GREEN, *THESE ARE THE WORDS*

Avodah: Service

The act of volunteering is an assertion of individual worth. The person who of his own free will decides to work on behalf of the good of his community is in effect saying, "I have gifts and talents which are needed. I am a person who accepts a responsibility, not because it is imposed upon me, but rather because I wish to be useful. My right to thus be used is a symbol of my personal dignity and worth as a citizen in a democracy."

Edward Lindeman

The motto of life is give and take. Everyone must be both a giver and a receiver. One who is not both is a barren tree.

Martin Buber

Avodah: The Story of the High Priest

As we begin to tell the story of the *Kohen Gadol,* let us think a minute about what a story is, and how a story should be told, and what the purpose is for telling a story.

By retelling the story of the *Kohen Gadol* and his sacrifice of the scapegoat in the Ancient Temple, we put ourselves into a certain frame of mind about the meaning of sacrifice, of atonement, and of this special Fast Day of the Jewish calendar.

Martin Buber, in his volume of *Hasidic Tales* (Early Masters, Preface) conveys the following about "how to tell a story."

> A rabbi, whose grandfather had been a disciple of the Baal Shem, was asked to tell a story. "A story," he said, "must be told in such a way that it constitutes help in itself." And he told: "My grandfather was lame. Once they asked him to tell a story about his teacher. And he related how the holy Baal Shem used to hop and dance while he prayed. My grandfather rose as he spoke, and he was so swept away by his story that he himself began to hop and dance to show how the master had done. From that hour on he was cured of his lameness. That's the way to tell a story!"

If a story "must be told in such a way that it constitutes help in itself," what assistance does the retelling of the *Avodah* give us? Let's think about the answer to that question as we read the *Avodah*.

                                                        Rabbi Dov Peretz Elkins

The Root of All Holiness

Each Sabbath is a reflection of the World to Come, and Yom Kippur is the Sabbath of Sabbaths. During the Sabbath the extra spirituality, *neshama yeseirah,* that descends enjoys the bodily pleasures that we have in honor of the Sabbath. Similarly, on Yom Kippur our soul elevates our body to the level of the World to Come. Our body is then able to perceive spiritual pleasures. Just as there is no eating, drinking, or physical pleasures in the World to Come, they are absent on Yom Kippur too. Although normally we can only imagine spiritual pleasure, on Yom Kippur we can actually perceive it.

Let us therefore leave our lusts and passions, our pleasures and physical yearnings for this one singular day of the year to soar as the angels who have but one heart and desire for the will of God. Then we will abandon all evil and stand before the Throne of God with truth and humility. Then we will be at the root of all holiness, of time and space, of spirit and soul, as the *Kohen Gadol* who enters the Holy of Holies on the holiest day of the year.

                                                        Moshe Braun

Being Better—Serving Better

The *Avodah* Service reminds us of the root meaning of *Avodah*—service to God.

Spiritual traditions of all ages have always combined service to God and humanity with service to self. In Judaism and other religious traditions, personal growth and community outreach are seen as one indivisible unit.

Abraham Maslow, late head of the Dept. of Psychology at Brandeis University, expressed this thought in the following words:

The empirical fact is that self-actualizing people, our best experiencers, are also our most compassionate, our great improvers and reformers of society, our most *effective* fighters against injustice, inequality, slavery, cruelty, exploitation (and also our best fighters *for* excellence, effectiveness, competence). And it also becomes clearer and clearer that the best 'helpers' are the most fully human persons. What I may call the bodhisattvic path is an *integration* of self-improvement and social zeal, i.e., the best way to become a better 'helper' is to become a better person. But one necessary aspect of becoming a better person is *via* helping other people. So one must and can do both simultaneously.

D.P.E.

The Meaning of *Avodah*

Avodah means service; an *eved,* coming from the same root, is a servant. *Avodah* can also mean ordinary physical labor. In Egypt, the back-breaking toil under the Pharaohs was called *avodat parech (parech* meaning breaking). On the eve of the Exodus, *avodah* acquires a new meaning. Moses summons the elders of Israel and says to them: "Go and pick out lambs for your families and slaughter the Passover offering.... And when your children ask you, 'What do you mean by this *avodah?'* you shall say, 'It is a Passover sacrifice to the Lord ...'" (Exodus 12:21–27). There is new meaning to the word *avodah.* The offering and eating of the paschal lamb become an *avodah* (sacrificial service) to God. When the Temple stood in Jerusalem, all of its sacrificial rites would be considered *avodah,* service to God.

After the destruction of the second Temple and the cessation of the sacrificial service, *avodah* took on two more new meanings.

Avodah means study [of Torah].... You ask, "Isn't *avodah* work?" Scripture says, "And God took Adam and placed him in the garden of Eden to work it...." (Genesis 2:15). *Avodah* [before the sin and curse cannot mean labor, so it] must mean study [i.e., work without sweat of the brow]. Or perhaps *avodah* is prayer.... You ask, "Isn't *avodah* Temple sacrifice?" Scripture says, "[Do *avodah*] with all your heart...." (Deuteronomy 11:13). Is there a Temple *avodah* in heart [literally]? Therefore, *avodah* means prayer. Just as the service of the altar is called *avodah,* so is [study or] prayer called *avodah (Sifre Devarim 41).*

Avodah is what we do to construct a world; it is how we order reality and secure its foundations. *Avodah* is the way we repair the daily fractures that weaken our relationship with God. This is what the sacrifice did for the First Temple Israelites and what study and prayer did for the rabbis.

In our own day, *avodah* has been used in a startling new way, particularly by early Zionist thinkers like A.D. Gordon. On the surface he seems to have just restored the original meaning of *avodah* as labor. But in a deeper way he too is describing the way the cosmos is ordered by human hands in sacred service.

"All this should teach us that from now on our chief ideal must be *avodah* (labor). *Avodah* will heal us. In the center of all our hopes we must place *avodah;* our entire structure must be founded on *avodah*....*Avodah* is a lofty human ideal, an ideal of the future" (A.D. Gordon, *People and Labor*).

Rabbi Steven Greenberg

Avodah—For Whom Do the Priests Pray?

During the elaborate and beautiful *Avodah* service we read again and again how the *kohanim* pray for themselves, their household, and the whole house of Israel.

The garments worn by the *Kohanim* during their service during the year reminded them of their obligation to bear the burdens of Israel.

The late Rabbi Pinchas Peli suggested that the Torah's description of the two stones on the shoulders of the *Kohen*, worn on a garment called the *"Ephod,"* containing the names of the 12 tribes of Israel, are meant "to teach us an important lesson about responsible leadership. There are many leaders, who, after they are elected or chosen for high office, swiftly forget the people whom they are supposed to represent. The names of the twelve tribes of Israel were to be carried on the shoulders of Aaron, so that he should never forget the burdens of their needs."

Indeed, an important lesson about leadership is learned from this section of the Yom Kippur liturgy, the *Avodah*, the ancient priestly worship in the Jerusalem Temples.

D.P.E.

Avodah—Community Service

"Service to others is the rent we pay for the space we occupy." We will discover that, by helping our neighbors, we are enriching ourselves. You know the adage, "What goes around comes around." Or as we read in the Bible, "Cast your bread upon the waters and in the length of days, it shall return to you" (Kohelet 11:1).

Rabbi Hillel E. Silverman

Avodah: Community Service—Serving Others, We Serve Ourselves

There is a story about a mountain climber who was lost in a terrible snowstorm. Blinded by snow and ice, exhausted and half-frozen, he knew that he would freeze to death if he stopped and fell asleep. As he attempted to walk to safety, he fell across a body in the snow. He didn't know what to do. If he paused, he would jeopardize his own life, and yet here was the semi-conscious form of a fellow human being. He began to massage the fallen man. After many minutes of exertion, the man started to revive, and the warmth of the victim's body began to rejuvenate the good Samaritan. They both stumbled to safety.

Who received the greater blessing? The recipient or the giver? Actually, both of them were blessed, because they helped each other.

Rabbi Hillel E. Silverman

The Ritual of the Goats—We Are Left with Words....

Our Torah reading [read during the *Avodah* Service] is something different. It describes in vivid detail the ritual of the two goats—one sacrificed to the Lord, the other sent as expiation for the people's sins to Azazel, into the wilderness.

For us this test is a strange one. We live in a world distant from sacrifice and this kind of ritual. But it is important to think of this Torah reading as more than the reciting of a peculiar rite. Think of it instead as a drama—a double, perhaps even a triple-edged experience.

The Leviticus reading tells an ancient story, a story that comes from far back in our people's origins. This is the ritual that Aaron performed, in deadly earnest and with great care, when the Israelites wandered in the desert. It is a mysterious event—no one knows why it succeeded in expiating sin. But this was God's decree and it worked. If performed with care, sin was expiated.

Yom Kippur is a double drama. Not only is the performance in the wilderness described in our Leviticus reading, but on Yom Kippur we hear the echo of another expiation service as well. This expanded and modified version of the same ritual, the ritual that was performed in the temple by the High Priest when the people were finally established in their land, is included in the *Avodah* section of the *musaf* service.

And there is a third story too. Our story. For us there is the memory of the Leviticus rite and the recounting of the Temple ritual. But we have no goat of sacrifice and no goat to send to Azazel. We, living after Aaron's time and after the Temple's destruction, have no drama of action. We do, however, have the repository of language. For us the repetition of the words and the challenge of prayer is the only route toward atonement. For us, then, Yom Kippur may be even more awesome, more frightening than for our ancient forebears. They could rely on Aaron and later on the priests.

They had the power of the deed. We are left only with the shadow of deeds—the offering called language.

Dr. Barry W. Holtz

Through Service to God *(Avodah)* I Add to the Good of the World

It is within my power
Either to serve God or not to serve God.
Serving God, I add to my own good
And the good of the whole world.
Not serving God,
I forfeit my own good
And deprive the world of that good,
Which was in my power to create.

Leo Tolstoy

Reciting the *Avodah* in the Diaspora

When the Jewish people lost their home (the land of Israel) and God lost his (the Temple), then a new way of being was devised, and Jews became the people of the book and not the people of the Temple or the land. They became the people of the book because they had nowhere else to live. That bodily loss is frequently overlooked, but for me it lies at the heart of the Talmud, for all its plenitude. The Internet, which we are continually told binds us all together, nevertheless engenders in me a similar sense of Diaspora, a feeling of being everywhere and nowhere. Where else but in the middle of Diaspora do you *need* a home page?

The Talmud tells a story that captures this mysterious transformation from one kind of culture to another. It is the story of Yochanan ben Zakkai, the great sage of the first century, who found himself living in besieged Jerusalem on the eve of its destruction by Rome. Yochanan ben Zakkai understood that Jerusalem and the Temple were doomed, so he decided to appeal to the Romans for permission to found a yeshiva outside Jerusalem. In order to get him out of Jerusalem without being killed by the Zealots—the Jewish revolutionaries— Yochanan's students hid him in a coffin and carried him outside the city walls. They did this not to fool the Romans but to fool the Zealots, who were killing anyone who wasn't prepared to die with the city.

Yochanan wasn't prepared to die with the city. Once outside its walls, he went to see the Roman general Vespasian and requested permission to set up a yeshiva in Yavneh. Vespasian consented, and it is thus in Yavneh that the study of the oral law flourished, in Yavneh that the Mishnah took shape, and in Yavneh that Talmudic culture was saved while Temple culture died. In a sense, Yochanan's journey in his coffin is the symbolic enactment of the transformation Judaism underwent when it changed from a religion of embodiment to a religion of the mind and of the book. Jews died as a people of the body, of the land, of the Temple service of fire and blood, and then, in one of the greatest acts of translation in human history, they were reborn as the people of the book.

I think about Yochanan ben Zakkai in his coffin when I think about how we are passing, books and people both, through the doors of the computer age, and entering a new sort of global Diaspora in which we are everywhere—except home....

Jonathan Rosen

Avodah: We Are Defined by Our Connections

In the *Avodah* ritual we read on Yom Kippur, the High Priest enters the Holy of Holies and prays in a widening circle of concerns, first for his family, then for his tribe, and then for the entire people. When he stands before God, he does so, not as a holy man but as the representative of a holy people. As an individual, he has no right to be there, no matter how pious he might be. As the representative of a community, he was welcome to enter, bearing the community's cares and concerns. He defined himself not by what he believed but by whom he belonged to.

So we define ourselves, not by our beliefs but by our human connections, our Jewish bonds, our family love.

When I have instructed candidates for conversion to Judaism, at the end of our study, I ask them, "Of everything you've read and experienced this year, what has impressed you the most about being Jewish?" And they all give the same answer: the warmth and closeness of the Jewish family.

They are overwhelmed by the degree to which Jews care about each other: family, Israel, Russian immigrants. They don't find that anywhere else in the world.

You can't be a complete human being alone, without your family and people. You don't join a synagogue the way you join a health club, because you've decided that you need what they have to offer. You join in order to make sure that there will be a Jewish facility in your town for all those who need it, even as years ago, other Jews created this synagogue so that it would be here for you.

Rabbi Matthew H. Simon

Service

The section of the Yom Kippur liturgy called the *Avodah* is about the way the *Kohanim* worshipped in the ancient Temple *(Bet HaMikdash).*

The word *avodah* in Hebrew means "service"—with the same double meaning in Hebrew as it does in English. *Avodah* means both "service" (or, services) in the sense of "worship," as well as in the sense of doing community service or public service.

These two ideas, of course, are closely intertwined, because when one *worships* God, one *serves* God. And when one renders service to another human being, one is also serving God.

Thus, during the *Avodah* Section of the High Holiday liturgy, we give thought to both meanings of the word—to serving God, and serving others.

A wise person once said about the importance of giving service: "Help someone up their mountain, and you can't help but get a little closer to the top yourself."

D.P.E.

Belonging

Service is closer to generosity than it is to duty. It connects us to one another and to life itself. When we experience our connectedness, serving others becomes the natural and joyful thing to do. Over the long run, fixing and helping are draining, but service is renewing. When you serve, your work itself will sustain you, renew you, and bless you, often over many years.

Rachel Naomi Remen, M.D.

Giving Generously of Ourselves

"Service" is not a word that we often use, but one that we might think about more. To serve means that we subordinate our own desires and expectations so as to give generously of ourselves for a larger good. Sometimes we may hesitate to do so, in part from the popular view of "servitude" as a kind of slavery or the compulsion to do things against our will. After all, as Jews, we annually celebrate our freedom from slavery; we've served too many "masters" to use the word "service" lightly.

But let us think anew about this concept. We can put aside our proclivity to be centered largely on our own needs, and reclaim "service" as a way to offer ourselves to those causes and ideals that bespeak our highest values and commitments.

Rabbi Lori Forman

Rise with Strength Renewed

We pray every year at this time to be written in the Book of Life for another year. One more year. Give me one more year. I'm not finished. Not yet. We're afraid. We don't want to die. But Yom Kippur is about dying. We enact the drama of our dying. We put on our *kittels*. We stop eating. It's over. How do I let go of this life? How do I let go of myself? How do I forgive everything, everyone, myself, and let my life fall? Bowing completely is falling down back into the womb of the earth, slowly, softly. Relaxing completely. Give up your little story.... Give back your small self. Sense that ground and through it the immensity of the Big Story, and from within it and behind it, feel its unknowable Author.... We are only halfway home. Bowing is not just about giving up and going down. It's about giving up and going down *in order to get back up. All the way up.* Up, more easily and further than you have ever been. Up, with fresh energy, power, openness. Up, with renewed purpose, and yes, up with a sense of authority. From where does our strength come? Our strength comes from God. But sometimes we've got to go down to get it. We rise with strength renewed.

Bruce Fertman

God and the *Kohen Gadol*

When children call their parents in the middle of the night, they just cry. They don't even call, "Mother, Father ... " They just cry.

How does it feel when your baby cries at night?

It's a taste of how God felt when the High Priest was calling God's name on Yom Kippur.

Reb Shlomo Carlebach

Avodah Service

It was in this morning's Torah reading that we first came across the notion of the scapegoat. Two goats were brought to the *Kohen Gadol,* one was offered as a sacrifice and one became the scapegoat. The sins of the people were laid on the horns of the goat, and the goat was then sent out to his death in the wilderness.

We have such problems with this ritual! The brutality in the treatment of the goat is our first problem, of course, but in addition, we have vague unrest with the whole notion of scapegoating.

We're Jews. How can we not? Our history is filled with instances where we were made a society's scapegoat, the reason for a nation's economic ills, where we were expelled from our homes and our countries—or worse.

But when you eliminate the involvement of living creatures, the ritual of the scapegoat, of Azazel, can be very healing.

Consider *Tashlikh.* We know that just because we've tossed some kinds of crumbs into the water, we're not off the hook. We still have to continue to work on our behavior. But there's something cathartic about investing those crumbs with all our mistakes, then tossing them into the river.

In the same way, I think there can be something very cathartic about taking all the baggage we carry with us, as individuals and as a community—the hurts, the losses, the uncertainty, fears and angers and frustrations—and somehow sending it off into the wilderness. Sort of like heading to Los Angeles and checking our bags to, say, Houston. And not bothering to ask the airline to trace them.

This year, I'm going to look for a goat. It will be a sugar bowl or a small jar or jug. It will have a top that is removable. And into it, I will put slips of paper on which I will have written all the difficulties that plague me as the year unfolds. I haven't yet decided what I'll do with those slips of paper at the end of the year, but there's one thing for sure. I won't read them again. Once I've given my hurts over to my goat, they will no longer be mine.

Rabbi Diane Cohen

Yom Kippur Customs

Yom Kippur, the 10th day of *Tishrey*, is the holiest and most awesome day on the Hebrew calendar. It is called a "Sabbath of Sabbaths"; all work that is forbidden on the Sabbath is forbidden on Yom Kippur as well. In addition, it is a full fast day, which means that there are five special prohibitions: against eating and drinking, sexual relations, bathing, wearing (leather) shoes, and wearing perfumes. The Talmudic (Talmud) tractate dealing with Yom Kippur is simply called "The Day."

RABBI ARTHUR GREEN, *THESE ARE THE WORDS*

The *Kittel*

[*The traditional white synagogue garment worn on Rosh Hashanah and Yom Kippur.*]

The *kittel,* a long, flowing, white, loose-sleeved linen robe, is the traditional Jewish garment worn by men during Rosh Hashanah and Yom Kippur services. The sources of this tradition date back to Talmudic times when, as described in the Jerusalem Talmud, a white garment was worn on the Sabbath and all solemn occasions.

The wearing of the *kittel*—the word is a Yiddish derivation of the German word for "smock"—is a tradition only among Ashkenazi Jews. Which congregant wears a *kittel,* however, has varied through the ages.

An engraving of a Rosh Hashanah service in Prague, Austria, in 1734, shows almost the entire congregation clad in a *kittel* and the traditional Jewish ruff, or collar of that period. Today, on Rosh Hashanah, usually only the rabbi, the *bal t'kiyah* (the person who blows the *shofar,* or ram's horn), the *bal koreh* (Torah reader) and the *hazzanim* (cantors) wear a *kittel* on Rosh Hashanah. In the 1930s and '40s in America, only a sprinkling of pious, older Jews wore a *kittel* on Yom Kippur. Today, however, the *kittel* is becoming increasingly prevalent on that holiday. In many Orthodox synagogues and in the yeshiva world, the majority of married men don a *kittel.*

The *kittel* is a very loose-fitting, practical garment. It is particularly comfortable during the long, often hot, day of the Yom Kippur service. The sleeves and collar of the *kittel* may be decorated with fancy stitching, but in most cases, it is fastened at the waist by a simple linen sash. In the 18th and 19th centuries, it was fashionable in European Ashkenazi communities to wear special silver belt buckles on the *kittel* sash. These usually were decorated with two rampant lions facing each other supporting a cartouche on which were inscribed the words from the Yom Kippur liturgy: "For on this day atonement shall be made to you to cleanse you from all your sins."

There is a great deal of symbolism inherent in the wearing of the *kittel.* The color white is associated with purity and the forgiveness of sins as embodied in the High Holy Day services. Pure white garments were worn by the High Priest during the Yom Kippur service in Temple times.

The *kittel* is also worn on occasions that symbolize a new beginning. On the *Yamim Noraim,* the Days of Awe, for example, we are given a chance to repent and to begin a new start in life. Many of the other occasions on which a *kittel* is worn reinforce this theme of new beginnings. Thus, a *kittel* is worn by a traditional bridegroom at his wedding to symbolize the new life beginning for him and his bride. At a circumcision, a *kittel* is often worn by the father as a proxy for his son who is being introduced into a new life.

On Passover, the leader of the seder service traditionally wears a *kittel* since the seder commemorates the new life of freedom and rebirth for the Jewish people. A *kittel* is worn by the *bal musaf,* the leader of the additional prayers on *Shemini Atzeret,* the eighth day of the Succot festival. The *tefilat geshem,* the prayers for the renewal of the rain cycle in Israel, are said at this time.

Even if a Jew does not wear a *kittel* during his lifetime, he will probably be buried in one upon his death, as the *kittel* is part of the traditional raiment in which the dead are clothed for burial. Another name for the *kittel,* the *sargenes,* is thought to derive from the German word *sarg,* or coffin. Death, which marks the passing into eternal life, may be the ultimate symbolic beginning which the wearing of the *kittel* commemorates.

Herb Geduld

A Meditation on Fasting

Fasting
Fasting might seem like a cruel test to see if we can deny our bodies food. Yet, at the heart of this practice is a desire to shift our attention away from the body's immediate needs and to focus on spiritual concerns. The logic goes something like this: when we fast, we are faced with admitting our frailty. In that weakened state, we examine the parts of ourselves that are fragile and strengthen them with meditations and supplications. Fasting together as a community, we examine our failings and resolve to strengthen one another in the weeks to come.

Meditation

When Rabbi Sheishet was fasting, he added these words to his daily prayers:

> Master of the worlds:
> We have learned that long ago,
> in the days when the Temple still stood,
> when people offered sacrifices as their atonement,
> they offered only the fat and the blood.
> That was sufficient to atone for them.
> And now, when the Temple no longer stands,
> I am fasting,
> and, as a result, parts of me will be diminished.
> *Ye'hi ratzon,*
> May it be Your will:
> To regard those parts of me that are diminished
> as if I had offered them up before You upon an altar,
> and may You show me favor.
> (Adapted from Babylonian Talmud: *Brakhot* 17a)

Ritual

As you fast, move slower than usual, staying focused on the purpose of your fast.

Blessing

(As you begin your fast)
> *Potei'ach et yadekhah, u'masbia l'khol chai ratzon.*
> Open Your hand and fulfill each creature's needs.

Teaching

Why, when we fasted, did You not see? ... This is My chosen fast: to loosen all the bonds that bind people unfairly, to let the oppressed go free, to break every yoke. Share your bread with the hungry, shelter the homeless, clothe the naked, and turn toward those in need. Then a cleansing light shall break forth like the dawn ... then you shall call and the Lord will answer.

(Adapted from Isaiah 58)

And they fast on this day to approach a resemblance to the angels, inasmuch as the fast is consummated by humbling themselves, lowering their heads, standing, bending their knees, and singing hymns of praise. Then all the physical powers abandon their natural functions and engage in spiritual functions, as though having no animal nature.

(Judah HaLevi, The Kuzari 3:5, as quoted in S.Y. Agnon, *Days of Awe*)

Penitence is inspired by the yearning of all existence to be better, purer, more vigorous and on a higher plane than it is. Within this yearning is a hidden life-force for overcoming every factor that limits and weakens existence. The particular penitence of the individual and certainly of the group draws its strength from this source of life, which is always active with never-ending vigor.

(Abraham Isaac Kook, *The Lights of Penitence*)

Rabbi Irwin Kula and Vanessa L. Ochs

Dress

In Spanish-Portuguese synagogues in the United States, known for their upper-class decorum, the men carry Torah scrolls during *Kol Nidrei* dressed in formal evening clothes, including high silk hats (the attire also worn in British synagogues). They followed the opening service with special prayers for the government, the congregation, the two Torah carriers, the congregations that established America's first synagogues, Jerusalem, those held in captivity, those traveling, the sick, and uniquely, women, for the work they had done in preparing the white clothes for the *Sifrei Torah, Aron Hakodesh,* and *bimah.*

In another example of the similarity between Yom Kippur and a wedding day, the Libyans had their young boys dress in their best clothes and sing wedding songs in the synagogue courtyard.

Lesli Koppelman Ross

(Alternative) Yom Kippur Chant

(for Neal)

> every year it's the same scramble ... search for new poems ...
> discover new melodies ... find the right words ... abracadabra
> open the heart (god knows we try) as we close our eyes
> retreat under our prayer shawls, listen for echoes
>
> we dress in white, (like priestly shrouds or angel garb)
> bare our feet ... a costume for a part in an ancient play
> we've almost forgotten
>
> only the children remember ... they bow, face east, fall *korim*
> touch the earth, return to their roots ... our children
> (those precious ones) closest to beginnings, they return
> to purity, while we grown-ups watch
>
> we all play dead, no food or drink, no sex or talk
> of everyday, only chants (sung in minor tones) those words
> we never understood (alone) we sing together
>
> we sacrifice our dailiness, leave reasoning minds behind
> raise clouds of song, (a new incense for Jerusalem)
> this *alternative service* "alters" our "native" selves
> we offer only what we have
>
> sighs (from those deeply hidden places) roused by the
> shofar's call, our tears flow in a cleansing rite
> that heals our aching fractured souls

Carol Rose

Why Fast?

Four main reasons are given for the command to fast on Yom Kippur.

Fasting as a penance: The most obvious reason for fasting on Yom Kippur is that by this means we show contrition for the wrongs we have done and the good we have failed to do. The man who "punishes himself" may be morbidly masochistic. But most people feel the need to give of themselves, to make some sacrifice, in order to demonstrate that their protestations of remorse mean something and are more than lip service. Self-affliction (Judaism does not encourage the excess of this) in moderation is an act affirming a man's sincerity. The man who fasts for his sins is saying in so many words, I do not want to be let off lightly; I deserve to be punished.

Fasting as self-discipline: Self-indulgence and lack of self-control frequently lead to sin. It is natural that repentance be preceded by an attempt at self-discipline. Disciplining oneself is never easy but all religious teachers have insisted on its value. It is true that history and literature abound in examples of the harm done by an overactive Puritan conscience, especially when it seeks to interfere with the behavior of others. Macaulay said that the Puritans objected to bear-baiting not because it gave pain to the bear but because it gave pleasure to the spectators! But the value of self-discipline must not be judged by its aberrations. The traditional Jewish character ideal is for a person to be harsh with himself but indulgent toward others. Fasting on Yom Kippur serves as a potent reminder for the need of self-discipline which leads to self-improvement.

Fasting as a means of focusing the mind on the spiritual: It has been noted frequently that Judaism frankly recognized the bodily instincts and the need for their legitimate gratification. This is best illustrated in the rabbinic comment on the verse in the Book of Genesis that God saw all that He had created and behold it was very good—not simply good, remark the rabbis, but very good. Good refers to the good inclination; very good, to the evil inclination. For, the rabbis go on to say, were it not for the bodily instincts life would be good but it would be a colorless, unvarying good. A man would have no ambitions, he would not build a house or marry, the world would be left desolate. And yet with all its recognition of the bodily needs, religion seeks to encourage and foster the spiritual side of man's life. By fasting on Yom Kippur the needs of the body are left unattended for twenty-four hours and the Jew gives all his concentration to the things of the spirit. This is the meaning of the references in Jewish tradition that Jews are compared to the angels on Yom Kippur when, clothed in white, they spend the whole day in prayer, contemplation and worship.

We must, of course, live in this world. "One world at a time" is sound Jewish doctrine. But unless our faith is to be denuded of its spirituality we must, from time to time, direct our thoughts to the non-physical side of existence. Scripture says that "no man shall be in the Tent of Meeting" (Leviticus 16.17) when the high priest enters to make atonement there on Yom Kippur. This is taken by the Midrash to mean that at that awful hour the high priest was "no man," his body become ethereal like that of the angels. This is what happens to every Jew who observes the day as it should be observed.

Fasting as a means of awakening compassion: By knowing what it means to go hungry, albeit for a day, our hearts are moved for those who suffer. But fasting we are moved to think of the needs of others and to alleviate their suffering. In the Yom Kippur morning *haftarah* this idea is given its classic expression. The prophet castigates his people for their neglect of the poor. Their fasting and their pretence of piety is not acceptable to God if it serves merely as a cloak for inhumanity.

Rabbi Dr. Louis Jacobs

We Are Clay in the Potter's Hands

"As clay in the hands of the potter ... so are we in Your hand O God of love ... "

This selection, taken from the evening service of Yom Kippur, has always struck a rather resonant chord for me amidst all the other giants of the High Holy Day liturgy. Its outstanding poetic images—God as potter, stone mason, craftsman, glassblower, draper and smelter—gently remind those of us made of stone hearts and set minds that we should be pliable, prepared to set out on a new spiritual course. The God who formed us can shape us again, provided we are prepared to turn to God and humble ourselves, temper our pride and place ourselves upon the Divine potter's wheel.

At first glance, the *piyyut* (liturgical poem) might seem to suggest that human beings are trapped by destiny and all is fatalistic; after all, clay cannot be a pot, no matter how much it might like to be, without the skilled hands of the potter.

However, what the poem teaches us is that although we are largely dependent on our God, we are also an indispensable part of that creation. We must bring good raw material, that which can be stretched, expanded and developed, to the job at hand.

I read recently of another great artist, Michelangelo, who, it is said, salvaged a certain piece of marble that had been discarded by other sculptors.

"What will that odd piece of marble ever yield?" he was asked. But Michelangelo did not see a long, narrow piece of marble; he saw a statue of David. And David, as we all know, has become a masterpiece.

When asked how he accounted for his amazing creative genius, Thomas Edison replied, "It's because I never think in words; I think in pictures." Orville and Wilbur Wright were laughed at—leave the flying to the birds, they were told. Give up experimenting with lightning—nothing could outdo the oil lamp, Ben Franklin was told. Edison, the Wright brothers and Franklin could see things not as they were, but how they might be....

Judaism, our shared strength and joy, has given us our High Holy Days so that we might be recast, shaped again and transformed into works of beauty.

The verdict is in our own hands as much as in the hands of the potter.

Rabbi Gary J. Robuck

Teshuvah: Forgiveness Walks

Try not to leap from engaging in an important or stressful activity directly into a *teshuvah* session. It is important to arrive centered, grounded, slowed down, and available to listen. Engaging in a meditation walk en route to a *teshuvah* session can be an excellent form of preparation. This practice is intended to help release your thoughts, expectations, and anxieties about the upcoming *teshuvah* session.

A meditation walk is done slowly enough that you become conscious of each part of every footstep. Let time slow down, important as the one in which you are engaged. As thoughts intrude, and they will, notice them with an internal "Ah yes, of course, someone in my position would be feeling that way," and release them gently, returning to your foot-centered consciousness. It is helpful to repeat a sacred phrase during such walks. I recommend a verse from Torah: *L'hithalekh lifnei Elohim*, which means to "Walk yourself before God."

Rabbi Goldie Milgram

La-Brit Habet—Recall Your Covenant

Essential to all Jewish theological viewpoints is the Covenantal relationship between God and the Jewish People, established in the days of the Bible and continued to our own day.

In the prayer *"Kee Hineh KaHomer"* we recite the refrain: Recall Your Covenant, and forgive our sin.

Rabbi Arthur Green (*Seek My Face*) defines the Covenant between God and Israel in a special way. To him Covenant is a commitment to keeping faith with the deepest Self that is within us. "It is a decision to live in such a way that allows" God to be revealed to others through us. "Covenant is our willingness to be a channel, to serve as a conduit of God's presence to those with whom we live."

D.P.E.

Never Lose Hope: *Uve-khen ... tikvah le-dor-shekha*

Grant hope to those who seek You and Confidence to those who await You ...

In the "*U've-khen*" prayers we beseech God to grant to all creatures the fundamental things that we need to survive—a sense of God's awesome power, a feeling of *kavod*, of honor and glory, and a knowledge that the righteous will triumph and rejoice.

One of the most important things we ask of God in this section of the liturgy is for *tikvah*, for hope. It is not surprising that Naftali Imber, author of the Jewish national anthem, selected the biblical word "*tikvah*," hope, as its cardinal theme. We ask God to grant "*tikvah le-dor-shekha*"— hope to those who seek You and confidence to those who await you.

Rabbi Nachman of Breslov, the famous Hasidic master, explained once why people don't always have enough faith in themselves, and confidence in their own ability to survive the perils of life.

The reason we often give up hope is because we look around us and see our contemporaries, and imagine them to be far worthier than they in fact are. In our imagination we put ourselves down, and put others on a pedestal. "If only I were like so-and-so," we say, "we could make it." The truth is that so-and-so is probably often wishing she were like us.

If we follow Rav Nachman's advice, and not idealize others, and give ourselves more credit, it will be easier for us to find the hope and faith we seek when we ask God for *tikvah*, to stand up to the thorny problems that life inevitably presents us.

Rabbi Dov Peretz Elkins

Ve-Yaya-su Kulam Agudah Ehat—The Importance of Community

But being part of a community is more than showing up in *shul* on Rosh Hashanah and Yom Kippur, as important as they are. What does it mean to be part of a community? In the fabled town of fools known as Chelm, there flowed a river through the middle of the town. It occurred to several merchants that a bridge would be good for business on both sides of the river. However, some of the younger people objected. They said: "Of course, it would be nice to build a bridge, but let's not do it because it would be good for business; we should build it solely for aesthetic reasons. We'll be glad to contribute to the building expenses for beauty's sake, but won't give a penny for the sake of business."

Still others, even younger people, argued, "A bridge! That's a good idea, but not for the sake of trade or beauty but to have someplace to stroll back and forth. We'll be glad to contribute money to build a bridge for strolling." And so the three groups began to quarrel, and they are quarreling still. And to the present day Chelm does not have a bridge.

Here is an example of what happens when a sense of community breaks down; when each component only views the benefit to itself. And sadly this is what is happening to our sense of Jewish communality. But it is the working on behalf of the community that is fundamental.

Author Unknown

Get a Life

I am madly addicted to reading Personal Ads. They tell you a lot about what people are looking for in their lives.

But this past summer, I found an ad in the *Berkshire Advocate*. The woman was not looking for a relationship. Or maybe she was. Maybe she was looking for a relationship ... that goes beyond relationships.

> I am a 58 year old woman with, doctors tell me, one year to live. I would like to spend that year doing something meaningful, interesting, and fun. I like C-span, Bill Moyers, *Times* crosswords, Nina Totenberg, Anna Quindlen, Mario Cuomo, Nevada. I don't like George Will, R.J. Reynolds, computer talk, fundamentalists, California. I have limited stamina and resources.
>
> Have you any ideas how I can spend this year making a difference?

I do not know if the woman is Jewish or not. But she managed to condense the entire Yom Kippur liturgy into eight lines in the back of a free weekly newspaper. "For what is our life, and what our vaunted strength? What can we say in Your presence?" She has re-written the *U'Netaneh Tokef*, asking in the pages of the *Advocate* what in our world might temper the Decree over which we have no control. This is the great, unspoken theme of Yom Kippur. It is why we fast. It is why we wear white. It is why tomorrow we will read of Jonah's sojourn in the belly of the whale. On Yom Kippur, we confront our own mortality. There is only one difference between the woman in the *Berkshire Advocate* and us. She gave voice to what we already, deep down in our hearts, know to be true.

Rabbi Jeffrey K. Salkin

The Origins of Yom Kippur

From the very beginning of the creation of the world, the Holy One, blessed be God, foresaw the deeds of the righteous and the deeds of the wicked. "And the earth was desolate" alludes to the deeds of the wicked; "And God said: Let there be light," to those of the righteous; "And God saw the light, that it was good," to the deeds of the righteous; "And God made a division between the light and the darkness:"

between the deeds of the righteous and those of the wicked; "And God called the light 'day'" alludes to the deeds of the righteous; "And the darkness God called night," to those of the wicked; "And there was evening," to the deeds of the wicked; "And there was morning," to those of the righteous; "One day:" the Holy One, blessed be God, gave them (the righteous) one day, and which is that? It is the Day of Atonement.

Bereshit Rabbah 3:10

Who Fasts?

Children do not fast on Yom Kippur, but they should train them one year or two years before they are of age, so that they will become well versed in the commandments.

If a pregnant woman smelled food and craved it, they may give her food until she regains her composure. One who is sick may be given food on the advice of skilled persons; and if no skilled persons are there, the patient may be given food at his or her own wish, until he or she says, "Enough!"

Mishnah Yoma 8:4–5

May We Rise Along with Our Prayers

In the *Ya-aleh* prayer we express our deep desire that our supplications and pleas, our voice, our atonement, our knocking at the gates, our confessions, rise to Heaven.

It is worth noting that Rabbi Samson Raphael Hirsch (19th century Germany), in his commentary on Leviticus (1:3), gives a novel interpretation to the type of offering known as the *olah*, usually translated as the "burnt-offering." Conventional exegesis assigns the sacrifice "olah" to the etymology of *going up*, or being burnt completely, and thus going up, as sacrifices offered on the altar would, to Heaven. It would therefore be a burnt offering, or one which is totally consumed on the altar, and its ashes "rise to Heaven."

Rabbi Hirsch gives a different interpretation. He explains that other offerings *(todah, sh'lamim, asham, hatat)* are not given names because of *how* they are offered, but rather according to the inducement for the offering, or the object of it.

So, in the case of the *olah,* the offering is made by one who wishes to *rise higher,* from the root *alah,* to go up (as in *aliyah* to the Torah). One who brings an *olah* offering, he explains, brings a consciousness that "greater progress toward goodness and godliness is necessary." Bringing an *olah* helps to raise one's moral state and bring God nearer. He thus translates *olah* as a "progress-offering," or an "elevation-offering."

So in the *Ya-aleh* prayer. it is not only our prayers, supplications, confessions and atonement that we wish to offer up, but we want to raise up our *selves,* raise our own moral state and become nearer to God.

As we offer our prayers to rise on high, so we try to lift ourselves, our souls and our spirits, to a higher level of holiness and sanctity, to live a life closer to God's presence.

Rabbi Dov Peretz Elkins

A New *Ya-aleh*

May our Zeal rise heavenward in the Evening
May our Yearnings reach God's throne in the Morning
May Your eXpectations be revealed in the Evening
May our Weariness rise heavenward in the Evening
May our Vanity reach God's throne in the Morning
May Your Unity be revealed in the Evening
May our Terror rise heavenward in the Evening
May our Sorrow reach God's throne in the Morning
May Your Relief be revealed in the Evening
May our Queries rise heavenward in the Evening
May our Prayers reach God's throne in the Morning
May Your Openness be revealed in the Evening
May our Neglect rise heavenward in the Evening
May our Misgivings reach God's throne in the Morning
May Your Love be revealed in the Evening
May our Kindness rise heavenward in the Evening
May our Justice reach God's throne in the Morning

May Your Imminence be revealed in the Evening
May our Hubris rise heavenward in the Evening
May our Greed reach God's throne in the Morning
May Your Forgiveness be revealed in the Evening
May our Errors rise heavenward in the Evening
May our Deeds reach God's throne in the Morning
May Your Consolation be revealed in the Evening
May our Bluster rise heavenward in the Evening
May our Arrogance reach God's throne in the Morning
May Your Answer be revealed in the Evening

                                    Rabbi Moshe Tutnauer

U'v'khen Ten Kavod Le-amekha—Give Dignity to Your People—*Kavod:* Honor Connected to Our Deepest Selves

Kavod means dignity, honor, weightiness, and comes from the root *k-b-d*. One can understand a community's *kavod* values by whom and what it considers worthy of *kavod*. There is a kind of honor communities bestow that depends on status, power and wealth that is often tied to a sense of self-importance. This type of honor is considered a limited resource, and people fight or vie for it, thinking of it as an award to be acquired or won. But there is another type of honor that is far weightier, one that depends on who we are and what we stand for, an honor that is connected to our deepest selves. Look at some of the words with which *kavod* is traditionally linked in the Jewish way:

kevod hamakom (God)

kevod hatzibur (community)

kevod hatorah (Torah)

kevod habriyot (human beings)

kevod morim (teachers)

kevod hameit (dead)

kevod harav (rabbi)

kevod Shabbat (Sabbath)

kevod horim (parents)

The range and depth of our culture's understanding of *kavod* is breath-taking. *Kavod* is a currency that flows back and forth between human beings and God. There is an infinite amount of this *kavod,* and kavod is of infinite value. Who is worthy of being treated with *kavod?* One who treats God's creatures with *kavod.* Human beings are capable of making *kavod* happen and worthy of receiving *kavod.* God gets *kavod* from us and we get it from each other. *Kavod* only exists if we give it to each other, and only if we give it to each other do we have it from God.

Rabbi Irwin Kula

Kavanah for the *Amidah—Devekut:* Clinging to God

Devekut is the process of merging with the Divine, going beyond yourself and your self-imposed boundaries. *Devekut* means being intimate with God as sunlight is to the sun. It is being comfortable and cozy with God, like honey on bread. The phrase "cozy with God" was first taught by Rabbi Zalman Schachter-Shalomi, and is now practiced in imaging by many of his students.

Devekut is an intimacy in which all thoughts and ideas are transparent between you and God. It is seeing God through the same eyes that God sees you through. It is synchronizing the rhythm of your heart with the Divine heartbeat of the universe.

Devekut is your body encoded in the body of God, your soul enveloped by God's soul, and your actions manifesting Divine performance.

Rabbi Shoni Labowitz

Introduction to the *Amidah*

[*This meditation of Rebbe Nachman of Breslov is an appropriate way for us to focus our spiritual attention on the* Amidah. *We might imagine in our mind's eye that we are in a beautiful outdoor setting, as we pray.*]

"Master of the universe, grant me the ability to be alone:
May it be my custom to go outdoors each day,
among the trees and grasses, among all growing things,

there to be alone and enter into prayer.
There may I express all that is in my heart,
talking with the One to whom I belong.
And may all grasses, trees, and plants
awake at my coming.
Send the power of their life into my prayer,
making whole my heart and my speech
through the life and spirit of growing things,
made whole by their transcendent Source.
O that they would enter into my prayer!
Then would I fully open my heart
in prayer, supplication and holy speech;
then, O God, would I pour out the words
of my heart before Your presence."

Rebbe Nachman of Breslov, adapted by Louis I. Newman

Ki Hineh KaHomer

I have always been troubled by this *piyyut*. It's just too passive for me.
If we are to search our souls and reconsider our choices in the year
just past, why are we asking God to make something wondrous of us?
Isn't that our job?

But some of my colleagues have been chatting about twelve-step
programs lately, and the notion of giving ourselves over to some
Higher Power, and now I wonder.

We are meant, I think, to walk a very fine line between two
extremes. The first is as an example of a human using free will, making choices in our behavior, sometimes for the good, often not.

The other extreme, however, is that of someone who is only
human, limited, flawed, in need of support and guidance. On the one
hand, we need to be open to the awareness of the hand of God guiding
us on the path of our lives. On the other hand, we need to know that
the hand will be there.

The Hasidim tell of a sage who would carry a piece of paper in his
pocket. On one side, when his soul felt battered, he would read "For
my sake was the world created." On the other side, when his humility

needed reinforcement, he would read "I am nothing but the dust of the earth."

When we are ready to blame anyone and everyone for our choices, we need to recall our responsibility for our own actions; perhaps "If it is to be, it is up to me." And when we feel as though change is impossible without help, we need to recall that God is our partner; perhaps "God, please make of me something wonderful."

Rabbi Diane Cohen

Hayom—The Opportunity of the Present Moment

On the morning of Yom Kippur, after we have confessed our shortcomings and have prayed for forgiveness, we will hear the Torah's words of challenge and comfort. We will be assured that the Torah's instruction for living "… is not too baffling for you, nor is it beyond reach…. No, the thing is very close to you, in your mouth and in your heart, to observe it" (Deut. 30:11,14).

But our personal experience sometimes belies this message. We have found it hard to change. Another year has passed, and we are back in the synagogue again. What is it that we still need to learn? If the Teaching is so "close," why does it continue to elude us?

A midrash from Yemen elaborates on this verse:

> They say to a person: "Go to a certain town and learn Torah there." But the person answers: "I am afraid of the lions that I will encounter on the way." So they say: "You can go and learn in another town that is closer." But the person replies: "I am afraid of the thieves." So they suggest: "There is a sage in your own city. Go and learn from him." But the person says: "I am afraid that people may harm me on the way." So they say: "There is a teacher in your own house. Go and learn from him." But the person replies: "What if I find the door locked, and I have to return to where I am?" So they say: "There is a teacher sitting and teaching right here in the chair next to you." But the person replies: "You know what? What I really want to do is go back to sleep!"

This is what Scripture refers to when it says (Proverbs 26:14): "The door is turning upon its hinges, and the lazy is still upon his bed" (Yalkut Midreshei Teiman).

Can we recognize ourselves in the person who says that he wants to gain insight and change but then lists a hundred and one reasons why he cannot? Perhaps we are afraid of "wild animals"—of our own intense feelings, of the unarticulated pain and hurt that we barely manage to keep under control. We do not want to leave ourselves vulnerable again. What if we find the door locked? Will we be worse off for having made the effort to change and not succeeded? Can we admit that despite the words that we have been saying all day in our prayers, there is a part of us that wants to remain asleep? Change is difficult. We do not want to get out of bed. So here we are again.

The Torah reminds us that the power to choose life and growth over fear and stagnation is in our hands. The words are already on our lips, and the teaching is already in our heart. But we need to be awake and be aware.

Rabbi Pinhas of Koretz often cited the words "A man's soul will teach him." And he emphasized them by adding, "There is no person who is not incessantly being taught by his soul." One of his students asked: "If this is so, why don't people obey their souls?" Rabbi Pinhas replied: "The soul teaches without ceasing but it never repeats" (from *Tales of the Chasidim* by Martin Buber).

This moment will never come again. The unique convergence of present factors: the place where we are standing in our life; our willingness to hear what we must do; our ability to understand the teaching within us; the strength to obey—all these will never come together again in quite the same way. This is the opportunity of the present moment.

Hayom Te'amtzenu: This day, may we have the strength:
Hayom Tevarchenu: This day, may we be blessed:
To hear the teaching of the heart; and also to do it.

Rabbi Tom Gutherz

Hayom—Today

Some of the saddest words too frequently spoken at the end of one's life go something like this: "He worked so hard all his life but never took the time to enjoy any pleasures. Now, when he could enjoy life, nit da kein yoren, he ran out of years." Whenever I hear this melancholy summary I always ask myself, "Why, why did he postpone the enjoyment of life? Why did he wait? Is it possible to enjoy at 60 the pleasures that are available only at 40? Does financial security enable us to retrace our steps and to do now what should have been done then and could only have been done then? Is there any way of rewinding and replaying the film of life?"

There is no future joy which can compensate us for the legitimate joys we needlessly deny ourselves today. God, our prayer book reminds us, is waiting—waiting for us to stop waiting and to proceed with all haste to begin to do now, this day, all the things for which this day was made.

Rabbi Sidney Greenberg

Aleinu—The Kabbalistic Origins of *Tikkun Olam*

[*We use the expression* Tikkun Olam *frequently to refer to the "repair of the world." Very few of us realize its complex theological origins in the Kabbalah of the Ari—Rabbi Yitzhak Luria, of 16th century Safed. Rabbi Diane Cohen explains this concept in clear and simple terms.*]

The kabbalistic tradition tells us that when God created the world, the primal light was too bright for mortal creatures, so God attempted to enclose the light in earthen vessels. The light shattered the earthen vessels, and sparks of pure light are now hidden, as it were, under broken pieces of pottery. The way we release a spark of divine light into the world, the way we break one of these shards of pottery, is to do a *mitzvah*. Perform a deed required by God. And each time we do a mitzvah, we release a spark of divine light and hasten the redemption of the world. The image reminds us that redemption is in our hands as well as in God's. It emphasizes the notion of human responsibility. From this idea we get the popular phrase—*tikkun olam*—repair of the world.

Rabbi Diane Cohen

Sim Shalom—A Prayer for Peace

Let us live in peace, God.

Let children live in peace, in homes free from brutality and
abuse.

Let them go to school in peace, free from violence and fear.

Let them play in peace, God, in safe parks, in safe neighborhoods; watch over them.

Let husbands and wives love in peace, in marriages free from
cruelty.

Let men and women go to work in peace, with no fears of
terror or bloodshed.

Let us travel in peace; protect us, God, in the air, on the seas,
along whatever road we take.

Let nations dwell together in peace, without the threat of war
hovering over them.

Help us, God. Teach all people of all races and faiths, in all
the countries all over the world to believe that the peace
that seems so far off is in fact within our reach.

Let us all live in peace, God. And let us say, Amen.

Rabbi Naomi Levy

Yaaleh—Let Us Rise in Torah Knowledge: Flying Words

Long, long ago, somewhere in Europe, there was a Jewish town which
was ruled by a tyrant who hated all people, especially the Jews.

One day, the tyrant ordered the Jews to burn all their holy books.
Further, they were forbidden to write new books or make copies of
those that were burned. But the Jews of the city were very pious and
learned. Each and every one of them knew the Torah by heart, so
they were able to continue to study the Torah and to teach it to their
children.

In order to keep up the custom of reading the Torah in the synagogue on the Sabbath, and yet not to disobey their ruler, the Jews of
the city prepared a scroll of the Torah made of the finest parchment,
but entirely blank inside. The cantor, who was blind, but who knew
every word of the Torah by heart, would take out the scroll every Sat-

urday morning, and though not a word was written inside, he would read aloud as if a real Torah scroll was before him.

Now there was another Jewish community not far from the first. But this town had a good and kind ruler, who granted the Jews all rights given other citizens. Yet, living in freedom, the Jews quickly forgot the Torah and lost interest in religious worship. Even on the Sabbath their ancient synagogue would remain closed. Only once a year, on Yom Kippur, would the Jews open the synagogue doors, and enter to hear a reading of the Torah.

On Yom Kippur Eve, the cantor in the second town unlocked the door and went in to prepare the services for the next day. Suddenly he saw the portals of the Ark which contained the scrolls open up as if by a hidden hand. Out of the darkness a cloud rolled, a cloud of words and letters. The words and letters lined up in solid rows and flew out of the window.

"The Torah has forsaken us," cried the cantor.

From inside the Holy Ark came an answer, "You have forsaken the Torah."

The next day, when all the Jews of the city gathered for the first time in a year, the Torah was taken out. The whole congregation saw that it was blank. There wasn't a single word written on it.

At the very same time, back in the first town where the Jews were oppressed, another miracle occurred. There, when the time came for reading the Torah, and the cantor began to unroll what everyone knew to be the blank scrolls … just then, a thick cloud of words and letters flew in through the window, spread itself across the scroll, with each word and letter finding its proper place.

Just as suddenly, the blind cantor regained his eyesight. With deep joy he began to read the miraculous words in front of him.

Sometime later a few Jews from the oppressed town traveled to the free town. They told their brethren about the miracle of the words on the scroll, and the Jews in the free town understood. The free Jews collected a great sum of money to bring their suffering fellow Jews to their own city. Together they established a great school where both old and new residents studied the Torah together. And in time, the whole city became known as a community of great Jewish scholars.

David Einhorn

Ve-yaa-su Khulam Agudah Ehat—Gathered Embers Generate Heat

The compelling need to foster closeness is encapsulated in a hasidic tale about a depressed student who sought counsel from his rabbi. Illness and a business setback compounded the student's feelings of abandonment.

The conversation is set against the backdrop of a fireplace. The fire is about to die out. Only scattered embers remain. Suddenly the flames flare up anew.

"Do you see," pointed out the rabbi, "what happened when I gathered the embers close together? They came back to life. When the coals were separated, they generated little heat; but when they came close together they received warmth from each other and the fire was renewed.

"It's the same with people. When we are alone and separated, our spirit is in danger of dying out. But when we stand close together we get warmth and comfort from one another, and hope is renewed."

Rabbi Harvey Meirovich

V'tivneha M'herah Ut'gadel K'vodah—Rebuild and Glorify Your Land

Rabbi Aryeh Levin, whose uplifting biography can be found in a book by Simcha Raz called *A Tzaddik in Our Time*, was one of the great saints of modern Jerusalem.

The day before his death in 1969, Reb Aryeh taught his students an explanation of the verse in Psalms 69:36–37, which tells us that God will deliver Zion and rebuild the cities of Yehudah.... And that those who honor God's name will dwell there.

Reb Aryeh explained that this verse lays out three stages of reset-tling *Eretz Yisrael*. First God saves Zion from its enemies, and the ene-mies of the Jewish People. Second the halutzim, the Zionist pioneers came and settled the Land, Jerusalem and the cities of Yehudah. We continue to rebuild Israel's cities throughout the land, north and south, east and west. We are now in the process of completing the sec-ond stage, of rebuilding, and creating peace.

Only when the first two stages have been fulfilled and completed, will we be ready for the third and final stage, when the cities of *Eretz Yisrael* will be filled with people who honor, cherish and love God's name.

For that reason we pray throughout the *Musaf* prayers, and in other places in the *Mahzor,* for God to restore Zion, and bring our People back to its Land, so that we can ultimately be filled with love of God and follow God's ways.

D.P.E.

Piyyutim: Liturgical Poetry

In a commentary on the High Holiday *Mahzor*, Rabbi Jeffrey Cohen writes that, "Prayer is to the spirit of the High Holy Days what *matzah* is to *Pesach* and the *sukkah* to the Festival of *Sukkot*. It is the basic essence of Rosh Hashanah and Yom Kippur." Rosh Hashanah commemorates no particular event in Jewish history, and we are engaged now in the major ritual activity associated with this holiday—seeking to wrest meaning and inspiration from the *Mahzor,* the High Holiday prayerbook.

Much of the liturgy for this day is familiar to daily and Shabbat davveners. A special feature are the many *piyyutim*, religious poems, which are inserted at various points in the service. The great age of the *piyyutim* ranges from the 3rd to the 12th centuries. Many have become classics that evoke from us the spirit of the day with their words and special melodies, however, the Rabbis were not universally thrilled with the theological liberties taken by the authors of these prayers. Maimonides, for example, wrote that, "Such authors compose things that are either pure heresy or which contain such absurdities that prompt the reader both to laugh and also to grieve that anyone could have the temerity to apply such references to God. Were it not that I pitied the authors for their defects, and bore them no malice, I would have cited examples from their works to expose their errors. I declare that they are guilty not only of ordinary sin, but also of profanity and blasphemy! This applies also to the multitude that listens to the prayers of such a foolish person."

Maimonides and those who felt as he did were not opposed to the concept of *piyyut,* but rather to particular compositions. We certainly should not let his opinion discourage us from our own liturgical compositions. I share his words with you, rather, as an encouragement to know that not every word in the prayerbook is to be taken literally, sacrosanct and immune from change or question. In a spirit of generosity, we should empathize with the efforts of the authors, while translating their words into metaphors which speak to our own hearts.

Rabbi Bonnie Koppell

JONAH AND HUMAN RESPONSIBILITY

Another great paradigm of *teshuvah* is the Biblical tale of Jonah. For this reason it is read in the synagogue on Yom Kippur afternoon, as the special season of *teshuvah* draws near to its close. God teaches the prophet Jonah not to be cynical, to always maintain faith in the possibility of human transformation, just as God does. The prophet, who had longed for God to destroy the wicked city of Nineveh, is reminded that the city contains "more than a hundred and twenty thousand people who do not know their right hand from their left, and much cattle" (Jonah 4:11). Most sinners are like fools or children, not knowing right from left, no more guilty than cattle. Their Creator does not want to destroy them, but to see them transform their lives by turning to God.

RABBI ARTHUR GREEN, *THESE ARE THE WORDS*

Jonah: Running Away from Ourselves

Not long ago, superstar Carl Lewis broke an incredible record. He ran the 100 meter dash in 9.92 seconds. In the Bible, we have our own runners. One of them is the prophet Jonah (or *Yonah* in Hebrew), about whom we read on the afternoon of Yom Kippur.

God commands Yonah to go into the ancient city of Nineveh and tell the people to change for the better or face destruction. Yonah, however, decides to ignore God and take a boat to Tarshish—which is in the opposite direction of Nineveh.

Now I've always liked reading the book of Yonah. . . because his story speaks to me and to you, for Yonah gives in to the temptation to run away from the right thing. Yonah is trying to run away from his better self.

But, as Rabbi Sidney Greenberg has noted in a book called *Words to Live By*, "wherever we go, we take ourselves along. God finds Jonah even in the belly of the whale. The only way to 'get away' from ourselves is to effect a change within ourselves. What we need is not a change of scene, but a change of soul."

As Yom Kippur approaches, let's try to end our running records. Maybe this will be the year when we end that long record of running from ourselves, from God, from one another.

In preparation for Yom Kippur, why don't you make a list of things that you've wanted to do to improve yourself? Then, narrow the list down and pick one item from that shorter list that you intend to pursue seriously during this new year.

Rabbi Hayim Herring

The Book of Jonah: A Lesson on Happiness

God, holidays, family and friends, *simhah shel mitzvah* [the joy of doing a *mitzvah*]. All sources of joy in Judaism, in sharp contrast to values that surround us. In TV land and in our streets, a more luxurious car, more fashionable jeans, a pumped-up sneaker, even the right cereal, are primary sources of happiness. In the Bible, *simhah* [joy] is almost never associated with material possessions. One of the few exceptions occurs in the Book of Jonah. After Jonah calls on the people of Nineveh to repent, he flees to the city outskirts and sits in the sun. God causes a large *kikayon* plant to grow. *V'yismah Yonah al hakikayon simhah gedolah.* Jonah is very happy about the *kikayon*. What happens next? The plant shrivels up and Jonah is unhappy again. Material possessions can make us comfortable, but they cannot give us the *simhah* that Torah and tradition offer us.

Rabbi Stephanie Dickstein

Jonah and Self-Change

For I know that you are a compassionate and gracious God, slow to anger, abounding in kindness, renouncing punishment.

(JONAH 4:2)

It's ironic. Sometimes we fear success even more than we fear failure. Jonah did. He had the unique honor of being the only prophet in the Bible to whom the people really listened. Yet he ran! He was angry. He wanted the people to be punished. Why? Because he lacked compassion for others. And himself. Fearing change in others, he also feared change in himself.

Jonah's bottom is about as low as you can go—the deep, dark depths of what seems to be a whale's belly. But Jonah's problem really is the fear in his own gut. Bachya Ibn Pakuda, the eleventh century Spanish moralist, wrote: "I'd be ashamed were God to see me fear anyone but God."

God can make compassionate changes, so can we. It sounds presumptuous, but not when we remember we were made in the Divine image, just a little lower than the angels.

Growth and Renewal: Self-change comes hard, but it can come if you work at it. Break up the change you want make into parts, then take it one part at a time. God will help you on the way.

Rabbi Kerry M. Olitzky

Jonah: A *D'var Torah*

The whale part of the story is easy. The real mystery is Jonah and the way he acts. Most people in the Bible are easy to understand and very easy to sympathize with. But not Jonah. Is there any other book of the Bible in which the hero is so rebellious and so unrepentant, even after he is given chance after chance to improve his ways?

Jonah is just a man living his life until, one day, God orders him to go to the great city of Nineveh to warn the people to repent or God will destroy them. Instead of obeying God, Jonah flees to Tarshish.

Later, as Jonah languishes in the belly of the large fish, we think, maybe, he sees the error of his ways. He sings God's praise and promises "What I have vowed I will perform."

Jonah keeps this vow. He goes to Nineveh and warns the people to repent. The response is breathtaking. The people of Nineveh instantly put on sackcloth. They fast and vow to turn from their evil ways. So sincere is their change of heart that God spares them.

Clearly, Jonah was a man with talent. Jonah, however, is not happy with his new calling. Quite the contrary. He is deeply troubled to have helped these people do *t'shuvah*/repentance. He complains to God that this is just what he had predicted and this is why he fled to Tarshish. He is so unhappy he even asks God to kill him.

When God refuses, Jonah goes to live in the desert to watch what will become of Nineveh. While in the desert, a plant grows over his hut, and Jonah loves the plant. God sends a worm and a hot wind to kill the plant in one night, and Jonah grieves for it.

God tries to use the plant and Jonah's feelings for it to make Jonah understand that God cares for the people of Nineveh. The story ends there. Jonah never gives any sign that he has changed.

The first key I tried to make sense of this story was to think about the significance of Jonah's name—Yonah/Dove. There is one other important dove in the bible—the dove in Noah. That dove also lives in a large vessel surrounded by water. That dove too is sent forth on an important mission that will determine human survival.

I thought, perhaps, understanding the dove can help explain Jonah. What is there about the dove that could shed light on Jonah? At first, there seems to be no help. The dove never speaks. We never know the dove's feelings.

We can guess that the dove didn't know or understand that it was being sent on an important mission. It didn't argue with Noah. It was just a bird. Human motivations were a mystery to it. All it could know was that it was taken from the safety of the Ark and thrown into the air, forced to fly over an enormous ocean. In the end it found a plant and some security for itself. Despite all this ill treatment, it faithfully fulfilled its mission and brought a message of deliverance to the people on the Ark.

How could Jonah be like the dove? He was a man. He speaks. God told him what he was to do and why. Jonah hears God and argues with God. Jonah is not an animal who could miss this clear message. But, then again, Jonah does behave as if he has no more understanding than did the dove. In many ways he's even worse. What can this mean?

The problem is that Jonah's story is told from God's point of view. That's why the instructions seem so clear and why Jonah's behavior seems so odd. Putting ourselves in Jonah's position makes it easier to understand.

This is Jonah's version of the story.

Jonah began having odd and frightening dreams. He dreamed God wanted him to go to Nineveh to tell the people there to repent. Nineveh? The greatest military power of the age? Nineveh—no friend of the Jews? He thought he must be going mad. He tried to act sanely, tried a change of scenery.

Finally, after the miraculous storm, the stay in the fish's belly, Jonah is a defeated man. He tries to give in to this calling. People will jeer at him. The city will not be destroyed in forty days. Then Jonah will have proved to himself that the voices are only in his head. He will have proved that he shouldn't listen to the voices. He will be able to go home—to ignore the voices even if they continue.

But the worst happens. The people listen to Jonah. Jonah is so frightened he runs away to the desert. He can never go home. He has really heard God's voice and can never live a normal life again.

From God's point of view, there was a very clear message of caring / rachmanut and an assurance that we can make mistakes and repent. From Jonah's point of view, there were only these confusing voices commanding him to do the oddest things. Here is a man who could have been the world's greatest prophet, but the job was too frightening.

We are so like Jonah and so unlike Moses. The thing we have to do might as well be in the heavens or across the seas. The commandments may be simple and in our mouths and in our hearts, but we don't know how to tell which are the true commandments and which are distractions.

As Jews, we are given many small commandments, most are not too hard to do. Doing these small mitzvot allows us to consecrate each moment and each space. There are so many commandments that to pay attention and to do them requires enormous concentration.

Perhaps what this means is that we should live our lives like a walking meditation, concentrating on these small mitzvot/commandments / blessings so that we do not step off the path. The kabbalists say we live in a shattered world. The path is hard to find. Every step is likely to be a misstep.

The normal way we have to live our lives is as a continual effort to return. In meditation, when attention wanders we must return to concentrating, without judgment or condemning our weakness. Judgment and regret become distractions. When we are distracted, we cannot return. When we truly return, we get a new chance to shoot the arrow and this time hit the target. The *het* [sin] is wiped out.

R. Adin Steinsaltz tells us that the Torah is a system of knowledge and insights to guide the individual Jew to reach his own selfhood. Halachah is not only the law, it is a guide for walking, for living. It guides us in our aloneness and searching so that we can find ourselves. When we do *teshuvah* we turn from a fixation on other objects to a concentration on God.

But even when our focus is elsewhere, God is not in the heavens or over the seas. We need no one to get the divine message and bring it back to us. We need to turn and to return, to go into the people we truly are.

Just as with Jonah, there is a constant answering in those moments of clarity. There are brief flashes when we do the right thing. And then the next moment we wander from the path, from our true selves. But then, in the next, we may find the way back.

If we could only see our lives from a cosmic vantage point, we would see that we spend most of our time running away, even—and especially—when we know what is right. Steinsaltz says that *teshuvah* is a lifelong journey, not guilt, but a sense of spiritual disquiet, a feeling that we are no longer the right person in the right place, that we are outsiders in a world whose meaning escapes us.

Return us to you, *Adonai,* and we will return. Renew our days as you have before.

                                                                Ellen Dannin

Jonah Learns about Love

Love is the active concern for the life and the growth of that which we love. Where this active concern is lacking, there is no love. This element of love has been beautifully described in the book of Jonah. God has told Jonah to go to Ninevah to warn its inhabitants that they will be punished unless they mend their evil ways. Jonah runs away from his mission because he is afraid that the people of Nineveh will repent and that God will forgive them. He is a man with a strong sense of order and law, but without love. However, in his attempt to escape, he finds himself in the belly of a whale, symbolizing the state of isolation and imprisonment which his lack of love and solidarity has brought upon him. God saves him, and Jonah goes to Nineveh. He preaches to the inhabitants as God had told him, and the very thing he was afraid of happens. The men of Nineveh repent their sins, mend their ways, and God forgives them and decides not to destroy the city. Jonah is intensely angry and disappointed; he wanted "justice" to be done, not mercy. At last he finds some comfort in the shade of a tree which God has made to grow for him to protect him from the sun. But when God makes the tree wilt, Jonah is depressed and angrily complains to God. God answers: "Thou hast had pity on the gourd for which thou hast not labored neither madest grow; which came up in a night, and perished in a night. And should I not spare Nineveh, that great city, wherein are more than six score thousand people that cannot discern between their right hand and their left hand; and also much cattle?" God's answer to Jonah is to be understood symbolically. God explains to Jonah that the essence of love is to "labor" for something and "to make something grow," that love and labor are inseparable. One loves that for which one labors and one labors for that which one loves.

Erich Fromm

The Book of Jonah: A Summary

Its primary theme is the universality of God who loves all and rules over all people, forgiving anyone who repents and acknowledges his wrongdoing.

The story begins with a call from God. Jonah is to go to the wicked city of Nineveh, to proclaim that imminent punishment upon it and those who live there, because of their great sins. Jonah, the reluctant prophet, tries to evade the mission. He is afraid and refuses to obey. In an attempt to flee from God's will, he embarks for Tarshish. On the high seas a terrible storm arises, threatening to engulf the ship and take the lives of all aboard. The storm rages more fiercely than ever and the lives of all are in danger. Meanwhile Jonah is fast asleep in the ship's hull. When Jonah is found he is roundly reprimanded and asked to pray to his God—"if it so be that God will think of us"—for immediate deliverance.

The mariners believe that someone on board ship is responsible for the violent tempest. They cast lots to discover the guilty one and it falls to Jonah, who admits he is running away from God's behest. They surround Jonah and question him:

"Tell us, we pray you, for whose cause this evil is upon us. What is your occupation? Where do you come from? What is your country? And what people are you?" And he said to them, "I am a Hebrew; and I fear the Lord, the God of heaven, who made the sea and the dry land."

The men now know that Jonah is fleeing from the presence of the Lord and therefore he is the cause of the storm. Jonah suggests because he is responsible, he be cast into the raging sea. He is thrown overboard, the storm subsides and the sea becomes calm.

Chapter II tells of the great fish sent to swallow up Jonah and imprison him for three days and three nights. As Israel prays for deliverance from the dark depths of exile and is rescued, so Jonah is saved from the whale so that he may continue on his mission to Nineveh.

In his despair, Jonah cries to God a magnificent prayer reminiscent of the Psalms:

I called out of my affliction
To God, and He answered me:
Out of the belly of the nether world I cried,
And You heard my voice.
For You cast me into the depth,
In the heart of the seas,
The flood was all around me;
And Your waves and billows
Passed over me.
Then I said, "I was cast out
From before Your eyes";
Yet I will look again
Toward Your holy temple.
The water encircled me all around,
Even to my very soul;
The deep embraced me;
The weeds were entwined around my head.
I went down to the bottoms of the mountains;
The earth with her bars closed upon me forever;
Yet, You brought up my life from the pit,
O Lord my God.
When my soul fainted within me,
I remembered the Lord;
And my prayer reached You,
In Your holy temple.
Those who regard lying vanities
Forsake their own good.
But I will sacrifice to You
With the voice of thanksgiving;
What I have vowed I will pay.
Salvation is of the Lord.

God hears Jonah's prayer and instructs the fish to cast him up on dry land. He has submitted to God's will and has learned his lesson of unquestioning obedience. Again, God commands him to go to Nineveh. Jonah proceeds unhesitatingly.

The inhabitants are impressed after listening to the warning uttered by God's prophet. They acknowledge their wrongdoing and repent. Their king dresses himself in sackcloth, proclaims a fast, and calls upon his people to cry mightily to God.

When God sees that the people are sincere, the contemplated punishment is rescinded. The city for the time being is saved. Jonah, however, is grieved because he feels he has failed in his mission and is angered because he had been sent to preach an imminent punishment which has not been fulfilled.

God rebukes Jonah and then Jonah goes out from the city. He sets up little booth and sits under it in the shade to see what will happen in Nineveh. A large, fast-growing plant, a gourd, rises to shelter him from the hot sun and gives Jonah great comfort. The next morning, however, the gourd plant has withered because God has sent a worm to injure it from within. When the sun rises, God prepares a hot east wind, and the sun beats on Jonah's head so that he is faint and begs that he may die. And here by analogy God teaches Jonah a lesson.

"You had pity on the gourd for which you did not labor nor make it grow, which came up in the night and perished in the night. Should I not have pity on Nineveh that great city, in which there are more than six score thousand people who cannot discern between their right hand and their left hand, and also much cattle?"

God feels compassion for the people. God is the God of all creatures. God will punish or save, depending on deeds. All may come to God for forgiveness and pardon.

Jonah questions whether the Ninevites are worthy of receiving the lofty messages of God's forgiveness, and he is taught by God that they, too, are worthy to receive God's love and compassion which extends to all. This explains why the entire Book of Jonah has been selected as the prophetic portion which is read in the synagogue at the afternoon service, *Minhah,* on Yom Kippur, the Day of Atonement.

Rabbi Alex J. Goldman

Why Are You Sleeping? *Mah Lekha, Nirdam?*— Jonah 1:6

Imagine that one morning you had an important appointment—perhaps an interview for a job, or a meeting or a plane to catch on your dream vacation trip around the world ... and you overslept!

As mortifying as that horrible prospect may sound, such a disappointment pales in comparison with an event on actual record. According to midrashic interpretation, on the morning when God was to reveal the Torah to them on Mount Sinai, the entire people of Israel overslept! For three days they prepared for the great theophany, and when the very special morning arrived, all the thunder and lightning and the blaring voice of the shofar were present in order to awaken the sleeping masses who had almost missed the entire event! (Exodus 19:16, Shir HaShirim Rabba 1:12)

Some authorities maintain that we should stay up all night on *Layl Shavuot* and study (*Tikkun Layl Shavuot*) to compensate for having overslept on the very first Shavuot. In addition, the Jerusalem Talmud informs us that we are not supposed to nap on Rosh Hashanah, the day of the blowing of the shofar, because "He who sleeps during the day of Rosh Hashanah, his *mazal* (fortune) falls asleep too." Other sources tell us that blowing the shofar makes us alert and awake, in more than the physical sense. In the biblical prophet Amos we read: "Shall the shofar be blown in the city and the people not tremble?" (Amos 3:6) In the medieval mystical book the *Zohar*, the *tekiah* blast is referred to as *Kol Lehitorerut*, a call to be alert and awake.

Perhaps this is where Maimonides, the great 12th century philosopher and law codifier, derived his popular interpretation of the shofar:

> Awake and remember your Creator, you who forget eternal truths by grasping the trifles of the hour. Look well into your deeds and return in repentance. You have lost your way pursuing vain desires. Think of your Creator, and heed the call of your souls. Return to the Lord, and God will have mercy upon you (*Mishneh Torah, Hilchot Teshuvah*, 3:4).

The Call to Awaken

What is the meaning of this call to awaken?

In many religious traditions, sleep implies a state of spiritual lethargy. In the *midrash* about Mount Sinai, the ancient rabbis were trying to say that the people were emotionally and spiritually unprepared for an event as great as Sinai, when God revealed the Torah to us. After all, it was a slave nation, with no experience of God except for what Moshe had told them. This simple, untutored folk was in no way ready for an experience of direct confrontation with the holy God!

Perhaps the message of the *midrash* is that often, when God speaks to us, or when great spiritual events occur around us, or when life manifests itself in some special sacred way, *we may sleep through it!* Therefore, we need the sound of the shofar to awaken us and bring us to a higher level of readiness. After all, who wants to sleep through a momentous occasion such as the giving of the Torah?

Missing the Peak Experiences of Life

We might say that B'nai Yisrael sleeping through the giving of the Torah is a metaphor for missing the peak experiences of life. "Sleep" is also the word the rabbis use to describe the routine response of the average person, in all his simplicity and banality, to life's sacred opportunities.

Rabbi James Ponet, in a meditation written to introduce the blowing of the shofar, tells us that: "We resist waking up, [we] yearn for a trancelike numbness, ... [and we] choose to stumble through our days as if in a dream. For we are inertial beings given to drifting with the tide, heedless of our destination. It takes an outside force to stun us ... to scare us out of our programmed fears, push us kicking out of the "four cubits" of dull, daily idolatry where, like sleepers, we have eyes but do not see, ears but do not hear, noses but do not smell, hands but do not feel.... God created Jews in order to keep newness in the world; it is the task of the Jew to awaken the dawn" (*Orim: A Jewish Journal at Yale*, Autumn, 1986, pp. 127–128).

A New Age

A new consciousness is emerging, a new Renaissance, awakening the slumbering giant of modern technological society from a deep sleep. Moshe received the Torah and brought a new awakening to a people who would rather have slept through life, radically changing their lives by giving it form, purpose, and direction. The Renaissance, the Awakening, shook up a people too long lying in the darkness of ignorance, poverty, squalor, and inequity. So, too, today, we are being awakened by a new generation which is seeking a higher quality of cultural and spiritual life: deeper relationships, better families, more effective education, justice for the poor, the sick and the hungry, more creative pursuits in the work place, and a redefined role for women that permits their real, full self to emerge. As Jean Houston states, "The depths start to rise, and the other side of the moon of ourselves haunts our becoming and demands its tribute. It is the first stirrings of the Rhythm of Awakening" (*The Possible Human,* p. xv). This is a new Renaissance era of personal fulfillment, self-realization, and higher spiritual evolution.

On Rosh Hashanah, the shofar arouses us from the "trance of ordinary life." It comes to prevent us from missing life by sleeping through it, like Rip Van Winkle who saw a picture of King George III when he went to sleep, and after he awoke saw a picture of George Washington. He had slept through a revolution. We dare not sleep through the revolution that is taking place in our own day, before our very eyes!

Too many of us sleep through life, with its many opportunities for growth, learning and development, by being couch potatoes and watching TV. The television is turned on in the average American household for seven hours a day! By the end of his life, John Doe of Main St., USA, will have spent ten years in front of the set. The blaring of the TV day and night makes us into passive zombies, glued to a screen portraying violence, sex, extra-marital affairs and dysfunctional families. It keeps us from getting to know members of our own family, reading a good book, and developing the art of conversation.

Two Mitzvot

Two mitzvot are indispensable to revive and reawaken Judaism in our generation: *Kashrut* and Shabbat. Let's take them one at a time.

1. *Kashrut* awakens our religious and ethical consciousness on many levels. As our consciousness expands regarding healthy eating habits, we should expand the meaning of Jewish dietary laws. New prohibitions could include preservatives, additives, artificial coloring, excessive amounts of sugar, salt, fat, or cholesterol—all the things

which we stuff into our mouths without thinking, poisoning our bodies, giving ourselves premature cancer or heart disease, and violating one of Judaism's sacred principles of treating our body with honor and respect.

The message comes to us via many avenues—the medical community, ecology groups, the government, even from our own children—yet we continue to pretend that we don't hear. We remain asleep while our bodies are destroyed. It's time to wake up, and stop putting caffeine, nicotine, and other pollutants into the sacred vessel which houses our soul.

Further, we need to pay more attention to the whole eating experience, and to elevate it, as Judaism demands, to a sacred act. We should say a prayer of gratitude before and after we eat, eat slowly and carefully, and share the surplus with the hungry instead of tossing it into the garbage. We can recycle our waste products instead of fouling the environment with them.

2. We also sleep through life by ignoring the regenerative power that Shabbat can bring to our lives and to our families.

There is an old and hallowed tradition that Shabbat afternoon is a wonderful time to catch some extra winks. Nevertheless, the remaining time during Shabbat we could be much more awake to the beauty of the constellation of its traditions: from Friday night candles, kiddush, blessing the children, family singing of *z'mirot* and *Birkat HaMazon*, to attending worship on Shabbat morning, *Seudah Shlishit* and *Havdalah* on Saturday night, and the myriad opportunities for friendship, study, and reflection that Shabbat offers.

If the Jewish people are to truly awaken to the magnificence of our priceless heritage, Shabbat observance must be a more vital part of our weekly routine. We shall have to sing more, be silent more, feel awe more, hope more, praise more and love more. If you observe Shabbat in some meaningful way for just a few months, your entire life will change. And the beauty of that one day a week will begin to penetrate and transform all the other days as well.

Increased Spirituality

Lastly, to be truly awake in this age of renewed consciousness, we need to devote more time and energy to our spiritual selves. Our young people have for too long been disillusioned with the spiritual emptiness of

Jewish institutional life, including the synagogue. We must find ways to bring more spiritual depth into our personal lives as well as into our synagogue experience.

We need to become more familiar with the majestic beauty of the *Siddur* and the *Mahzor,* with the poetic phrases and ideas that have the power to awaken us from our spiritual slumber and lethargy, and call forth within us a new appreciation of life's blessings.

So much of the underlying theology of Rosh Hashanah points in the direction of being born again, of awakening on the morning of the New Year to a new life and a new way of life. *Hayom Harat Olam*—this is the birthday of the world. This is the first day of the rest of our lives. It is the time to awaken to the infinite possibilities latent within our souls. The pious Jew finds this invitation in the first sentence of the 16th century Code of Jewish Law, the *Shulchan Arukh*: Arise like a lion in the morning for the service of the Creator!

Hayom Harat Olam! As Thomas Paine stated in his call to arms: "We have it in ourselves to begin the world again." In 18th century France, Count de Saint Simon instructed his valet to wake him every morning with these words: "Wake up, monsieur, you have great things to do today." The shofar calls to each of us: Wake up! You have great things to do this year!

Amen!

Rabbi Dov Peretz Elkins

Of What People Are You?—I Am a Hebrew (Jonah 1:8–9)

Jonah was a stowaway on a storm-tossed boat. He was fleeing from God, from his people, from his country, from his duty. All his ties were snapped; all his bridges burnt. Then the storms of life began to rage and the hurricanes of existence to howl. His fellow travelers, who up to then ignored his presence, suddenly became aware of him. "Tell us," they said, "are you not to blame for this trouble? What is your occupation, where do you come from, what land is yours, what is your people?"

How many times in our sad history were these questions asked? Who are you? To retain our equilibrium, to preserve our balance, our mental health and our emotional stability, let us answer this question without hesitation, without fear—and with pride. I am a Jew! Take it or leave it. I am a Jew! Whatever the consequences, my dignity is intact; my faith is firm; my honor unsullied; my pride is strong.

This is what a sense of belonging means. O Lord, "cast us not away from Thy presence."

Rabbi Joseph H. Lookstein

Choosing to Change

On Yom Kippur, we recognize our aloneness and seek to repair our relationships to others. Central to this is our relationship to God. God says to us, "Turn toward me and I will turn toward you." We ask that our days be renewed as of old (*Hadesh yameinu ke-kedem*). Literally, this means "Make our days new as of old"—a paradox that captures the sense of a reconnection to the way we were or at least the way we should be. We try to make the old new, not to discard it. We go back to go forward. By repairing the breach between ourselves and the Divine Other, we can also begin to repair the many breaches between ourselves and the myriads of people with whom we have relationships.

Yom Kippur calls for profound reexamination of our self-definition and our relationship to the rest of the world. The tradition recognizes the difficulty of this process and sets aside the day of Yom Kippur specifically and this whole period more generally to force us to focus on a subject we prefer to avoid. All of us are like Jonah, ready to flee to some exotic Tarshish rather than face the reality of who we are and, even more threatening, the possibility that we could become different.

Ironically, Jonah is the only successful prophet in the whole Bible, the only one whom people listen to and who causes them to actually change their ways. Yet it is his knowledge that he will succeed, not doubts about a possible failure, that causes Jonah to flee. Jonah is not afraid that the people of Ninevah will dismiss him as a quack; rather, he knows that they will repent. As he says: "O Lord! Isn't this just what I said when I was still in my own country? That is why I fled beforehand to Tarshish. For I know that You are a compassionate and gracious God.... Please, Lord, take my life, for I would rather die than live."

Rather than face that possibility, he flees. To the end, Jonah resists any sense of responsibility for the fate of the world or his own fate.

Jonah lacks compassion for the people of the city, a compassion found in everyone else in the story, including the sailors, who are extremely reluctant to throw Jonah overboard. Lacking compassion for others, he lacks compassion for himself. Fearing *teshuvah* and change in others, he fears change in himself and flees the truth, only to find it at least for a moment in the dark depths of the whale.

Rosh ha-Shanah and Yom Kippur together affirm the chance for positive change; for no matter how old or routine, there is hope for new birth and new ways. Each year these days ask us, "Which shall it be, Tarshish or Ninevah? Darkness or light? Death or life?"

Rabbi Michael Strassfeld

The Book of Jonah—Whose Story Are We Telling?

When we read the Book of Jonah
Whose story are we really telling?

Are we telling the story
of Jonah Ben Amittai, God's prophet?
God sends Jonah to pass judgment
on the city of Nineveh
But Jonah tries to flee from God
And lands up in the belly of a big fish.
And even when he comes to Nineveh
He begrudgingly preaches to the people.
Are we telling the story of an angry man who doesn't under-
      stand the importance of forgiveness?

Or are we telling the story of the wicked city of Nineveh?
Though the Ninevites are
The mortal enemies of ancient Israel
God sends his prophet to call
Upon them to turn in repentance
And give up their evil ways.
 When they do God immediately forgives them.
No one is beyond the call of atonement.
Are we really telling God's story?
Is this the story of the One of whom we say,

"He is compassionate and gracious....
Yet he does not forgo punishment; rather He visits iniquity ...
    unto the third and fourth generation.
Is this Jonah's God really the same as the angry God we read
    about in the book of Exodus?
It's no wonder that Jonah is confused—
the God He knew about from Exodus
sounds different from the one
who called Him to service in his own generation.
Here we find a God who is forgiving
Who is big enough to change His mind
And forgive the most wicked of people.
So which one is it?
Whose story do we read on Yom Kippur Afternoon?

I would suggest that we read all of them
and none of them.

We are really reading our own story.

We are the ones who flee from God,
Who are often so angry
that we cannot forgive those who hurt us.
We are the ones who live in the great city of Nineveh
and must learn to listen
and answer the call for repentance.

And we must strive to be like the One
Who is big enough to overcome indignation
and who is not so proud that He can't change His mind.

On Yom Kippur afternoon as the day grows late we pause to
    look at ourselves and to ask ourselves:

What are we fleeing from?

How can we change?

Who do we follow?

                            Rabbi Mark B. Greenspan

CLOSING THE GATES

The concluding service of Yom Kippur is called *ne'ilah*, the "closing" or "locking" of gates. It is recited during the final hour of Yom Kippur, between dusk and nightfall. Its atmosphere combines passion, urgency, and exhaustion in the final effort of atonement. The various special lines within the *'amidah*, recited from Rosh Hashanah through Yom Kippur, that call upon God to "inscribe" us in the book of life, are now changed to a plea that God "seal" us for life, since the heavenly books are sealed as Yom Kippur ends.

There is some debate among the commentators as to just what "closing of the gates" is meant by the name of this service. It would seem to refer to the heavenly gates through which prayer is received, and which are about to close with the end of the day. The problem with this reading is that heaven's gates don't really close. If the angels did try to close them at the end of Yom Kippur, we humans could always turn to tears (which some do anyway during *ne'ilah*) and the Talmud explicitly says that "the gates of tears are never closed." Other commentators therefore said that these were the gates of the earthly Temple; *ne'ilah* is recited at the hour when the Temple gates were usually closed.

That is an interesting fact, but hardly very impressive. Why should this prayer of the synagogue be timed to the closing of the Temple gates? It makes more sense to say that the prayer refers to the gates of

our hearts, which are about to close up because we have reached the
end of our ability to keep them open. The entire season of Rosh
Hashanah and Yom Kippur has made great emotional demands on
us. We stand face-to-face with our mortality, we examine the value
of our lives, we pray for others who are dear to us. In this final hour, as
we realize the inner gates will have to close, we begin to turn from
supplication toward making peace. We start on the road to accepting
the new year, whatever our fate in it will be.

RABBI ARTHUR GREEN, *THESE ARE THE WORDS*

The Gates Are Open—God Accepts All

The open gates are a metaphor for many things. All wayward souls have an opportunity to march through the gates of forgiveness and acceptance. God is prepared to accept all.

Another interpretation, particularly relevant for our time, is the notion that all are welcome in the synagogue family. The gates of the Synagogue, and the gates of Judaism, are open at all times for all people. Many synagogues today sponsor outreach programs, to encourage those who are married to non-Jews to feel at home in the congregation, and to make those who have chosen to be Jews feel completely at home.

An ancient Midrash establishes firm precedent for God's willingness to be ready to accept all within the House of God:

> There is no creature whom the Blessed Holy One rejects.
> God accepts all.
> The gates are open at every hour.
> All who wish to enter may enter.
> Therefore it is written in Scripture:
> "My doors I open to the wanderer" (Job 31:32).
> Meaning, the Blessed Holy One accepts all creatures as one.
> (Exodus Rabbah 19:4.)

Rabbi Dov Peretz Elkins

Pidyonenu Ad Arev—May Redemption Come to Us at Dusk

When I.B. Singer gave his Nobel lecture in December 1978, he startled the audience in Stockholm by suddenly breaking into Yiddish. He said the Swedish Academy was also honoring *"loshen fun golus, ohn a land, ohn grenitzen, nish gshtitzt fun kein shum meluchoh"* ["a language of exile, without a land, without frontiers, not supported by a government"]; a language which possesses no words for weapons, ammunition, military exercises, war tactics; a language that was despised by both "gentiles and emancipated Jews."

When the poet entertains, Singer continued, he " ... is searching for eternal truth, for the essence of being. In his own fashion he tries to solve the riddle of time and change, to find an answer to suffering, to reveal love in the abyss of cruelty and injustice."

D.P.E.

Walking through Different Kinds of Doors— Judge Us Not for What We Were, but for What We Can Be

The following prayer was written by a prisoner in jail:

"Please God, when I ride home on the train, help me to keep myself straight and strong as those tracks of steel. Help me to remember, God, when I walk in my front door, how many times I walked through a different kind of door—3" door with bars of steel. When I walk through the park and breathe fresh air and hear the laughter of kids, help me, God, to appreciate how sweet freedom is. When I cash my first paycheck and stop on my way home to buy a shirt or maybe shoes, help me, God, to appreciate my independence. That's about it, God, and if you don't mind my asking, please don't judge me for what I was, but for what I can be."

That little phrase captures the dramatic mood of *N'eilah*. We spent a whole day enumerating our sins and transgressions in the *Al Het*. We told God what we were; we described our black record. At the same time, we do not surrender to despair and hopelessness and declare that all is lost, sin is irremedial, and that we are doomed. We want to be judged for what we can be, not for what we were in the past.

Rabbi Gilbert S. Rosenthal

Is It Too Late?

The Hebrew poet laureate of early 20th century *Eretz Yisrael*, Hayim Nachman Bialik, tells this lovely legend of "King David in the Cave."

There were two pious young Torah students learning about the Messiah, and they dreamed of Redemption. One night, an old man with a white beard came to them in a dream and said *David Ha-Melekh Hai!*—King David Lives! He told them to go to a certain cave and there they would find him. They searched and finally found him. The same old man was there, guarding the entrance. It was the prophet Eliyahu. Eliyahu told them to enter and pour water on King David's hands the minute he awakens. Then he will rise and bring the Redemption.

They saw David sleeping but were dazzled and fascinated by the gold and jewels and marble around him. When the King arose for a moment and spread his hands to be washed, they were too preoccupied. He sighed and went back to sleep.

Alas, it was too late!

N'eilah is our last opportunity for repentance. Our last chance to help hasten the redemption. Will we miss our chance?

Retold by Rabbi Gilbert S. Rosenthal

N'eilah—The Closing of the Gates

During this final service of the *Yamim Noraim*, it is not strange that we should feel pensive and contrite. The sun descends, the Gates of heaven and repentance begin to close. There is the even stronger feeling that we are nearing a fateful decision. There is a powerful urge to hold back the closing of the Gates. Maybe we have not really prayed well, prayed enough, prayed sincerely. There is a feeling of remorse we all share as these Days of Awe draw to a close. The refrain of a hymn in an early Reform *Union Hymnal* describes it simply and accurately:

> The sun goes down, the shadows rise,
> The day of God is near its close.
> Lord, crown our work before the night:
> At eventide let there be light.

Anyone at all familiar with Jewish religious literature knows the fascination we Jews have had for the "gates" through which we all must pass. Every classic edition of the Jerusalem and Babylonian Talmuds has title pages adorned with drawings of a gate. These are known as the *Sha'ar Blat*, Yiddish for "gate pages." Most European prayer books published before the Holocaust decorated their title pages with a rendering of a gate and used the word GATE in their titles, such as *Gates of Prayer, Gates of Judah,* etc.

A brief survey of some of the older prayers reveals some 75 prayer phrases referred to as "gates": "Gates of Wisdom," "Gates of Mercy,"

"Gates of Forgiveness," etc. A little-known women's penitential prayer *(tehinah)*, recited before the Sabbath *Havdalah*, contains 65 "Gates of …" in alphabetical order. Another prayer, *Sha'arey Armon* (Gates of the Temple), recited early in the *N'eilah* service, speaks of the closing of the gates of prayer as the final opportunity to pray for mercy.

It is the custom in many Synagogues for the Ark to remain open for the entire *N'eilah* service, during which some congregants remain standing. In other synagogues, the Ark remains open, but congregants sit, except for certain special *Selihot* where local custom dictates whether to stand or not.

Hazzan Samuel Rosenbaum

The Final Shofar Blast

The stirring sound of the shofar as Yom Kippur ends has many different explanations. Some say that the practice recalls the giving of the Torah at Sinai (when the shofar was blown). Others say that the shofar signals the triumph of Israel over its sins for another year and heralds the possible coming of the Messiah. Finally, there is a superstitious belief that the shofar confuses Satan at a time when he might be tempted to harm the Jewish people.

The numerical equivalent of the Hebrew *HaSatan* (Satan) is 364. A midrash interprets this as indicating that Satan can harm the Jewish people every day of the year, except on Yom Kippur.

Rabbi Daniel B. Syme

Closing Gates, New Beginning

Yom Kippur 1945 in Berlin. It was, of course, the first of the Yomim Noraim to be marked in that shattered city following the end of World War II. After V-E Day in May 1945, I was transferred from my job as a Third Army rifleman to the US Control Council, later to be known as the Office of Military Government (US). I was stationed first in Hoechst, the site of IG Farben headquarters right outside of Frankfurt and then in Berlin, when OMG (US) moved there. We were billeted in Zehlendorf, a leafy suburban Scarsdale-like place near Lake

Wansee where monstrous things had been conceived and directed, although none of this was known to this 21-year-old infantry corporal—now assigned to the Economics Division of OMG (US).

It was September 1945 and somehow word passed to those troops stationed in Berlin that High Holiday Services for Jewish personnel would be held in a place called Goethe Hall. Berlin at that time, unlike Gaul, was divided into four "Sectors"—US, British, French and Russian. At that time, personnel of any one of those sectors could move freely into the others. My recollection is that Goethe Hall was not in the US sector. (When I returned to Berlin about five years ago I tried unsuccessfully to find Goethe Hall. I don't know if it still stands.)

But the Yom Kippur Service was held under US auspices in a large auditorium, filled with uniformed personnel of the United States and our allies. It was stunning—and thrilling—to be part of this unlikely congregation, gathered from the victorious forces with uniforms of all ranks and nationalities, The Baal Korei was a young officer from the 82nd Airborne Division with, to me, a distinctly Yeshiva-ish intonation—a fluent and experienced reader of the Torah. A handful of German civilians—the remnants, we were told, of the "Judische Gemeinde"—were present. Their stories were unknown to me then, nor I think were most of us fully aware at that early time, long before the word *Shoah* was used, what those stories would turn out to be.

There was a Yom Kippur appeal. The currency at that time, "occupation currency," in denominations of marks, but issued by the respective victorious governments, was square-ish paper currency and when empty GI food ration cartons were circulated, they became giant receptacles for gifts of currency.

That at least is how I remember it. In 1995, at the Holocaust Museum in Washington, there was a celebration called "Liberation '45," with the insignia, ribbons and flags of the military units that had participated in the ending of that terrible time. My wife and I visited the Exhibition and there, in the basement of the Museum in Washington, were photographs of that Service and of some of those young men and women who had lived to see that day, including, for me, that memorable paratroop officer who led the Service.

I don't remember how long the Service lasted. Did it last right through to the end of Yom Kippur? Almost certainly not. But as I now imagine it—see it—as Ne'ilah approached that day and the Gates were closing, did I sense—did I dream—that this was a New Beginning? I hope so.

Maurice S. Spanbock

Shofar

Under the British mandate, the area in front of the Kotel did not look as it does today. Only a narrow alley separated the Kotel and the Arab houses on its other side. The British instituted the following ordinances, designed to humble the Jews at the holiest place of their faith: it is forbidden to pray out loud, lest one upset the Arab residents; it is forbidden to read from the Torah; it is forbidden to sound the *shofar* on Rosh Hashanah and Yom Kippur.

On Yom Kippur of 1930, Rabbi Moshe Segal was praying at the Kotel. He thought to himself: "Can we possibly forgo the sounding of the shofar that accompanies our proclamation of the sovereignty of God? Can we possibly forgo the sounding of the shofar, which symbolizes the redemption of Israel?"

Rabbi Segal opened the drawer in the prayer stand and slipped the shofar into his shirt. He wrapped himself in a tallit and thought, "All around me, a foreign government prevails, ruling over the people of Israel even on their holiest day and at their holiest place, and we are not free to serve our God; but under this *tallit* is another domain. Here I am under no dominion save that of my Father in Heaven; here I shall do as He commands me, and no force on earth will stop me." When the closing verses of the *ne'ilah* prayer were proclaimed, Rabbi Segal took the shofar and blew a long, resounding blast. Before he had finished, the British Police had grabbed him. He was immediately arrested. Chief Rabbi Abraham Isaac Kook intervened with the High Commissioner to obtain his release.

For the next eighteen years, until the Arab conquest of the Old City in 1948, the shofar was sounded at the Kotel at the end of every Yom Kippur. The British well understood the significance of this blast; they knew that it would ultimately demolish their reign over our land as the walls of Jericho crumbled before the shofar of Joshua, and they did everything in their power to prevent it. But every Yom Kippur, the shofar was sounded by men who know they would be arrested for their part in staking our claim on the holiest of our possessions. By men who believed in the impossible.

Author Unknown

The Gates Clang Shut—*Neilah*

Twice a year during the days of the Great Temple, on Tisha B'Av and on Yom Kippur, there was a service at the end of the day, called *Neilah*, or closing, because it was performed as the Temple gates were clanging shut. We still perform this service on Yom Kippur, and we still call it *Neilah*, only now it is not the closing of the Temple gates that we are referring to, but rather the closing of the gates of heaven.

This is generally a very well-attended service. At my synagogue, people throng to the *Neilah* service. Most of them have been in synagogue all day long. Since far more people come to our Yom Kippur services than we can accommodate in a single sanctuary sitting, we have many services going on at once all day long. We have staggered services, alternative services, parallel services out in the social hall, several seatings in the main sanctuary. But by the afternoon service, all the people begin to trickle into the main sanctuary at once. The seats fill up quickly, then people start sitting on the floor in the aisles. People stand at the back of the room. People sit on the steps up in the balcony and pack themselves into the foyer just outside the sanctuary. As *Neilah* begins, I look out over a sea of faces tightly pressed together. The sanctuary is filled to more than double its capacity. I always feel a thrill of fear at this moment. Our synagogue is very old, and the main sanctuary is up on the second floor. What if the floor should collapse from the weight of all this overload? What if an earthquake were suddenly to hit? What makes these thousands of people so desperately want to crowd into a space meant to hold only a fraction of that number?

The Hasidic master Levi Yitzchak of Berditchev said that it isn't just that the gates of heaven are open during the Ten Days of *Teshuvah;* what is far more significant is that an energy, an attractive force, passes through this opening during these days. This is a very subtle energy, and for most of the Ten Days, when the gates are wide open, we don't even notice it. But during the *Neilah* service, as the gates begin to close and the opening becomes narrower and narrower, this attractive energy becomes more and more intense, more and more noticeable. It is precisely this energy which draws us to the *Neilah* service so intensely, and which inspires us to pray so fervently once there. The prayer we utter at *Neilah* is that most urgent of all human prayers, the prayer of the last chance. The gates of heaven are closing. We only have a few minutes left.

Rabbi Alan Lew

N'eilah

"Open for us the gates even as they are closing" (High Holiday Prayerbook). The sun is low, the hour is late, let us enter the gates at last. When a person begins life, countless gates stand waiting to be opened. But as we walk through the years, gates close behind us, one by one. Remember the unopened gates, and open them before they are locked. The gates do not stay open forever. And, at the end, they are all closed, except the one final gate which we must enter. Do not remain standing at the outer gate. Gates are made to be entered and opened. The sun is low, the hour is late. Let us enter the gates at last.

Each one of us is standing before his or her own unopened gates. Each of us is conscious of other gates that have closed forever. For many, the gates of youth and the blush of early life have closed forever. For some, the gates of stormy adolescence are just opening. For others, the gates of parenthood have been closed while the gates of becoming grandparents have not yet opened. Soon-to-be brides and grooms anxiously await the gates of marriage, while others feel locked within the gates of loneliness and solitude. Undoubtedly, there are some who feel that all the gates are locked, while others see only open gates in all directions.

It is good that we feel hunger. Perhaps never in the history of humanity have so many women and children and men been hungry. Not just on this Yom Kippur. Millions of our fellow human beings suffer from hunger, living the fast of Kippur every day of their lives without any of its saving characteristics, without any of the spiritual elation that comes along with the crescendo of our prayers and, above all, without the certainty that upon going home, they will be able to break their fast. Hunger is not a shame or a scourge; it is, pure and simple, a scandal, an obscenity, one of humanity's grossest irresponsibilities. This is a gate for which we do have the key.

But what of those gates that have closed? Isn't it true that there is always a second chance? No, my friends, it is not true. With all the money in the world, you cannot buy yesterday! Yom Kippur is all but over. We cannot go back to last night's *Kol Nidre* ever again, except in the recesses of memory.

One of the most urgent challenges of life is to come to terms with the gates that have closed forever. This requires a keen and honest reading of one's life, and that is what this day is all about. But we must be very careful not to make the error of declaring a gate shut forever that still can and must be opened. If we are to change the rhythm and content of our human relations, then we simply must find the keys to open the gates to our own selves. We must find a way to reach those parts of our selves that have been languishing and have atrophied. To exercise those capacities we must exorcise those false gates—of self-deception, selfishness, fear, timidity, bashfulness—that we have permitted to rust on their hinges. We can only love by opening our hearts all the way, and this is no simple task! It is much easier to let those gates remain closed, because sometimes it hurts to force a gate open.

Is there ever a moment in life when there are no further gates to be opened? No, not while one is alive. Living implies that there are always gates to be opened, at all ages, at all moments. What is required are the strength and the commitment necessary to search for the right key for the right lock. One must also be aware that upon opening the next gate, we may see things that are not very pleasant. No one can know beforehand what is behind every gate. There are gates that lead to Dante's *Inferno,* and there are gates that lead to God's resplendent Presence. It is simply risky to open gates. But it is more tragic to live one's whole life locked into one little antechamber surrounded by gates that we don't have the courage to risk opening.

Before we begin the *Neilah* Service, let us decide if we want to look for the keys. Assuming we have the keys, do we want to open up new gates?

Shall we open the gate of compassion?

The gate of social justice?

The gate of love?
The gate of commitment to Judaism?
The gate of serious Torah study?
The gate of meditation?
The gate of prayer?
The gate of daring to lead more meaningful lives?
The gate of personal righteousness and more ethical living?
The gate of risking to love more deeply the people we say we love?
The gate of courage?
The gate of action?
The gate of empathic living?

Rabbi Marshall I. Meyer

A Meditation before *Neilah*

In just a few moments we'll begin *Neilah,*
the special service which brings
Yom Kippur to an end.

The word, *Neilah*, means closing,
as in the closing of a gate or a door.
In the time of the Holy Temple
People drew closer to the temple precincts
at the end of Yom Kippur.
As the sun set, the *Kohanim,*
the descendants of Aaron,
began to close the Temple gates.

For our people filled with a
sense of awe and humility at this sacred hour,
cleansed of their sins
and weakened by the fast,
the gates of the Temple
were the very gates of Heaven.

They were now closing …
What had the people accomplished?
What prayers remained unstated?

What secret thoughts were not yet expressed?
The closing of the gates
conveyed a sense of urgency.
What did they wish to do
before the closing of the gates?

For us the gates are also closing.
The old year is gone and a new one
Is about to begin.
We ask to be sealed in the book of life,
to be given another chance,
to pass through the gates
and find the potential that lies within us
and before us.

We ask for one more opportunity
to recite the Sheheyanu,
To thank God for sustaining us
and bringing us to this moment.
We know, however, that there will never
be enough moments to satisfy us.
The gates are closing and we know that
someday they'll close one last time.
Each moment is therefore precious.

At this time I'd like to ask you
to close your eyes and imagine
the gate that you now must enter.
Sit quietly for a moment
and as you do, relax your muscles
Beginning with your neck,
your shoulders,
your arms,
your chest,
your stomach,
your thighs,
your legs,
and allow yourself
to be completely comfortable.

Breathe in and out
In and out,
in and out.
Breathe deeply through your nose
and out through your mouth
and feel the tensions and worries
of the past year slowly slip away.

Picture the gate before you.
What does it look like?
Is it inviting or threatening?
Is there light or darkness beyond the lintel?
Is it still open or has it already closed?

Where will this gate take you?
You reach out and touch the knob.
It's cool.
Your arm is loose as you hold it—
you neither pull the door open nor slam it shut.

This is the door you must now enter.

Where will it take you?
What do you leave behind?

You feel a mix of emotions: fear, anticipation,
excitement, yearning.

You cannot wait much longer.
You must enter now.
Where would you like to go?
Who would you like to be?

Before the closing of the gate,
Before the door is shut,
It is up to you to enter....

Rabbi Mark B. Greenspan

Displaced Persons

It is the *Neilah* service of Yom Kippur, the last opportunity for prayer before the Gates of Mercy are slammed shut for the year, our last chance to implore God to inscribe our names in the Book of Life. I am standing next to my father in the crowded men's section of his Orthodox synagogue, feeling the soft brush of his yellowed prayer shawl against the sleeve of my arm as we sway and rock to the prayers, feeling a communion with him and with the lost world from which he came. My father's yellowed talis amid the garbled singsong of desperate, hurried prayer by stale-smelling old European Jews has always been my touchstone to faith in God. That is why it took me years to grow comfortable with the polished veneer of modern liberal synagogues.

It has become a personal tradition of mine to forgo my own synagogue for this one prayer service and pray alongside him. It began as a convenient way to attend the postfast dinner given every year by my sister, whose home is a few blocks from his, but now I insist upon it. So does my brother, who is standing on my father's right flank. How many more times, after all, will there be to pray alongside my father? Five? Ten? The Yom Kippur question of who will live and who will die grows increasingly sobering as my father ages and declines.

What mystifies me year after year is why my father is standing here at all. Here is a man whose entire family was slaughtered by the Nazis, who almost overnight lost his home, his town, his way of life. Yet he has never stopped believing entirely in a tender, sheltering God. He grew up in a pious farmer's home and from the age of thirteen daily prayed by fastening to his arm and forehead the straps of *tefillin*—the contraption of two leather boxes concealing slips of Scripture. I asked him once what happened to the *tefillin* when he was drafted into the Soviet army. He seemed eager to answer the question, as if he had thought about it many times.

"I had them until 1942," he said. "They sent us out on maneuvers. When I came back they were stolen."

That indignity did not rattle his faith. Sometime after the gathering of Holocaust survivors in Jerusalem, I showed him slides I had taken of my mother and him at a ceremony in front of the Western Wall. One shot showed him sitting solemnly next to my mother in the crowd of seven thousand survivors. I asked him what he was thinking.

"I was angry with God," he said more forthrightly than I ever remember his saying anything. "I was asking him why he killed my mother and father and my sisters."

Yet he has kept his faith, and in the last decades of his life he has become even more religious. He long ago gave up work on Saturday and now refuses to drive. He and my mother have made their home kosher. He walks in his leafy neighborhood with a yarmulke. My mother tells me he prays three times a day and says Psalms in between. In this synagogue, my reticent father may not be one of the more prestigious members, but he is known by everyone, one of the stalwarts who help make up the daily minyanim of at least ten Jews.

I think of a central Torah reading of the High Holidays, the binding of Isaac that is read on the second day of Rosh Hashanah. God asked Abraham to sacrifice his son, his only son, Isaac, on an altar as a test of his faith. Abraham, otherwise a master bargainer, did not quibble, rising early to do God's bidding and leading Isaac to the crest of Mount Moriah to bind him upon an altar, upon which he planned to slaughter and burn him. Only an angel's intercession stopped him from slitting Isaac's throat. Abraham's trust in God was such that he was ready to believe even after God asked him to perform such a horrific act. My father's trust is such that he continues to believe even after the horrific sacrifice of his kin. His grudging, patient faith has brought him a kind of reparation, even a squaring of the debt—his two sons standing at his sides, his wife and daughter and daughters-in-law in the women's section across the dividing curtain, grandchildren capering on the fringes of the service. The Holocaust was a watershed in his long life, but it was only a watershed. His life went on. A new family was formed; other ones will splice off from that. Death did not defeat him. He not only survived, he thrived. For his faith in God promised that there would yet be other days and moments worth holding on for.

Joseph Berger

NEXT YEAR IN JERUSALEM

Yerushalayim or Jerusalem is the city chosen by God to be His holy place. Other specific places may be holy because of ancient events, settlements, or associations. But only Jerusalem is "the city of God, His holy mountain; beautiful sight, joy of all the earth" (Psalm 48:2–3). Jerusalem is the center of Judaism's universal vision, spoken by the prophets of ancient Israel. The transformation of the world is to come forth from there:

> It shall be at the end of days
> That the mountain of the Lord's house
> Shall be established above all mountains,
> Exalted over all the hills.
> All nations shall flow there as rivers
> And many peoples shall go and say:
> "Come let us go to the mountain of the Lord
> To the house of the God of Jacob.
> He will teach us His ways
> And we shall walk in His paths."
> For teaching shall go forth from Zion
> And the word of the Lord from Jerusalem.
> He shall judge between the nations
> And decide among many peoples.
> They shall beat their swords into plowshares

And their spears into pruning hooks.
Nation shall not lift up sword against nation,
Neither shall they learn war any more. (Isaiah 2:2–4)

Jerusalem thus lies at the very heart of Judaism's most universal vision, the vision of peace. This love for a particular holy place, a love we proclaim to be shared by God with countless generations of Jews, is an essential part of our spiritual identity. There is no under-standing of Jews or Judaism without it. While we know full well that God is everywhere, accessible "to all who call upon God in truth" (Psalm 145:18), whoever and wherever they are, this city maintains a unique and central place in our religious imagination. Its welfare and especially its peace are of special concern, a regular object of Jewish prayer, both ancient and contemporary. The cry "Next year in Jerusalem!" with which we conclude both Yom Kippur and the *Pesah seder,* is our fondest hope, our cry for redemption. Since the days of the prophets the redemption of Israel and the rebuilding of Jerusalem have been thoroughly identified with one another: "Break forth and rejoice together, O ruins of Jerusalem, for God has consoled His peo-ple, redeemed Jerusalem" (Isaiah 52:9).

RABBI ARTHUR GREEN, *THESE ARE THE WORDS*

Jerusalem Rebuilt—This Year in Jerusalem!

[*The overpowering sense of the fulfillment of the Divine promise has come through perhaps nowhere as poignantly as in the inspired words of the late Chief Rabbi Shlomo Goren, spoken in the heat of passion as he stood at the just-conquered Western Wall in the reunited Jerusalem in June 1967.*]

Soldiers of Israel, beloved of your people, crowned with valor and victory! God be with you, valiant warriors!

I am speaking to you from the Western Wall, remnant of our Holy Temple. Comfort ye, comfort ye My people, sayeth your God.

This is the day for which we have hoped, let us be glad and rejoice in His salvation.

The dream of all the generations has been fulfilled before our eyes. The City of God, the Temple site, the Temple Mount, the Western Wall—the symbol of the Jewish people's Messianic Redemption—have been delivered this day by you, heroes of the Israel Defense Forces.

This day you have redeemed the vow of the generations: "If I forget thee, O Jerusalem, may my right hand wither." We did not forget thee, Jerusalem our Holy City, home of our glory. And it is your right hand, the Right Hand of God, that has wrought this historic deliverance.

Whose is the heart that will not exult at hearing these tidings of redemption! Henceforth the gates of Zion and of Old Jerusalem, and the paths of the Western Wall, are open for the prayers of their children, their builders and their liberators in *Eretz Yisrael,* and to the Jews of the Dispersion who may now come there to pray. The Divine Presence, which has never forsaken the Western Wall, is now marching in the van of the legions of Israel in a pillar of fire to illuminate our path to victory, and is emblazoning us with clouds of glory before the Jewish people and the entire world. Happy are we that we have been privileged to earn this, the most exalted hour in the history of our people!

To the nations of the world we declare: We shall respectfully protect the holy places of all faiths, and their doors shall be open to all.

Beloved soldiers, dear sons of our people, to you has fallen the greatest privilege of Jewish history. There is now being fulfilled the prayer of the ages and the vision of the Prophets: For thou, O God, didst destroy her in fire, and Thou wilt surely build her up again in fire, as it is written *(Zechariah* 2:5): "For I, saith the Lord, will be unto her a wall of fire round about, and will be the glory in the midst of her." Blessed art Thou, O Lord, consoler of Zion and builder of Jerusalem.

And to Zion and to the remnant of our Temple we say: Your children have returned to their borders. Our feet now stand within thy gate, Jerusalem: city bounded together once more with the New Jerusalem; city that is perfect of beauty and joy of the whole earth; capital city of the eternal State of Israel.

In the name of the entire community of Jewry in Israel and in the Diaspora, and with joy sublime, I herewith pronounce the blessing:

Blessed art Thou, O Lord our God, King of the Universe, for having kept us alive and sustained us and brought us to this day.

This year in rebuilt Jerusalem.

Rabbi Shlomo Goren

Next Year in Jerusalem—Guide Our Steps

And now these precious Days of Awe move finally to a close. The gates have almost swung shut, and only a crack of light still shines to guide us home. In these last moments, we affirm afresh what we will at our best affirm each day of this newly unfolding year. It is up to us to listen for the divine voice, up to us to re-enthrone God. The shofar's blast here marks not only the end of the fast. It marks also the redeeming revelation that can guide our steps as the gate clangs shut.

Rabbi David A. Teutsch

From the Shofar

We hear so much in the final blast of the shofar—the royal sovereign is present, messianic hope is evoked, the ram has been substituted, we are awake, aroused from our slumber, we are called to continuous struggle, we are celebrating and rejoicing, we are crying and releasing everything that has transpired in this long day.

Rabbi Sheila Peltz Weinberg

Suspended between Heaven and Earth

One of the ultimate Jerusalem experiences is the early morning of Shavuot. Around 4 a.m., men, women, and even children start making their way to the Kotel. They've been up all night, learning Torah in shuls, study houses and homes all over the city, and now they're on their way to daven *Shaharit* at the Wall. A trickle grows to a stream and then a flood. They come on foot down every street that connects the Old City with the new, flowing together into one vast current as they pass the War of Independence memorial. As one they move on down what was once an ancient donkey path into the Valley of Hinnom. The scene is surreal; people move with purpose and pleasure; it's cool and still dark, but the day ahead will be hot and they're wearing hats and light summer clothes. As they course through the valley and begin their ascent of Mount Zion on the other side, the spirit of Jerusalem's ancient pilgrimage festivals is alive before your eyes. The link with our forefathers is vibrant and strong. Thousands, perhaps tens of thousands of us, stand before the Western Wall. Shaharit begins, and we pray as one. When we reach the *Amidah,* the long silent prayer, a sudden hush falls over the great mass. It's at this instant that dawn streaks the dark sky. For a long breathless moment, you feel suspended between heaven and earth.

Aloma Halter

La-shanah Ha-ba-ah (Ha-zot!) B'yerushalayim— Whatever We Have Lost, We Can Find in Jerusalem

When I went to Elementary School there was a spot in the secretaries' office called the Lost and Found Department. It was a table covered with a single mitten here, a forlorn hat there, a lonely pencil case in the corner. Any student who suddenly realized he was missing something could repair to the Lost and Found in the hope that it would be sitting there waiting for him.

The Talmud tells us that in ancient Jerusalem there was a large stone. Whoever lost an article went there and whoever found an article did likewise. The latter stood and announced what he discovered; the former described what he was missing with its uniquely identifiable features and got it back (Baba Metzia 28b).

Taken at face value, the Talmudic account would merely inform us that the notion of a Lost and Found Department goes back at least a couple of millennia. That might intrigue historians but would mean little to most of us.

I, however, believe that the Talmudic story hints at something more. It comes to tell us that since time immemorial, Jerusalem has been a place where Jews have gathered to recover their most precious possession: their sacred heritage. Countless are the stories of men and women who never expected to be moved by a trip to Israel who were shaken to their roots by a visit to our ancient capital. People who never identified with the Jewish community and never longed for a taste of the Torah have been changed by a visit to this remarkable city.

As we celebrate ... Jerusalem's [continued] reign as the spiritual and political heart of our people, let us remember that whatever we have lost can be rediscovered there.

Rabbi Bruce Ginsburg

La-shanah Ha-ba-ah B'Yerushalayim—How Seriously Do We Mean It?

The rebbe of Ger taught, "The mitzvah of dwelling in the land depends on ability and possibility." The usual reading of his advice is that "ability" means our own wherewithal, and "possibility" denotes favorable outside circumstances. So where we are able to move and where circumstances permit it, we should indeed go there. But I read him as reflecting the tradition of Maimonides: The question is whether we have the ability within and the possibility without to live Jewish lives where we are. If we live in a place where we cannot be the Jews we ought to be, we should move to a place where we can; and for many of us, that place will be Israel.

Rabbi Lawrence A. Hoffman

Moshe Dayan at the *Kotel*—This Year in *Yerushalayim!*

[*Yael Dayan, daughter of the famous one-eyed General, Moshe Dayan, wrote a brief reminiscence immediately following the Six Day War in 1967 when the city of Yerushalayim was reunited under Israeli control. She wrote about her experience toward the end of the War.*]

While with combat troops in the Sinai, I got hold of a newspaper dated June 7. On the front page was a picture of my father on Mount Scopus. The fight for the old city was on, and the first soldiers had arrived at the Wailing Wall. Jerusalem, the whole of it, was again ours. I didn't envy him his first visit to the Wall with the chief of staff, I. Rabin, wearing helmets—and walking through the Lion's Gate. I knew I'd be there too one day. But I envied those who went with him. He knows how to lend the moment its true significance.

Friends who were with him at the Wall said: He walked proudly rather than victoriously; it was not a moment of victory but of fulfillment. The city wasn't safe yet, snipers weren't cleared, but it would have been unnatural for him not to have been there. He approached the old stones of the Wall in silence and stared, then took out a notebook, scribbled a few lines on a paper and wedged it among the stones. Later, asked what was on the paper, he replied: "It is an old custom to insert pleas in the Wall. I wrote: 'Would there be peace upon the house of Israel.'"

From among the stones, he plucked a flower and kept it with him. "Imagine," he said, "flowers sprouting from the Wailing Wall." He walked away and went down.

When the war was truly over, he went back to the Wall. He objected to a "victory parade" of any sort. Instead, he took the Chief of Staff and the brigadier generals of the army to the Temple Mount and the Wall. Once again, a group of lifelong friends—Arik, Shaike, Uzi, Eizer, Moti—back from battles in the south, north and east. A small group of people to whom he owed everything. They faced the Wall, and he asked the Chief of Staff to read the Order of the Day to the army. He followed with his own Order, and the generals read theirs. Thus the war ended, not in trumpets and drums but in the holy silence of a liberated compound of stories representing eternity.

Yael Dayan

Next Year in *Yerushalayim!*—Finding a Way to Return

During Napoleon's campaign against Russia, as he passed through a small Jewish shtetl, he expressed a desire to see the inside of a synagogue. By chance it was the fast of the Ninth of Av (Tisha B'Av), and the Jews were sitting in darkness on the floor weeping as they prayed.

When it was explained to Napoleon that the reason for the weeping was for the destruction of the Temple, he asked, "When did this happen?"

"Two thousand years ago," he was told.

Upon hearing this, the Emperor declared, "A people who knows how to remember its land for two thousand years will certainly find the way to return."

Dov Noy

Next Year in *Yerushalayim*

Thomas Friedman, in his best-selling book *From Beirut to Jerusalem*, reports a visit to Israel by the astronaut Neil Armstrong, a devout Christian.

When the astronaut was taken for a tour of the city of Jerusalem and the Temple Mount, he said to Meir Ben-Dov, an Israeli archeologist who was his guide:

"I have to tell you, I am more excited stepping on these stones than I was stepping on the moon."

The accurate perception of most people is that Jerusalem today is an extension of biblical Israel. It is the focal point of all the hopes, dreams and aspirations of not only the Jewish People, but of people throughout the world who see Israel and *Yerushalayim* as the realization of an ancient dream.

It is no surprise, therefore, that we proclaim the following statement twice each year, after the Pesah Seder and at the end of Yom Kippur:

La-shanah ha-ba-ah b'Yerushalayim! Next year in *Yerushalayim!*

D.P.E.

La-shanah Ha-ba-ah B'yerushalayim!—To Jerusalem

One does not travel to Jerusalem
One returns
One ascends
the road taken by generations,
the path of longing
on the way to redemption.
One brings rucksacks
stuffed with memories
to each mountain
and each hill.
In the cobbled white alleyways
one offers a blessing
for memories of the past
which have been renewed.
One does not travel to Jerusalem.
One returns.

Yitzhak Yasinowitz—
Translated from Yiddish by Miriam Grossman

La-shanah Ha-ba-ah B'Yerushalayim

According to Rabbi Avraham Yitzhak Kook, first Chief Rabbi of *Eretz Yisrael* (d. 1935), *Teshuvah*, the major theme of these Ten Days of Return, "*Aseret Y'may Teshuvah*," refers not only to returning to God and to our best selves, but in his view it also refers to returning home— to *Eretz Yisrael*. It is a personal quest as well as "a communal mandate to establish a land that is different from all others. A land that is a light to the nations of the world; a land that marks the dawn of redemption, a land of peace." (Rabbi Avi Weiss).

As we recite the final words of this Yom Kippur, let us hope for complete peace for Israel, the entire Middle East and the entire universe.

Rabbi Dov Peretz Elkins

Sources

"Personal correspondence" includes e-mails, postings on rabbinic message boards and other nonarchived electronic communications.

Abramowitz, Adina. "Prayer of the Hidden Jews," in *Kol Haneshamah: Prayerbook for the Days of Awe*. Elkins Park, Pa.: Reconstructionist Press, 1999.

Adler, Morris. "Watch Out for the 'Little' Sins," in *The Voice Still Speaks*. New York: Bloch, 1969.

———. *"Yizkor,"* in *May I Have a Word with You?* New York: Crown, 1967.

Agnon, S. Y. "Before the *Kaddish:* At the Funeral of Those Who Were Killed in the Land of Israel," in *The Works of S. Y. Agnon,* Vol. X, 5th edition. Translated from the Hebrew by Judah Goldin (adapted). Tel-Aviv, Israel: Schocken Books, 1959.

Appel, Yehuda. *"Kohen Gadol* Could Not Enter Holy of Holies Wearing Gold," *Cleveland Jewish News,* April 30, 1993.

Artson, Bradley Shavit. *"...B'Dibbur Peh—*Leprosy of Irresponsible Speech." Personal correspondence.

Baeck, Leo. "Judaism and Atonement," in *The Essence of Judaism*. New York: Schocken Books, 1948.

Balser, Henry B. *"Ve-khol Ma-aminim—*Emulating God's Attributes." Personal correspondence.

Bamberger, Bernard. J. *"Kedoshim Tih'yu—*Be Holy!" in *The Torah: A Modern Commentary*. Edited by W. Gunther Plaut. New York: UAHC Press, 1991.

Berenbaum-Grinblat, Ilana. "What Does God Ask of Women?" in *The Women's Haftarah Commentary*. Edited by Elyse Goldstein. Woodstock, Vt.: Jewish Lights, 2004.

Berger, Joseph. "Displaced Persons," in *Displaced Persons*. New York: Scribner, 2002.

Bergman, Samuel Hugo. "Death Does Not Exist," in *Faith and Reason*. New York: Schocken Books, 1968.

———. *"Shema:* God and God's World," in *Faith and Reason*. New York: Schocken Books, 1968.

Blumenthal, Rena. "God's Book of Life," *Reconstructionist Rabbinical Association Newsletter*.

Braun, Moshe. "Man and Beast Will Be Saved By God," in *The Jewish Holy*

Days: Their Spiritual Significance. Northvale, N.J.: Jason Aronson, 1996.

———. "The Root of All Holiness," in *The Jewish Holy Days: Their Spiritual Significance.* Northvale, N.J.: Jason Aronson, 1996.

Buber, Martin. "*Avodah:* Service," in *Tales of the Hasidim.* New York: Schocken Books, 1991.

Cohen, Diane. "Alternative *Al Het.*" Personal correspondence.

———. "*Aleinu*—The Kabbalistic Origins of *Tikkun Olam.*" Personal correspondence.

———. "*Avodah* Service." Personal correspondence.

———. "*Ki Hineh KaHomer.*" Personal correspondence.

Cohen, Kenneth L. "Can Love Be Commanded?" Personal correspondence.

———. "Good Grief." Personal correspondence.

Cohen, Seymour J. "The Power of Words." Personal correspondence.

Cramer, Irving. "Is This the Fast I Have Chosen?—It Wasn't My Turn." Personal correspondence.

Dannin, Ellen. "Jonah: A *D'var Torah.*" Personal correspondence.

Davis, Avram. "*Ve-khol Ma-aminim*—All Believe," in *The Way of Flame: A Guide to the Forgotten Mystical Tradition of Jewish Meditation.* Woodstock, Vt.: Jewish Lights, 1999.

Davis, Maurice. "Where God Can't Enter." Personal correspondence.

Dayan, Yael. "Moshe Dayan at the *Kotel*—This Year in *Yerushalayim!*" *Look* magazine, August 22, 1967.

Dickstein, Stephanie. "The Book of Jonah: A Lesson on Happiness." Personal correspondence.

Dorff, Elliot N. "Sources on Forgiveness." Multiple sources; see piece.

Edelman, Marian Wright. "On Justice, for All Children," in *Guide My Feet: Prayers and Meditations on Loving and Working for Children.* Boston: Beacon Press, 1995.

Eisen, Arnold. "Remember Us unto Life," in *The Jewish Holidays: A Guide and Commentary.* By Michael Strassfeld. New York: Harper & Row, 1985.

Fackenheim, Emil. "Martyrology—The 614th Commandment."Judaism, 16, no.3, Summer, 1967.

Feld, Merle. "*Yizkor,*" in *A Spiritual Life.* Albany: State University of New York Press, 1999.

Fertman, Bruce. "Rise with Strength Renewed," in *Kol Haneshamah: Prayerbook for the Days of Awe.* Elkins Park, Pa.: Reconstructionist Press, 1999.

Fields, Harvey J. "Yom Kippur and the 'Scapegoat'—Seeking Meaning for the Strange Ritual of the Scapegoat," in *A Torah Commentary for Our Times, Vol. II: Exodus and Leviticus.* New York: UAHC Press, 1991.

Forman, Lori. "*Al Het … B'timhon Levav*—By Confusion of Values, by Spoiling our Planet." Personal correspondence.

———. "Giving Generously of Ourselves." Personal correspondence.

————. *"Shema:* God's Oneness." Personal correspondence.

Freeman, Tzvi. *"U-Teshuvah…"* in *Bringing Heaven Down to Earth: 365 Meditations of the Rebbe.* Berkeley, Calif.: Class One Press, 1998.

————. *"… U-tzedakah*—Make Your Home a Wellspring of Charity." Personal correspondence.

Friedman, Debbie. "Returning to Ourselves," in *Lifecylces, Vol. 2: Jewish Women on Biblical Themes in Contemporary Life.* Edited by Debra Orenstein and Jane Rachel Litman. Woodstock, Vt.: Jewish Lights, 2000.

Fromm, Erich. "Jonah Learns about Love," in *The Art of Loving.* New York: Harper & Bros., 1956.

Frydman-Kohl, Baruch. "Torah Reading—Yom Kippur." Personal correspondence.

Geduld, Herb. "The *Kittel." Cleveland Jewish News,* September 25, 1992.

Gerson, Bernard R. *"Shema*—The Lord Is *One:* Hear, O Israel, *Adonai* Is Our God, *Adonai* Alone." Personal correspondence.

Gillman, Neil. "Like a Fading Flower, a Passing Shadow, a Fugitive Cloud and a Vanishing Dream." *Jewish Week,* September 10, 1999.

————. *"Teshuvah:* A New Factor in the Divine Relationship," in *The Way Into Encountering God in Judaism.* Woodstock, Vt.: Jewish Lights, 2004.

Ginsburg, Bruce. *"La-shanah Ha-ba-ah (Ha-zot!) B'yerushalayim*—Whatever We Have Lost, We Can Find in Jerusalem." Personal correspondence.

————. "Our Vows Are Not Vows." Personal correspondence.

Gluskin, Shai. "The Goat's Journey to the Desert," from www.jrf.org, 2004.

Gold, Michael. "From Beyond the Grave Our Loved Ones Reach Out and Touch Us." Personal correspondence.

————. "How Do We Abolish Sin?" Personal correspondence.

————. *"Parshat Nitzavim:* Choose Life." Personal correspondence.

Goldberg, Hillel. *"Kol Nidre:* Nothing Affects the Human Being More Than Music," *Intermountain Jewish News,* April 16, 1993.

Goldman, Alex J. "The Book of Jonah: A Summary," in *The Eternal Books Retold: A Rabbi Summarizes the 39 Books of the Bible.* Northvale, N.J.: Jason Aronson, 1999.

Goldstein, Elyse. *"U'netaneh Tokef."* Personal correspondence.

Goldston, Rob and Ruth Goldston. "Sweetening the Evil." Personal correspondence.

Golinkin, Noah. *"Ashamnu*—We Have Sinned." Personal correspondence.

Goodman, Arnold M. "Who Will Recite the *Shema* with Our Grandchildren?" Personal correspondence.

Graetz, Michael. "A Memoir of the Yom Kippur War." From "A Yom Kippur War Diary," *Conservative Judaism* XXIX, no. 4, Summer, 1975.

Green, Arthur. All Section Introductions from *These Are the Words: A Vocabulary of Jewish Spiritual Life.* Woodstock Vt.: Jewish Lights, 1999.

————. "Homecoming and *Teshuvah,"* in *Seek My Face: A Jewish Mystical Theology.* Woodstock, Vt.: Jewish Lights, 2003.

———. *"Sh'ma,"* in *Seek My Face: A Jewish Mystical Theology.* Woodstock, Vt.: Jewish Lights, 2003.

———. *"Teshuvah* and the Sacred Year," in *Seek My Face: A Jewish Mystical Theology.* Woodstock, Vt.: Jewish Lights, 2003.

Greenberg, Irving. "Sins Are Parts of Us Yet to Complete." Personal correspondence.

Greenberg, Sidney. "A *Kaddish* for the Children," *Jewish Exponent,* November 8, 1991.

———. "The Common Lot of All of Us." Personal correspondence.

Greenberg, Steven. "The Meaning of *Avodah,"* in *Sacred Days, 1995–1996.* New York: CLAL, The National Jewish Center for Learning and Leadership, 1995.

Greenspan, Mark B. "The Book of Jonah—Whose Story Are We Telling?" Personal correspondence.

———. "Celebrating and Revealing the Invisible—Yom Kippur Torah Reading." Personal correspondence.

———. "Just When…. An Introduction in Poetry, to the Haftarah of Yom Kippur Morning." Personal correspondence.

———. "A Meditation before *Neilah.*" Personal correspondence.

Greenspoon, David and Steve Kerbel. *"Ashamnu*—A to Z." Personal correspondence.

Gutherz, Tom. *"Hayom*—The Opportunity of the Present Moment." Personal correspondence.

Haber, Geoffrey J. *"U'Tzedakah."* Personal correspondence.

Halter, Aloma. "Suspended between Heaven and Earth." Personal correspondence.

Herring, Hayim. "Jonah: Running Away from Ourselves." Personal correspondence.

Heschel, Abraham Joshua. "Preface to the *Amidah,"* in *Man's Quest for God.* Santa Fe: Aurora Press, 1998.

Hirsh, Richard. "Forgiving as an Essential Human Attribute—To Make Peace with Ourselves, and with Others, To Move Forward With Hope." *Jewish Exponent,* December 18, 1992.

Hoffman, Lawrence A. *"La-shanah Ha-ba-ah B'Yerushalayim*—How Seriously Do We Mean It?" Personal correspondence.

Holtz, Barry W. "The Ritual of the Goats—We Are Left with Words…." Personal correspondence.

Jacobs, Louis. "Can a Sinner Dare to Pray?" in *Hasidic Thought.* New York: Behrman House, 2000.

———. "Why Fast?" in *The Book of Jewish Belief.* New York: Behrman House, 1995.

Jacoby, Jeff. *"Ve-al Dibbur Peh* … Sins of the Tongue" *Boston Globe,* March 11, 1999.

Jezer, Daniel A. *"Al Het* for our Age of Violence." Personal correspondence.

Karff, Samuel E. "A Jew Cannot Be Without God." Personal correspondence.

Karp, Abraham J. "Repentance, Prayer and *Tzedakah.*" Personal correspondence.

Kedar, Karyn D. "Forgive Yourself," in *God Whispers: Stories of the Soul, Lessons of the Heart.* Woodstock, Vt.: Jewish Lights, 2000.

Kessler, Martin. "A Martyr's Prayer for the New Year." Personal correspondence.

Klotz, Myriam. "The High Priest: An Eager Servant Awaiting Rebirth," in *The Women's Haftarah Commentary.* Edited by Elyse Goldstein. Woodstock, Vt.: Jewish Lights, 2004.

Kook, Abraham Isaac. "The Glory of Life," in *Abraham Isaac Kook: The Light of Penitence, The Moral Principles, Lights of Holiness, Essays, Letters, and Poems.* Translated by Ben Zion Bokser. New York: Paulist, 1978.

Koppell, Bonnie. *"Avinu Malkenu."* Personal correspondence.

———. *"Piyyutim:* Liturgical Poetry" Personal correspondence.

Kravitz, Harold J. *"Musaf—V'ye-e-tayhu."* Personal correspondence.

Kula, Irwin. "Martyrology—9/11 and Lamentations." Interview by Helen Whitney, *Frontline,* PBS, Winter 2002.

———. *"U'v'khen Ten Kavod Le-amekha—*Give Dignity to Your People—*Kavod:* Honor Connected to Our Deepest Selves," in *Sacred Days, 1995–1996.* New York: CLAL, The National Jewish Center for Learning and Leadership, 1995.

———, and Vanessa L. Ochs. "A Meditation on Fasting," in *The Book of Jewish Sacred Practices.* Woodstock, Vt.: Jewish Lights, 2001.

Kushner, Lawrence. "Sweetening the Evil in Yourself," in *God was in this place and I, i did not know.* Woodstock, Vt.: Jewish Lights, 1994.

Labovitz, Annette and Eugene Labovitz. *"Shema Yisrael,"* in *A Touch of Heaven: Eternal Stories for Jewish Living.* Northvale, N.J.: Jason Aronson, 1990.

Labowitz, Shoni. *"Kavanah* for the *Amidah—Devekut:* Clinging to God," adapted from *Miraculous Living.* New York: Simon & Schuster, 1996.

Lang, Jory. "The Cab Ride." Personal correspondence.

Levin, Moshe. *"Al Het—*Is it Possible to Change?" Personal correspondence.

Levy, Naomi. "Saving God's Life," in *Talking to God: Personal Prayers for Times of Joy, Sadness, Struggle, and Celebration.* New York: Knopf, 2003.

———. *"Sim Shalom—*A Prayer for Peace," in *Talking to God: Personal Prayers for Times of Joy, Sadness, Struggle, and Celebration.* New York: Knopf, 2003.

Lew, Alan. "The Gates Clang Shut—*Neilah,"* in *This Is Real and You Are Completely Unprepared.* New York: Little, Brown, 2003.

———. "Moving toward the Light of God," in *This Is Real and You Are Completely Unprepared.* New York: Little, Brown, 2003.

Lewis, Theodore. "On the Doorposts of Your House—Two Approaches to Life," in *Bar Mitzvah Sermons at Touro Synagogue.* Brooklyn, N.Y.: Theodore Lewis, 1989.

Listfield, Stephen Chaim. "Let Them Fix Their Errors." Personal correspondence.

Lookstein, Joseph H. "Of What People Are You?—I Am a Hebrew" (Jonah 1:8–9). Personal correspondence.

Lubavitcher Rebbe. *"Teshuvah* Is Not Repentance, *Tefillah* Is Not Prayer, and *Tzedakah* Is Not Charity," in *Torah Studies.* Brooklyn, N.Y.: Kehot, 1996.

Luria, Yaacov. "There Is One Synagogue Left in Kiev," in *Blood to Remember: American Poets of the Holocaust.* Edited by Charles Fishman. Lubbock: Texas Tech University, 1991.

Maller, Allen S. "So Too Does the Soul Evolve." Personal correspondence.

———. "Why Do We Fast?" Personal correspondence.

Mandell, Sherri. "Why We Stay in Israel." Personal correspondence.

Maslow, Abraham. "Being Better—Serving Better," in *Religions: Values and Peak Experiences.* New York: Viking, 1970.

Meier, Levi. *"Ve-khol Ma-aminim*—Trying to Believe," in *Seven Heavens: Inspirational Stories to Elevate Your Soul.* New York: Devora, 2002.

Meirovich, Harvey. *"Ve-yaa-su Khulam Agudah Ehat*—Gathered Embers Generate Heat." Personal correspondence.

Meyer, Marshall I. *"N'eilah,"* in *You Are My Witness: The Living Words of Rabbi Marshall I. Meyer.* Edited by Jane Isay. New York: St. Martin's Press, 2004.

Milgram, Goldie. "Repenting for Those Who Cannot," in *Reclaiming Judaism as a Spiritual Practice.* Woodstock, Vt.: Jewish Lights, 2004.

———. *"Teshuvah:* Forgiveness Walks," in *Reclaiming Judaism as a Spiritual Practice.* Woodstock, Vt.: Jewish Lights, 2004.

Milgrom, Shira. "Where Is God?" Sermonic material.

———. "Yom Kippur and Memory." Sermonic material.

Nelson, David W. "Inclusion in the Covenant." From www.clal.org, 2001.

Noy, Dov. "Next Year in *Yerushalayim!*—Finding a Way to Return," in *Golah ve-Eretz Yisrael.* Jerusalem, Israel: Hotsa'at Sha'ar, 1959.

Olitzky, Kerry M. "Jonah and Self-Change," in *100 Blessings Every Day.* Woodstock, Vt.: Jewish Lights, 1993.

———. "Penitence," in *100 Blessings Every Day.* Woodstock, Vt.: Jewish Lights, 1993.

Palmer, Joanne. *"Vidui*—An Annotated Report." Personal correspondence.

Patterson, David. "Introduction to the *Amidah*—God's Presence Vibrates on Our Lips," in *The Greatest Jewish Stories Ever Told.* Middle Village, N.Y.: Jonathan David, 1997.

Piercy, Marge. *"Shema,"* in *The Art of Blessing the Day: Poems with a Jewish Theme.* New York: Knopf, 1999.

Peli, Pinchas. *"Lashon Ha-Ra*—Traditional Sources," in *Torah Today.* Washington, D.C.: B'nai B'rith Books, 1987.

Plavin, Richard. "The Ritual of the Goats." Personal correspondence.

Polish, David. "An Elegy for the Six Million," in *Kol Haneshamah: Prayerbook for the Days of Awe.* Elkins Park, Pa.: Reconstructionist Press, 1999.

Polster, Sarah. "Aaron's God—and Ours." *Tikkun: A Bimonthly Interfaith Critique of Politics, Culture & Society.*

Prinz, Deborah R. *"Kol Nidre:* Drawn Into Heaven's Womb." Personal correspondence.

Raz, Simcha. "Fasting: Who Can and Who Has To?" Personal correspondence.

———. "Repentance as *Halakhah."* Personal correspondence.

Rebbe Nachman of Breslov. "Introduction to the *Amidah,"* in *The Hasidic Anthology.* Edited by Louis I. Newman. New York: Schocken Books, 1963.

Remen, Rachel Naomi, MD. "All in the Family," in *My Grandfather's Blessings: Stories of Strength, Refuge, and Belonging.* New York: Riverhead Books, 2000.

———. "Belonging," in *My Grandfather's Blessings: Stories of Strength, Refuge, and Belonging.* New York: Riverhead Books, 2000.

Reuben, Steven Carr. "Driving Sorrow Out of Your Life." Personal correspondence.

Ridberg, Yael. "On Eagles' Wings." *Reconstructionism Today,* Autumn, 2004.

Riskin, Shlomo. *"Dibbur Peh … Leshon Ha-ra—*Even if True, Gossip Is Still a Sin." *Jerusalem Post,* June 1, 1991.

———. "We Will Outlive You, Globochnik!" *Jerusalem Post,* December 26, 1992.

Robuck, Gary J. "We Are Clay in the Potter's Hands," *Cleveland Jewish News,* September 25, 1992.

Rose, Carol. "(Alternative) Yom Kippur Chant," from *Mahzor Hadesh Yameinu: Renew Our Days.* Edited by Rabbi Ronald Aigen. Hampstead, Quebec, Canada: Congregation Dorshei Emet, The Reconstructionist Synagogue of Montreal, 2001.

Rosen, Jonathan. "Reciting the *Avodah* in the Diaspora," in *The Talmud and the Internet: A Journey between Worlds.* New York: Picador, 2001.

Rosenbaum, Samuel. *"N'eilah*—The Closing of the Gates," in *Mahzor 101: A Guide to the Prayer Book for the High Holy Days.* New York: The Cantors Assembly, 1997.

———. "What Did We Lose?" in *Mahzor 101: A Guide to the Prayer Book for the High Holy Days.* New York: The Cantors Assembly, 1997.

Rosenblum, Leon T. "Who Are the *Avaryanim?* Permission to Pray with the Iberians(?)" Personal correspondence.

Rosenthal, Gilbert S. "Is It Too Late?" Personal correspondence.

———. "Walking through Different Kinds of Doors—Judge Us Not for What We Were, but for What We Can Be." Personal correspondence.

Rosman, Steven M. *"U-tzedakah—*There Is a Healing Power in Doing Good," in *Jewish Healing Wisdom.* Northvale, N.J.: Jason Aronson, 1997.

Ross, Lesli Koppelman. "Dress," in *The Complete Jewish Holidays Handbook.* Northvale, N.J.: Jason Aronson, 1994.

Rubin, Yehoshua. *"Al Het—*Yom Kippur, a Loving Laundromat." Personal correspondence.

Salkin, Jeffrey K. "Get a Life." Personal correspondence.

Saltzman, Steven. "Judaism's Advice for a Meaningful Life." Personal correspondence.

Schachter-Shalomi, Zalman. "Getting Rid of the Mud," in *Wrapped in a Holy Flame: Teachings and Tales of the Hasidic Masters*. San Francisco: Jossey-Bass, 2003.

Scheinberg, Robert. "Forgive and Forget!" Personal correspondence.

Schorsch, Ismar. *"Lashon Ha-ra:* Judaism Is, Above All, a Love of Language," from www.jtsa.edu.

Schwartz, Dannel I. "Together We Can Stand Anything." Personal correspondence.

Segal, Benjamin J. "Azazel and Magic." Personal correspondence.

Shalvi, Alice. "A *Techine* for Yom Kippur," in *Beginning Anew: A Woman's Companion to the High Holy Days*. Edited by Gail Twersky Reimer and Judith A. Kates. New York: Touchstone, 1997.

Shapiro, Rami M. "Bold, Humble, Daring," in *Kol Haneshamah: Prayerbook for the Days of Awe*. Elkins Park, Pa.: Reconstructionist Press, 1999.

———. "Time Out—Life is Temporary." Personal correspondence.

Sherman, Andrew. *"Al Chet."* Personal correspondence.

Siegel, Danny. *"Tzedakah:* How Important a Value for Us?" in *Gym Shoes and Irises*. Pittsboro, N.C.: Town House Press, 1987.

Siegel, Michael S. "The Jew Must Stand for Something." Personal correspondence.

Silverman, Hillel E. *"Avodah*—Community Service." Personal correspondence.

———. *"Avodah:* Community Service—Serving Others We Serve Ourselves." Personal correspondence.

Silverstein, Mordechai. *"Shalom Shalom La-rahok Ve-la-karov."* Personal correspondence.

Simon, Matthew H. *"Avodah:* We Are Defined by Our Connections." Personal correspondence.

Simon, Sidney B. and Suzanne Simon. "What Forgiveness Is," in *Forgiveness: How to Make Peace With Your Past and Get on with Your Life*. New York: Warner Books, 1991.

Spanbock, Maurice S. "Closing Gates, New Beginning." Personal correspondence.

Strassfeld, Michael. "Choosing to Change," in *The Jewish Holidays: A Guide and Commentary*. New York: Harper & Row, 1985.

Syme, Daniel B. "The Final Shofar Blast," in *The Jewish Home: A Guide for Jewish Living*. New York: URJ Press, 2004.

———. *"Kol Nidrei:* Why Three Times?" in *The Jewish Home: A Guide for Jewish Living*. New York: URJ Press, 2004.

Tarlow, Peter. "And You Shall Afflict Your Souls...." Personal correspondence.

———. "The Basis of Sin: Self-Deception." Personal correspondence.

Teplitz, Saul. *"Shema*—Teach Them Well To Your Children." Personal correspondence.

Teutsch, David A. "Next Year in Jerusalem—Guide Our Steps," in *Kol Haneshamah: Prayerbook for the Days of Awe*. Elkins Park, Pa.: Reconstructionist Press, 1999.

Tutnauer, Moshe. "A New *Ya-aleh.*" Personal correspondence.

Twerski, Abraham J. "Forgiveness on *Kol Nidre,*" in *Not Just Stories: The Chassidic Spirit through its Classic Stories.* New York: Artscroll, 1997.

Weil, Andrew. *"U-Tefilah* … Can Prayer Heal?" from "Can Spirituality Heal?" *Self Healing,* January, 2000.

Weinberg, Dudley. "How Prayer Leads to Morality," in *The Efficacy of Prayer.* New York: UAHC pamphlet.

Weinberg, Sheila Peltz. "The Body/Mind Connection," in *Kol Haneshamah: Prayerbook for the Days of Awe.* Elkins Park, Pa.: Reconstructionist Press, 1999.

———. "From the Shofar," in *Kol Haneshamah: Prayerbook for the Days of Awe.* Elkins Park, Pa.: Reconstructionist Press, 1999.

———. *"Kavanah* for *Kol Nidre,*" in *Kol Haneshamah: Prayerbook for the Days of Awe.* Elkins Park, Pa.: Reconstructionist Press, 1999.

Weiss, Eric. "Spiritual Flutterings." Personal correspondence.

Weiss, Howard. "Don't Be Judgmental." Personal correspondence.

Wolpe, David. "Golden Silence," *Jewish Week,* April 23, 1999.

———. *"Ve-Shenantam Le-Venekha*—The Tradition of Study," *Jewish Week,* December 24, 1999.

Wolpe, Gerald I. *"Avinu Malkenu, Kotvaynu Be-Sefer Z'khuyot*—Don't Just Ask—Tell God: Send Me!" Personal correspondence.

Woznica, David. "A *Yizkor* Guided Imagery Exercise." From a *Yizkor* sermon; based on the teachings of Rabbi Elie Spitz.

Yehuda, Zvi. *"Ve-Khof Et Yitzrenu Le-Hishtabed Lakh*—Direct our Impulses [*Yetzer*]…" *Cleveland Jewish News,* October 18, 2001.

Zevin, Shlomo Y. "Is Reciting *Al Het* Reason to Rejoice?" in *A Treasury of Chassidic Tales on the Festivals.* New York: Artscroll, 1991.

Zevit, Shawn Israel. "Memory and *Teshuvah.*" Sermonic material.

Traditional Material

Aleichem, Sholom. "My People Are Being Consumed," upon fleeing Russia after the Kishinev pogrom of 1903.

Ansky, S. "…*B'timhon Levav*—By Confusion of Values," from his drama "The Dybbuk."

"Blessing the Children Yom Kippur Eve."

Carlebach, Shlomo. "God and the *Kohen Gadol,*" in *Ecstasy for the Soul.* The Rabbi Shlomo Carlebach Center.

Einhorn, David. *"Yaaleh*—Let Us Rise in Torah Knowledge: Flying Words."

Einstein, Albert. "A Short Visit—For a Divine Purpose." Traditional quotation.

"Gossip"

Kagan, Yisrael Meir. "Gossip: A Chronic Infectious Disease."

Lindeman, Edward. *"Avodah:* Service."

Maimonides. "Maimonides' Eight Degrees of Charity."

"Sins of the Tongue—… *B'Dibbur Peh, …B'Siah Siftotenu, …B'Leshon Ha-Ra."*

"A Special Prayer for Those Not Saying *Yizkor* for Parents." Adapted from a South African *Mahzor.*

Tolstoy, Leo. "Through Service to God [*Avodah*] I Add to the Good of the World." Traditional quotation.

"Whose Vows—Ours or God's?"

"Yetzer Ha-Ra—For the Sin of the Evil Impulse."

Yasinowitz, Yitzhak. *"La-shanah Ha-ba-ah B'yerushalayim!*—To Jerusalem." Translated from Yiddish by Miriam Grossman.

Yitzhak, Levi of Berditchev. "When God Is High Above, Awe Comes; When God Is Close, Love Comes—Peace to the Far, Peace to the Close" (Isaiah 57:19), in *Sefer Kedushat Levi, Mishpatim,* p. 139 (adapted).

Hasidic Tales and Teachings

"No Time for Sin."

"Quoting God."

"Radiance and Light—*Pirkei Avot* 2:13." Hasidic adaptation.

"Recognize Our Own Flaws."

"Remembering, Not Forgetting."

"Shema—And You Shall Love *Adonai* Your God.…"

"U-teshuvah.…—How to Cleanse Ourselves"

"When Words Enter the Heart."

Sources from Midrash

"Acts of Lovingkindness." From *Avot D'Rabbi Natan* 4.

"Atonement and Repentance." From *Avot D'Rabbi Natan* 29.

"The Origins of Yom Kippur." From *Bereshit Rabbah* 3:10.

"Lashon Ha-Ra—Be Careful of Unnecessary Words!" From *Derekh Eretz Zuta.*

"Atonement in the Desert." From *Eliyahu Zuta* 4.

"Forgiving Debts." From *Leviticus Rabbah* 30:17.

"I Am Canceling My Word and Fulfilling Yours—The Thirteen Divine Attributes." From *Leviticus Rabbah* 19:20.

"Punished for Being Jewish." From *Mekhilta of Rabbi Ishmael,* Tractate *Bahodesh,* chap. 7.

"Peace between People." From *Pesikta Rabbati* 50:6.

"Remaking Yourself." From *Pesikta Rabbati* 40:4.

"Teach Them Diligently to Your Children—Jacob and Esau." From *Pesikta de-Rav Kahana,* 121A.

Sources from Mishnah

"Bless God Even for Evil." From *Berakhot* 9:5.

"Celebrating Yom Kippur in the Past." From *Taanit* 4:8.

"Chance to Repent." From *Yoma* 8:9.

"Who Fasts?" From *Yoma* 8:4–5.

Sources from Talmud

"Can You Cross the River?" From *Talmud Yerushalmi, Demai* 22a.

"How Fortunate Are You, Rabbi Akiva." From *Talmud Bavli, Berakhot* 61b.

Sources from Unknown Authors

"An Interview with God."

"The Capture and Release of the *Yetzer Ha-Ra.*"

"God's Questions."

"Let's Forgive Each Other—Unlocking the Gates of Forgiveness: A Personal Prayer."

"The Plan of the Master Weaver."

"A Sabbath of Sabbaths."

"Shofar."

"*Ve-Yaya-su Kulam Agudah Ehat*—The Importance of Community."

"What We Have Lost."

Previously Existing Material Adapted by Rabbi Dov Peretz Elkins (Attributed to D.P.E.)

"*Al Het…. B'timhon Levav*—For the Sin … of Confusion of Values."

"*Avinu Malkenu*—A Tenacious Link."

"*Avodah*—For Whom Do the Priests Pray?"

"The Consequences of Sin and the Meaning of Evil."

"Day of Reconciliations," from *Jerusalem Post*, October 5, 2003.

"Deciding for God or for Azazel."

"Forgiveness in Hebrew Scriptures."

"Is Not This the Fast I Have Chosen … To Feed the Hungry, Clothe the Naked…."

"Jerusalem Rebuilt—This Year in Jerusalem!"

"*La-Brit Habet*—Recall Your Covenant."

"Lesson from the *Titanic*—Love Flows Continuously," from *National Jewish Post & Opinion*, May 6, 1998.

"Live, Read, Grow, and Be a Mensch!"

"Looking Into Our Own Hearts," from the *New York Times*, 1961.

"Next Year in *Yerushalayim.*"

"Pidyonenu Ad Arev—May Redemption Come to Us at Dusk."

"The Rest is Up To Me…"

"Service."

"Shema: One Universe."

"Shema: Ve-shenantam le-vanekha—A Jew Must Learn!"

"Sh'ma—Teach Them Diligently to Your Children."

"Still Warm from an Old Jacket."

"Teshuvah, Tefilah and Zedakah—Judaism Is a Religion of Action More Than Thought."

"The United States Holocaust Memorial Museum: Opening Ceremonies," from the *New York Times,* 1993.

"U'Tzedakah—God Makes Opportunities for Redemption."

"V'tivneha M'herah Ut'gadel K'vodah—Rebuild and Glorify Your Land."

"Ve-tiftah et Sefer Ha-Zikhronot….—You Record and Seal, Count and Measure…."

"We Humans Are Cracked Vessels: *Ashamnu, Bagadnu, Gazalnu*—We Have Sinned, We Have Dealt Treacherously…"

"Widening Our Circle of Compassion."

"You Shall Teach Them Diligently to Your Children—Weaving the Loom of Future Years."

"Zakhor—Never Forget."

"Zedakah: Money, Money, Money."

About the Contributors

Adina Abramowitz contributed to *Kol Haneshamah: Prayerbook for the Days of Awe* (Reconstructionist Press, 1999).

Rabbi Morris Adler was spiritual leader of Shaarey Zedek Congregation in Southfield, Michigan.

Shmuel Yosef Agnon was a Nobel Laureate in literature, and lived in Jerusalem.

Sholom Aleichem was a famous Yiddish writer in Russia in the late nineteenth and early twentieth century.

S. Ansky was a Russian Jewish writer and folklorist.

Rabbi Yehuda Appel teaches at Aish HaTorah in Cleveland, Ohio.

Rabbi Bradley Shavit Artson is dean of the Ziegler School of Rabbinic Studies and vice president of the University of Judaism.

Rabbi Leo Baeck was a leading German liberal rabbi, theologian and community leader. Imprisoned by the Nazis, he survived the war and was active in the reconstruction of European Jewry.

Rabbi Henry B. Balser is a spiritual leader and educator in Canada.

Rabbi Bernard J. Bamberger was a rabbi in Westchester, New York, and one of the contributors to the Plaut *Humash* of the Reform movement.

Rabbi Ilana Berenbaum-Grinblat serves at Temple Beth Shalom, Long Beach, California.

Joseph Berger writes for the *New York Times*.

Samuel Hugo Bergman was a philosopher and professor at the Hebrew University of Jerusalem.

Rabbi Rena Blumenthal is advisor to Jewish students at Vassar College.

Moshe Braun is a teacher and author.

Martin Buber was a philosopher and professor at the Hebrew University in Jerusalem.

Reb Shlomo Carlebach was a song writer, storyteller, traveling minstrel and teacher whose spirituality influenced thousands throughout the world.

Rabbi Diane Cohen is a Conservative rabbi who has served in pulpits in New Jersey, Philadelphia, Memphis and elsewhere.

Rabbi Kenneth L. Cohen is executive director of American University Hillel in Washington, D.C.

Rabbi Seymour J. Cohen served before his death at the Anshe Emet Synagogue in Chicago.

326   ABOUT THE CONTRIBUTORS

Irving Cramer was founding executive director of MAZON: A Jewish Response to Hunger.

Ellen Dannin is a professor of law at Wayne State University Law School, Detroit, Michigan.

Dr. Avram Davis is a teacher of Jewish meditation and spirituality, and the founder and codirector of an independent renewal center for Jewish learning and meditation, Chochmat HaLev in Berkeley, California.

Rabbi Maurice Davis was a Reform rabbi in White Plains, New York, known for deprogramming cult victims.

Yael Dayan, daughter of Moshe Dayan, is a journalist and a former member of the Knesset.

Rabbi Stephanie Dickstein serves at the New York Jewish Healing Center.

Rabbi Elliot N. Dorff is rector and Distinguished Professor of Philosophy at the University of Judaism in Los Angeles.

Marion Wright Edelman is president of the Children's Defense Fund.

David Einhorn was a writer in the nineteenth century.

Albert Einstein was a physicist and Nobel Prize laureate at the Institute for Advanced Studies in Princeton, New Jersey.

Arnold Eisen is Daniel E. Koshland Professor in Jewish Culture and Religion at Stanford University.

Rabbi Emil Fackenheim taught Jewish philosophy in Canada and Jerusalem.

Merle Feld is a poet and teacher in Northampton, Massachusetts.

Bruce Fertman contributed to *Kol Haneshamah: Prayerbook for the Days of Awe* (Reconstructionist Press, 1999).

Rabbi Harvey J. Fields served as senior rabbi of the Wilshire Boulevard Temple in Los Angeles, California.

Rabbi Lori Forman teaches at the Bergen County High School for Jewish Studies in Hackensack, New Jersey.

Rabbi Tzvi Freeman is a writer and teacher.

Debbie Friedman is a well known composer and singer.

Erich Fromm was an author and psychologist.

Rabbi Baruch Frydman-Kohl is senior rabbi at Beth Tzedec Congregation in Toronto, Ontario, Canada.

Herb Geduld is a writer who lives in Cleveland, Ohio.

Rabbi Bernard R. Gerson serves at Congregation Rodef Shalom in Denver, Colorado.

Dr. Neil Gillman is professor of Jewish philosophy at The Jewish Theological Seminary of America in New York City.

Rabbi Bruce Ginsburg serves at Congregation Sons of Israel, Woodmere, Long Island, New York.

Rabbi Shai Gluskin is the special assistant to the executive vice president of the Jewish Reconstructionist Federation.

Rabbi Michael Gold serves at Temple Beth Torah, Tamarac, Florida.

Rabbi Hillel Goldberg is executive editor of *Intermountain Jewish News,* Denver, Colorado.

Rabbi Alex J. Goldman was rabbi emeritus at Temple Beth El, Stamford, Connecticut.

Rabbi Elyse Goldstein is director of Kolel: The Adult Center for Liberal Jewish Learning in Toronto.

Ruth Goldston is a clinical psychologist practicing in Princeton, New Jersey. Her husband Rob Goldston is director of the Princeton Plasma Physics Laboratory.

Rabbi Noah Golinkin was rabbi emeritus at Beth Shalom Congregation in Columbia, Maryland, and was the founder of the Institute for Hebrew Literacy.

Rabbi Arnold M. Goodman served in congregations in the United States and is now retired in Jerusalem.

Rabbi Shlomo Goren was the fourth chief rabbi of Israel.

Rabbi Michael Graetz serves at Congregation Magen Avraham, Omer (Beersheba), Israel.

Rabbi Arthur Green is professor of Jewish philosophy and religion at Hebrew College, Boston, and dean of the rabbinical school.

Rabbi Irving Greenberg is director of Jewish Life Network, New York City, and a well known speaker and author.

Rabbi Sidney Greenberg was rabbi emeritus at Temple Sinai, Dresher, Pennsylvania, and author or editor of over 35 books.

Rabbi Steven Greenberg writes and teaches at CLAL (Center for Leadership and Learning) in New York City.

Rabbi Mark B. Greenspan serves at Oceanside Jewish Center, Oceanside, New York.

Rabbi David Greenspoon serves at Congregation Knesset Israel in Pittsfield, Massachusetts.

Rabbi Tom Gutherz works in Jewish education at Congregation Beth Israel in Charlottesville, Virginia.

Rabbi Geoffrey J. Haber serves at Temple Emanu-El, Closter, New Jersey.

Rabbi Yisrael Meir HaKohen lived and taught in Poland in the late nineteenth and early twentieth century.

Aloma Halter is a poet who resides in Jerusalem.

Rabbi Hayim Herring, PhD, is executive director of STAR (Synagogues: Transformation and Renewal) in Minneapolis.

Rabbi Abraham Joshua Heschel was professor of Jewish mysticism and philosophy at the Jewish Theological Seminary, and author of many books on Jewish thought.

Rabbi Richard Hirsh is director of the Reconstructionist Rabbinical Association.

Rabbi Lawrence A. Hoffman teaches at Hebrew Union College–Jewish Institute of Religion in New York City.

Dr. Barry W. Holtz is the Theodore and Florence Baumritter Professor of Jewish Education at The Jewish Theological Seminary.

Rabbi Dr. Louis Jacobs is rabbi emeritus at New London Synagogue, London, England, and author of many books on Jewish thought.

Jeff Jacoby is a syndicated columnist for the *Boston Globe*.

Rabbi Daniel A. Jezer is rabbi emeritus of Congregation Beth Sholom, Dewitt, New York.

Rabbi Samuel E. Karff is rabbi emeritus of Congregation Beth Israel in Houston, Texas.

Rabbi Abraham J. Karp was professor of Jewish studies at the University of Rochester, and research professor in American Jewish history at the Jewish Theological Seminary.

Rabbi Karyn D. Kedar is senior rabbi at B'nai Jehoshua Beth Elohim in Glenview, Illinois.

Steve Kerbel is a Jewish educator in the Washington, D.C. area.

Rabbi Martin Kessler serves a congregation in Pennsylvania.

Rabbi Myriam Klotz is on the faculty of the Institute for Jewish Spirituality and a spiritual director with the Reconstructionist Rabbinical College.

Rabbi Abraham Isaac Kook was first chief rabbi of *Eretz Yisrael*. He died in Jerusalem in 1935.

Rabbi Bonnie Koppell served for many years in a congregation in Chandler, Arizona.

Rabbi Harold J. Kravitz serves at Adath Jeshurun Congregation, Minnetonka, Minnesota.

Rabbi Irwin Kula is director of CLAL, the Center for Leadership and Learning, in New York.

Rabbi Lawrence Kushner is Emanu-El Scholar at Congregation Emanu-El in San Francisco and author of many books on Jewish spirituality.

Rabbi Eugene Labovitz and Dr. Annette Labovitz are storytellers and authors who travel and share their wisdom throughout North America.

Rabbi Shoni Labowitz is one of the spiritual leaders of Temple Adath Or, Ft. Lauderdale, Florida, a Jewish Renewal congregation.

Rabbi Jory Lang serves as Beth Moshe Congregation in North Miami, Florida.

Rabbi Moshe Levin serves at Congregation Ner Tamid, San Francisco, California.

Rabbi Levi Yitzhak of Berditchev was a famous Hasidic rebbe in Poland.

Rabbi Naomi Levy is spiritual leader of Nashuva, a groundbreaking soulful community in Los Angeles.

Rabbi Alan Lew served at Congregation Beth Sholom, San Francisco, California.

Rabbi Theodore Lewis was rabbi at Touro Synagogue in Newport, Rhode Island.

Edward Lindeman is an author, educator, and speaker.

Rabbi Stephen Chaim Listfield serves at Agudath Israel Synagogue, Montgomery, Alabama.

Rabbi Joseph H. Lookstein was rabbi at Congregation Kehilath Jeshurun, New York City.

Yaakov Luria is a columnist for the *Jewish World Review*.

Maimonides (Rabbi Moshe ben Maimon, or Rambam) was the greatest Jewish philosopher of the Middle Ages. He lived in the twelfth century in Spain and Egypt.

Rabbi Allen S. Maller serves at Temple Akiba in Culver City, California.

Sherri Mandell teaches and writes in Tekoa, Israel.

Rabbi Levi Meier is the Jewish chaplain at Cedar Sinai Medical Center, Los Angeles, California, and a clinical psychologist in private practice.

Rabbi Harvey Meirovich teaches and lives in Jerusalem.

Rabbi Mendl of Kotzk was a famous Hasidic master.

Rabbi Marshall I. Meyer served for many years at Communidad Bet El in Buenos Aires, Argentina, and later at Congregation B'nai Jeshurun in New York City.

Rabbi Goldie Milgram is an author and directs ReclaimingJudaism.org.

Rabbi Shira Milgrom serves at Congregation Kol Ami, White Plains, New York.

Rebbe Nachman of Breslov was the great grandson of the Baal Shem Tov, the founder of the Hasidic movement.

Rabbi David W. Nelson, PhD, was senior teaching fellow at CLAL, and is now the associate director of ARZA, The Association of Reform Zionists of America.

Dov Noy is an authority on Jewish stories, and lives in Jerusalem.

Vanessa L. Ochs, PhD, is director of Jewish studies at the University of Virginia.

Rabbi Kerry M. Olitzky is executive director of the Jewish Outreach Institute in New York City.

Joanne Palmer, a former Jewish journalist, is director of the department of public affairs at the United Synagogue of Conservative Judaism.

David Patterson is Distinguished Professor and director of the University of Memphis Honors Program. He converted to Judaism in 1990.

Rabbi Pinchas Peli was professor of Jewish studies at Ben Gurion University, Beersheba, Israel.

Marge Piercy is a poet, novelist and essayist. She has published fifteen books of poetry.

Rabbi Richard J. Plavin serves at Temple Beth Sholom, Manchester, Connecticut.

Rabbi David Polish was a seminal figure in Reform Judaism and is credited with being the leader who first turned the movement toward Zionism.

Sarah Polster was the religion editor at Jossey-Bass.

Rabbi Deborah R. Prinz serves at Temple Adat Shalom, Poway, California.

Rabbi Simcha Raz is a well known scholar, writer and teacher in Jerusalem, who has published dozens of books on Jewish literature in Hebrew, English and other languages.

Rachel Naomi Remen is a psychiatrist and author living in Mill Valley, California.

Rabbi Steven Carr Reuben serves at Kehillat Israel in Pacific Palisades, California.

Rabbi Yael Ridberg serves at West End Synagogue in New York City.

Rabbi Shlomo Riskin is chief rabbi of Efrat, Israel.

Rabbi Gary J. Robuck serves at North Shore Temple Emanuel, Chatswood, Sydney, Australia.

Carol Rose is a writer, educator and counselor. Her poetry collection won the Jewish Book Award for Poetry in 1998.

Jonathan Rosen, a novelist, is the editorial director of Nextbook.

Hazzan Samuel Rosenbaum was *hazzan* at Temple Beth El, Rochester, New York, and executive director of the Cantors Assembly.

Rabbi Leon T. Rosenblum serves Congregation Beth Shalom in Coconut Creek, Florida.

Rabbi Gilbert S. Rosenthal was executive vice president of the New York Board of Rabbis, and is now director of the National Council of Synagogues.

Rabbi Steven M. Rosman, PhD, serves in the department of complementary medicine, Lake Success, New York.

Lesli Koppelman Ross is a writer and artist whose works have appeared nationally. She has devoted much of her time to the causes of Ethiopian Jewry and Jewish education.

Rabbi Yehoshua Rubin is an Israeli teacher, storyteller, workshop leader, author and minstrel.

Rabbi Jonathan Sacks is chief rabbi of Great Britain.

Rabbi Jeffrey K. Salkin serves at The Temple in Atlanta, Georgia.

Rabbi Steven Saltzman serves at Adath Israel Congregation, North York, Ontario, Canada.

Rabbi Zalman Schachter-Shalomi is the "guru" and founder of the Jewish Renewal Movement. Currently he teaches at the Nairopa Institute in Boulder, Colorado.

Rabbi Robert Scheinberg serves at the United Synagogue of Hoboken, New Jersey.

Rabbi Ismar Schorsch is chancellor of the Jewish Theological Seminary, New York City.

Rabbi Dannel I. Schwartz serves at Temple Shir Shalom in West Bloomfield, Michigan.

Rabbi Benjamin J. Segal is former president of the Schechter Institute of Jerusalem, and is now head of Melitz Center for Jewish Zionist Education, Jerusalem.

Professor Alice Shalvi is a prominent Israeli academic, and former chairperson of the Schechter Institute in Jerusalem.

Rabbi Rami M. Shapiro is a frequent writer on Jewish spirituality.

Andrew Sherman is a member of Congregation B'nai Jeshurun in Manhattan where he volunteers as a musician in the weekly childrens' services.

Danny Siegel is a teacher, poet, and expert on *zedakah*. He founded and directs the Ziv Zedakah Fund.

Rabbi Michael S. Siegel serves at The Anshe Emet Synagogue in Chicago, Illinois.

Rabbi Hillel E. Silverman is rabbi emeritus, Temple Sholom, Greenwich, Connecticut.

Rabbi Mordechai Silverstein teaches at the Conservative Yeshiva in Jerusalem.

Rabbi Matthew H. Simon is rabbi emeritus, Bnai Israel Congregation, Rockville, Maryland.

Dr. Sidney B. Simon and Suzanne Simon are workshop leaders in the personal growth movement.

Maurice S. Spanbock is a past president and member of the board of directors of Lincoln Square Synagogue in New York City, and an officer and trustee of Ohr Torah Institution of Israel.

Susan Stone is an award-winning professional storyteller.

Rabbi Michael Strassfeld serves at the Society for the Advancement of Judaism in New York City.

Rabbi Daniel B. Syme serves at Temple Beth El, Bloomfield Hills, Michigan.

Rabbi Peter Tarlow is Hillel rabbi at Texas A&M.

Rabbi Saul Teplitz is rabbi emeritus at Congregation Sons of Israel, Woodmere, New York.

Rabbi David A. Teutsch was president, and is now professor, at the Reconstructionist Rabbinical College in Philadelphia.

Leo Tolstoy was a Russian writer, famous for short stories and novels.

Rabbi Moshe Tutnauer teaches all over the world. His home is in Jerusalem.

Rabbi Abraham J. Twerski is a psychiatrist who specializes in substance abuse, and is author of dozens of books on Judaism and psychology.

Dr. Andrew Weil is director of the Center for Integrative Medicine at the University of Arizona and editor of a health newsletter, *Dr. Andrew Weil's Self Healing*.

Rabbi Dudley Weinberg served a Reform congregation in Milwaukee, Wisconsin.

Rabbi Sheila Peltz Weinberg is a Reconstructionist rabbi, teacher of meditation to Jews, outreach director and senior faculty member of the Institute for Jewish Spirituality.

Rabbi Eric J. Weiss serves at the Bay Area Jewish Healing Center, San Francisco, California.

Rabbi Howard Weiss is a spiritual leader and teacher.

Rabbi Stewart Weiss is an educator in Raanana, Israel, and writes regularly for the *Jerusalem Post*.

Rabbi David Wolpe serves at Sinai Temple in Los Angeles, California.

Rabbi Gerald I. Wolpe is rabbi emeritus at Har Zion Temple, Penn Valley, Pennsylvania.

Rabbi David Woznica is rabbi at Stephen S. Wise Temple in Los Angeles.

Yitzhak Yasinowitz was a Yiddish poet.

Rabbi Zvi Yehuda was a teacher and writer at the Siegel College of Jewish Studies in Cleveland, Ohio, and is now retired in Boca Raton, Florida.

Rabbi Shlomo Y. Zevin was a prolific writer on Jewish themes.

Rabbi Shawn Israel Zevit serves at the Jewish Reconstructionist Federation in Elkins Park, Pennsylvania.

Credits

Jewish Women on Biblical Themes in Contemporary Life © 1997 Debra Orenstein and Jane Rachel Litman (Woodstock, VT: Jewish Lights Publishing). $19.95 + $3.95 s/h. Order by mail or call 800-962-4544 or on-line at www.jewishlights.com. Permission granted by Jewish Lights Publishing, P.O. Box 237, Woodstock, VT 05091.

Neil Gillman, *"Teshuvah:* A New Factor in the Divine Relationship," excerpt from *The Way into Encountering God in Judaism* © 2000 Neil Gillman (Woodstock, VT: Jewish Lights Publishing). $21.95HC or $18.99PB + $3.95 s/h. Order by mail or call 800-962-4544 or on-line at www.jewishlights.com. Permission granted by Jewish Lights Publishing, P.O. Box 237, Woodstock, VT 05091.

Hillel Goldberg, *"Kol Nidre:* Nothing Affects the Human Being More Than Music." Copyright © 2005 by Hillel Goldberg. Reprinted from the *Intermountain Jewish News,* April 16, 1993.

Arthur Green, "Homecoming and *Teshuvah," "Sh'ma"* and *"Teshuvah* and the Sacred Year," excerpts from *Seek My Face: A Jewish Mystical Theology* © 2003 Arthur Green (Woodstock, VT: Jewish Lights Publishing). $19.95 + $3.95 s/h. Order by mail or call 800-962-4544 or on-line at www.jewishlights.com. Permission granted by Jewish Lights Publishing, P.O. Box 237, Woodstock, VT 05091.

Arthur Green section introductions excerpted from *These Are the Words: A Vocabulary of Jewish Spiritual Life* © 1999 Arthur Green (Woodstock, VT: Jewish Lights Publishing). $18.95 + $3.95 s/h. Order by mail or call 800-962-4544 or on-line at www.jewishlights.com. Permission granted by Jewish Lights Publishing, P.O. Box 237, Woodstock, VT 05091.

Abraham Joshua Heschel, "Preface to the *Amidah,"* copyright Susannah Heschel, Executor.

Karyn D. Kedar, "Forgive Yourself," excerpt from *God Whispers: Stories of the Soul, Lessons of the Heart.* © 1999 Karyn D. Kedar (Woodstock, VT: Jewish Lights Publishing). $15.95 + $3.95 s/h. Order by mail or call 800-962-4544 or on-line at www.jewishlights.com. Permission granted by Jewish Lights Publishing, P.O. Box 237, Woodstock, VT 05091.

Myriam Klotz, "The High Priest: An Eager Servant Awaiting Rebirth," excerpt from *The Women's Haftarah Commentary: New Insights from Women Rabbis on the 54 Weekly Haftarah Portions, the 5 Megillot & Special Shabbatot* © 2004 Elyse Goldstein (Woodstock, VT: Jewish Lights Publishing). $39.99 + $3.95 s/h. Order by mail or call 800-962-4544 or on-line at www.jewishlights.com. Permission granted by Jewish Lights Publishing, P.O. Box 237, Woodstock, VT 05091.

Irwin Kula, *"U'v'khen Ten Kavod Le-amekha*—Give Dignity to Your People— *Kavod:* Honor Connected to Our Deepest Selves," © 1995–1996 CLAL— The National Jewish Center for Learning and Leadership.

Irwin Kula and Vanessa L. Ochs, "A Meditation on Fasting," excerpt from *The Book of Jewish Sacred Practices: CLAL's Guide to Everyday & Holiday Rituals & Blessings* © 2001 CLAL (Woodstock, VT: Jewish Lights Publishing).

$18.95 + $3.95 s/h. Order by mail or call 800-962-4544 or on-line at www.jewishlights.com. Permission granted by Jewish Lights Publishing, P.O. Box 237, Woodstock, VT 05091.

Lawrence Kushner, "Sweetening the Evil in Yourself," excerpt from *God Was In This Place and I, i Did Not Know* © 1994 Lawrence Kushner (Woodstock, VT: Jewish Lights Publishing). $16.95 + $3.95 s/h. Order by mail or call 800-962-4544 or on-line at www.jewishlights.com. Permission granted by Jewish Lights Publishing, P.O. Box 237, Woodstock, VT 05091.

Naomi Levy, "Saving God's Life" and *"Sim Shalom*—A Prayer for Peace," from *Talking to God: Personal Prayers for Times of Joy, Sadness, Struggle, and Celebration.* 2003 Knopf, New York.

Alan Lew, "The Gates Clang Shut—*Neilah*" and "Moving toward the Light of God," from *This Is Real and You Are Completely Unprepared.* Copyright © 2003 by Alan Lew. By permission of Little, Brown and Co., Inc.

"Looking Into Our Own Hearts" excerpt copyright © 1961 by The New York Times Co. Reprinted with permission.

Goldie Milgram, "Repenting for Those Who Cannot" and *"Teshuvah:* Forgiveness Walks," excerpts from *Reclaiming Judaism as a Spiritual Practice: Holy Days and Shabbat* © 2004 Goldie Milgram (Woodstock, VT: Jewish Lights Publishing). $19.99 + $3.95 s/h. Order by mail or call 800-962-4544 or on-line at www.jewishlights.com. Permission granted by Jewish Lights Publishing, P.O. Box 237, Woodstock, VT 05091.

Shira Milgrom, "Where is God?" and "Yom Kippur and Memory" © Rabbi Shira Milgrom.

David W. Nelson, "Inclusion in the Covenant," originally written for CLAL—The National Jewish Center for Learning and Leadership. Reprinted with permission.

Kerry M. Olitzky, "Jonah and Self-Change" and "Penitence" excerpted from *100 Blessings Every Day: Daily Twelve Step Recovery Affirmations, Exercises for Personal Growth & Renewal Reflecting Seasons of the Jewish Year* © 1993 Kerry M. Olitzky (Woodstock, VT: Jewish Lights Publishing). $15.99 + $3.95 s/h. Order by mail or call 800-962-4544 or on-line at www.jewishlights.com. Permission granted by Jewish Lights Publishing, P.O. Box 237, Woodstock, VT 05091.

Joanne Palmer, *"Vidui*—An Annotated Report," copyright 2005 Joanne Palmer. All rights reserved.

Marge Piercy, *"Shema,"* from *The Art of Blessing the Day* by Marge Piercy, copyright © 1999 by Middlemarsh, Inc. Used by permission of Alfred A. Knopf, a division of Random House, Inc.

Sarah Polster, "Aaron's God—and Ours," reprinted from *TIKKUN: A Bimonthly Interfaith Critique of Politics, Culture & Society.*

Rachel Naomi Remen, MD, "All in the Family" and "Belonging," from *My Grandfather's Blessings,* copyright © 2000 by Rachel Naomi Remen, M.D. Used by permission of Riverhead Books, an imprint of Penguin Group (USA) Inc.

Bar/Bat Mitzvah

The JGirl's Guide: The Young Jewish Woman's Handbook for Coming of Age *By Penina Adelman, Ali Feldman and Shulamit Reinharz* This inspirational, interactive guidebook helps pre-teen Jewish girls address the many issues surrounding coming of age. 6 x 9, 240 pp, Quality PB, 978-1-58023-215-9 **$14.99** *For ages 11 & up*
Also Available: **The JGirl's Teacher's and Parent's Guide**
8½ x 11, 56 pp, PB, 978-1-58023-225-8 **$8.99**

Bar/Bat Mitzvah Basics, 2nd Edition: A Practical Family Guide to Coming of Age Together *Edited by Helen Leneman; Foreword by Rabbi Jeffrey K. Salkin*
6 x 9, 240 pp, Quality PB, 978-1-58023-151-0 **$18.95**

The Bar/Bat Mitzvah Memory Book, 2nd Edition: An Album for Treasuring the Spiritual Celebration *By Rabbi Jeffrey K. Salkin and Nina Salkin*
8 x 10, 48 pp, 2-color text, Deluxe HC, ribbon marker, 978-1-58023-263-0 **$19.99**

For Kids—Putting God on Your Guest List, 2nd Edition: How to Claim the Spiritual Meaning of Your Bar or Bat Mitzvah *By Rabbi Jeffrey K. Salkin*
6 x 9, 144 pp, Quality PB, 978-1-58023-308-8 **$15.99** *For ages 11–13*

Putting God on the Guest List, 3rd Edition: How to Reclaim the Spiritual Meaning of Your Child's Bar or Bat Mitzvah *By Rabbi Jeffrey K. Salkin*
6 x 9, 224 pp, Quality PB, 978-1-58023-222-7 **$16.99**; HC, 978-1-58023-260-9 **$24.99**
Also Available: **Putting God on the Guest List Teacher's Guide**
8½ x 11, 48 pp, PB, 978-1-58023-226-5 **$8.99**

Tough Questions Jews Ask: A Young Adult's Guide to Building a Jewish Life *By Rabbi Edward Feinstein* 6 x 9, 160 pp, Quality PB, 978-1-58023-139-8 **$14.99** *For ages 11 & up*
Also Available: **Tough Questions Jews Ask Teacher's Guide**
8½ x 11, 72 pp, PB, 978-1-58023-187-9

Bible Study/Midrash

The Modern Men's Torah Commentary: New Insights from Jewish Men on the 54 Weekly Torah Portions *Edited by Rabbi Jeffrey K. Salkin* A major contribution to modern biblical commentary. Addresses the most important concerns of modern men by opening them up to the messages of Torah.
6 x 9, 368 pp, HC, 978-1-58023-395-8 **$24.99**

The Genesis of Leadership: What the Bible Teaches Us about Vision, Values and Leading Change *By Rabbi Nathan Laufer; Foreword by Senator Joseph I. Lieberman*
6 x 9, 288 pp, Quality PB, 978-1-58023-352-1 **$18.99**

Hineini in Our Lives: Learning How to Respond to Others through 14 Biblical Texts and Personal Stories *By Rabbi Norman J. Cohen, PhD* 6 x 9, 240 pp, Quality PB, 978-1-58023-274-6 **$16.99**

A Man's Responsibility: A Jewish Guide to Being a Son, a Partner in Marriage, a Father and a Community Leader *By Rabbi Joseph B. Meszler*
6 x 9, 192 pp, Quality PB, 978-1-58023-435-1 **$16.99**

Moses and the Journey to Leadership: Timeless Lessons of Effective Management from the Bible and Today's Leaders *By Rabbi Norman J. Cohen, PhD*
6 x 9, 240 pp, Quality PB, 978-1-58023-351-4 **$18.99**; HC, 978-1-58023-227-2 **$21.99**

Righteous Gentiles in the Hebrew Bible: Ancient Role Models for Sacred Relationships *By Rabbi Jeffrey K. Salkin; Foreword by Rabbi Harold M. Schulweis; Preface by Phyllis Tickle* 6 x 9, 192 pp, Quality PB, 978-1-58023-364-4 **$18.99**

The Triumph of Eve & Other Subversive Bible Tales *By Matt Biers-Ariel* 5½ x 8½, 192 pp, Quality PB, 978-1-59473-176-1 **$14.99** *(A book from SkyLight Paths, Jewish Lights' sister imprint)*

The Wisdom of Judaism: An Introduction to the Values of the Talmud *By Rabbi Dov Peretz Elkins* 6 x 9, 192 pp, Quality PB, 978-1-58023-327-9 **$16.99**
Also Available: **The Wisdom of Judaism Teacher's Guide**
8½ x 11, 18 pp, PB, 978-1-58023-350-7 **$8.99**

Congregation Resources

Empowered Judaism: What Independent Minyanim Can Teach Us about Building Vibrant Jewish Communities
By Rabbi Elie Kaunfer; Foreword by Prof. Jonathan D. Sarna
Examines the independent minyan movement and the lessons these grassroots communities can provide. 6 x 9, 224 pp, Quality PB, 978-1-58023-412-2 **$18.99**

Spiritual Boredom: Rediscovering the Wonder of Judaism *By Dr. Erica Brown*
Breaks through the surface of spiritual boredom to find the reservoir of meaning within. 6 x 9, 208 pp, HC, 978-1-58023-405-4 **$21.99**

Building a Successful Volunteer Culture
Finding Meaning in Service in the Jewish Community
By Rabbi Charles Simon; Foreword by Shelley Lindauer; Preface by Dr. Ron Wolfson
Shows you how to develop and maintain the volunteers who are essential to the vitality of your organization and community. 6 x 9, 192 pp, Quality PB, 978-1-58023-408-5 **$16.99**

The Case for Jewish Peoplehood: Can We Be One?
By Dr. Erica Brown and Dr. Misha Galperin; Foreword by Rabbi Joseph Telushkin
6 x 9, 224 pp, HC, 978-1-58023-401-6 **$21.99**

Inspired Jewish Leadership: Practical Approaches to Building Strong Communities
By Dr. Erica Brown 6 x 9, 256 pp, HC, 978-1-58023-361-3 **$24.99**

Jewish Pastoral Care, 2nd Edition: A Practical Handbook from Traditional & Contemporary Sources *Edited by Rabbi Dayle A. Friedman, MSW, MAJCS, BCC*
6 x 9, 528 pp, Quality PB, 978-1-58023-427-6 **$30.00**; HC, 978-1-58023-221-0 **$40.00**

Rethinking Synagogues: A New Vocabulary for Congregational Life
By Rabbi Lawrence A. Hoffman, PhD 6 x 9, 240 pp, Quality PB, 978-1-58023-248-7 **$19.99**

The Spirituality of Welcoming: How to Transform Your Congregation into a Sacred Community *By Dr. Ron Wolfson* 6 x 9, 224 pp, Quality PB, 978-1-58023-244-9 **$19.99**

Children's Books

What You Will See Inside a Synagogue
By Rabbi Lawrence A. Hoffman, PhD, and Dr. Ron Wolfson; Full-color photos by Bill Aron
A colorful, fun-to-read introduction that explains the ways and whys of Jewish worship and religious life. 8½ x 10½, 32 pp, Full-color photos, Quality PB, 978-1-59473-256-0 **$8.99**
For ages 6 & up (A book from SkyLight Paths, Jewish Lights' sister imprint)

Because Nothing Looks Like God
By Lawrence Kushner and Karen Kushner Introduces children to the possibilities of spiritual life. 11 x 8½, 32 pp, Full-color illus., HC, 978-1-58023-092-6 **$17.99** *For ages 4 & up*
Board Book Companions to *Because Nothing Looks Like God*
5 x 5, 24 pp, Full-color illus., SkyLight Paths Board Books *For ages 0–4*

  How Does God Make Things Happen? 978-1-893361-24-9 **$7.95**

  What Does God Look Like? 978-1-893361-23-2 **$7.99**

  Where Is God? 978-1-893361-17-1 **$7.99**

The Book of Miracles: A Young Person's Guide to Jewish Spiritual Awareness
Written and illus. by Lawrence Kushner
6 x 9, 96 pp, 2-color illus., HC, 978-1-879045-78-1 **$16.95** *For ages 9 & up*

In God's Hands *By Lawrence Kushner and Gary Schmidt* 9 x 12, 32 pp, Full-color illus., HC, 978-1-58023-224-1 **$16.99**

In Our Image: God's First Creatures *By Nancy Sohn Swartz*
9 x 12, 32 pp, Full-color illus., HC, 978-1-879045-99-6 **$16.95** *For ages 4 & up*

Also Available as a Board Book: **How Did the Animals Help God?**
5 x 5, 24 pp, Full-color illus., Board Book, 978-1-59473-044-3 **$7.99** *For ages 0–4*
(A book from SkyLight Paths, Jewish Lights' sister imprint)

The Kids' Fun Book of Jewish Time
By Emily Sper 9 x 7½, 24 pp, Full-color illus., HC, 978-1-58023-311-8 **$16.99**

What Makes Someone a Jew? *By Lauren Seidman*
Reflects the changing face of American Judaism.
10 x 8½, 32 pp, Full-color photos, Quality PB, 978-1-58023-321-7 **$8.99** *For ages 3–6*

Ecology/Environment

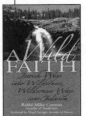

A Wild Faith: Jewish Ways into Wilderness, Wilderness Ways into Judaism
By Rabbi Mike Comins; Foreword by Nigel Savage 6 x 9, 240 pp, Quality PB, 978-1-58023-316-3 **$16.99**

Ecology & the Jewish Spirit: Where Nature & the Sacred Meet
Edited by Ellen Bernstein 6 x 9, 288 pp, Quality PB, 978-1-58023-082-7 **$18.99**

Torah of the Earth: Exploring 4,000 Years of Ecology in Jewish Thought
Vol. 1: Biblical Israel & Rabbinic Judaism; Vol. 2: Zionism & Eco-Judaism
Edited by Rabbi Arthur Waskow Vol. 1: 6 x 9, 272 pp, Quality PB, 978-1-58023-086-5 **$19.95**
Vol. 2: 6 x 9, 336 pp, Quality PB, 978-1-58023-087-2 **$19.95**

The Way Into Judaism and the Environment *By Jeremy Benstein, PhD*
6 x 9, 288 pp, Quality PB, 978-1-58023-368-2 **$18.99**; HC, 978-1-58023-268-5 **$24.99**

Graphic Novels/History

The Adventures of Rabbi Harvey: A Graphic Novel of Jewish Wisdom and Wit in the
Wild West *By Steve Sheinkin* 6 x 9, 144 pp, Full-color illus., Quality PB, 978-1-58023-310-1 **$16.99**

Rabbi Harvey Rides Again: A Graphic Novel of Jewish Folktales Let Loose in the
Wild West *By Steve Sheinkin* 6 x 9, 144 pp, Full-color illus., Quality PB, 978-1-58023-347-7 **$16.99**

Rabbi Harvey vs. the Wisdom Kid: A Graphic Novel of Dueling
Jewish Folktales in the Wild West *By Steve Sheinkin*
Rabbi Harvey's first book-length adventure—and toughest challenge.
6 x 9, 144 pp, Full-color illus., Quality PB, 978-1-58023-422-1 **$16.99**

The Story of the Jews: A 4,000-Year Adventure—A Graphic History Book
By Stan Mack 6 x 9, 288 pp, Illus., Quality PB, 978-1-58023-155-8 **$16.99**

Grief/Healing

Facing Illness, Finding God: How Judaism Can Help You and Caregivers
Cope When Body or Spirit Fails *By Rabbi Joseph B. Meszler*
Will help you find spiritual strength for healing amid the fear, pain and chaos of
illness. 6 x 9, 208 pp, Quality PB, 978-1-58023-423-8 **$16.99**

Midrash & Medicine: Healing Body and Soul in the Jewish Interpretive
Tradition *Edited by Rabbi William Cutter, PhD*
Explores how midrash can help you see beyond the physical aspects of healing to
tune in to your spiritual source. 6 x 9, 240 pp (est), HC, 978-1-58023-428-3 **$24.99**

Healing from Despair: Choosing Wholeness in a Broken World
By Rabbi Elie Kaplan Spitz with Erica Shapiro Taylor; Foreword by Abraham J. Twerski, MD
5½ x 8½, 208 pp, Quality PB, 978-1-58023-436-8 **$16.99**

Healing and the Jewish Imagination: Spiritual and Practical Perspectives on
Judaism and Health *Edited by Rabbi William Cutter, PhD*
6 x 9, 240 pp, Quality PB, 978-1-58023-373-6 **$19.99**; HC, 978-1-58023-314-9 **$24.99**

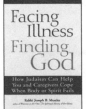

Grief in Our Seasons: A Mourner's Kaddish Companion *By Rabbi Kerry M. Olitzky*
4½ x 6½, 448 pp, Quality PB, 978-1-879045-55-2 **$15.95**

Healing of Soul, Healing of Body: Spiritual Leaders Unfold the Strength & Solace
in Psalms *Edited by Rabbi Simkha Y. Weintraub, CSW*
6 x 9, 128 pp, 2-color illus. text, Quality PB, 978-1-879045-31-6 **$16.99**

Mourning & Mitzvah, 2nd Edition: A Guided Journal for Walking the Mourner's
Path through Grief to Healing *By Anne Brener, LCSW*
7½ x 9, 304 pp, Quality PB, 978-1-58023-113-8 **$19.99**

Tears of Sorrow, Seeds of Hope, 2nd Edition: A Jewish Spiritual Companion for
Infertility and Pregnancy Loss *By Rabbi Nina Beth Cardin*
6 x 9, 208 pp, Quality PB, 978-1-58023-233-3 **$18.99**

A Time to Mourn, a Time to Comfort, 2nd Edition: A Guide to Jewish
Bereavement *By Dr. Ron Wolfson; Preface by Rabbi David J. Wolpe*
7 x 9, 384 pp, Quality PB, 978-1-58023-253-1 **$19.99**

When a Grandparent Dies: A Kid's Own Remembering Workbook for Dealing
with Shiva and the Year Beyond *By Nechama Liss-Levinson, PhD*
8 x 10, 48 pp, 2-color text, HC, 978-1-879045-44-6 **$15.95** *For ages 7–13*

Life Cycle
Marriage/Parenting/Family/Aging

The New Jewish Baby Album: Creating and Celebrating the Beginning of a Spiritual Life—A Jewish Lights Companion
By the Editors at Jewish Lights; Foreword by Anita Diamant; Preface by Rabbi Sandy Eisenberg Sasso
A spiritual keepsake that will be treasured for generations. More than just a memory book, *shows you how—and why it's important*—to create a Jewish home and a Jewish life. 8 x 10, 64 pp, Deluxe Padded HC, Full-color illus., 978-1-58023-138-1 **$19.95**

The Jewish Pregnancy Book: A Resource for the Soul, Body & Mind during Pregnancy, Birth & the First Three Months *By Sandy Falk, MD, and Rabbi Daniel Judson, with Steven A. Rapp* Medical information, prayers and rituals for each stage of pregnancy. 7 x 10, 208 pp, b/w photos, Quality PB, 978-1-58023-178-7 **$16.95**

Celebrating Your New Jewish Daughter: Creating Jewish Ways to Welcome Baby Girls into the Covenant—New and Traditional Ceremonies *By Debra Nussbaum Cohen; Foreword by Rabbi Sandy Eisenberg Sasso* 6 x 9, 272 pp, Quality PB, 978-1-58023-090-2 **$18.95**

The New Jewish Baby Book, 2nd Edition: Names, Ceremonies & Customs—A Guide for Today's Families *By Anita Diamant* 6 x 9, 336 pp, Quality PB, 978-1-58023-251-7 **$19.99**

Parenting as a Spiritual Journey: Deepening Ordinary and Extraordinary Events into Sacred Occasions *By Rabbi Nancy Fuchs-Kreimer, PhD* 6 x 9, 224 pp, Quality PB, 978-1-58023-016-2 **$16.95**

Parenting Jewish Teens: A Guide for the Perplexed
By Joanne Doades Explores the questions and issues that shape the world in which today's Jewish teenagers live and offers constructive advice to parents.
6 x 9, 176 pp, Quality PB, 978-1-58023-305-7 **$16.99**

Judaism for Two: A Spiritual Guide for Strengthening and Celebrating Your Loving Relationship *By Rabbi Nancy Fuchs-Kreimer, PhD, and Rabbi Nancy H. Wiener, DMin; Foreword by Rabbi Elliot N. Dorff*
Addresses the ways Jewish teachings can enhance and strengthen committed relationships. 6 x 9, 224 pp, Quality PB, 978-1-58023-254-8 **$16.99**

The Creative Jewish Wedding Book, 2nd Edition: A Hands-On Guide to New & Old Traditions, Ceremonies & Celebrations *By Gabrielle Kaplan-Mayer* 9 x 9, 288 pp, b/w photos, Quality PB, 978-1-58023-398-9 **$19.99**

Divorce Is a Mitzvah: A Practical Guide to Finding Wholeness and Holiness When Your Marriage Dies *By Rabbi Perry Netter; Afterword by Rabbi Laura Geller* 6 x 9, 224 pp, Quality PB, 978-1-58023-172-5 **$16.95**

Embracing the Covenant: Converts to Judaism Talk About Why & How
By Rabbi Allan Berkowitz and Patti Moskovitz 6 x 9, 192 pp, Quality PB, 978-1-879045-50-7 **$16.95**

The Guide to Jewish Interfaith Family Life: An InterfaithFamily.com Handbook
Edited by Ronnie Friedland and Edmund Case
6 x 9, 384 pp, Quality PB, 978-1-58023-153-4 **$18.95**

A Heart of Wisdom: Making the Jewish Journey from Midlife through the Elder Years
Edited by Susan Berrin; Foreword by Rabbi Harold Kushner
6 x 9, 384 pp, Quality PB, 978-1-58023-051-3 **$18.95**

Introducing My Faith and My Community: The Jewish Outreach Institute Guide for the Christian in a Jewish Interfaith Relationship
By Rabbi Kerry M. Olitzky 6 x 9, 176 pp, Quality PB, 978-1-58023-192-3 **$16.99**

Making a Successful Jewish Interfaith Marriage: The Jewish Outreach Institute Guide to Opportunities, Challenges and Resources *By Rabbi Kerry M. Olitzky with Joan Peterson Littman*
6 x 9, 176 pp, Quality PB, 978-1-58023-170-1 **$16.95**

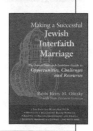

A Man's Responsibility: A Jewish Guide to Being a Son, a Partner in Marriage, a Father and a Community Leader *By Rabbi Joseph B. Meszler*
6 x 9, 192 pp, Quality PB, 978-1-58023-435-1 **$16.99**

So That Your Values Live On: Ethical Wills and How to Prepare Them
Edited by Rabbi Jack Riemer and Rabbi Nathaniel Stampfer
6 x 9, 272 pp, Quality PB, 978-1-879045-34-7 **$18.99**

Meditation

Jewish Meditation Practices for Everyday Life
Awakening Your Heart, Connecting with God
By Rabbi Jeff Roth
Offers a fresh take on meditation that draws on life experience and living life with greater clarity as opposed to the traditional method of rigorous study.
6 x 9, 224 pp, Quality PB, 978-1-58023-397-2 **$18.99**

The Handbook of Jewish Meditation Practices
A Guide for Enriching the Sabbath and Other Days of Your Life
By Rabbi David A. Cooper Easy-to-learn meditation techniques.
6 x 9, 208 pp, Quality PB, 978-1-58023-102-2 **$16.95**

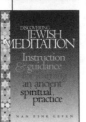

Discovering Jewish Meditation: Instruction & Guidance for Learning an Ancient
Spiritual Practice *By Nan Fink Gefen, PhD*   6 x 9, 208 pp, Quality PB, 978-1-58023-067-4 **$16.95**

Meditation from the Heart of Judaism: Today's Teachers Share Their Practices,
Techniques, and Faith *Edited by Avram Davis*
6 x 9, 256 pp, Quality PB, 978-1-58023-049-0 **$16.95**

Ritual/Sacred Practices

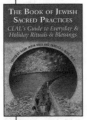

The Jewish Dream Book: The Key to Opening the Inner Meaning of
Your Dreams *By Vanessa L. Ochs, PhD, with Elizabeth Ochs; Illus. by Kristina Swarner*
Instructions for how modern people can perform ancient Jewish dream practices and dream interpretations drawn from the Jewish wisdom tradition.
8 x 8, 128 pp, Full-color illus., Deluxe PB w/ flaps, 978-1-58023-132-9 **$16.95**

God in Your Body: Kabbalah, Mindfulness and Embodied Spiritual Practice
By Jay Michaelson
The first comprehensive treatment of the body in Jewish spiritual practice and an essential guide to the sacred.
6 x 9, 272 pp, Quality PB, 978-1-58023-304-0 **$18.99**

The Book of Jewish Sacred Practices: CLAL's Guide to Everyday &
Holiday Rituals & Blessings *Edited by Rabbi Irwin Kula and Vanessa L. Ochs, PhD*
6 x 9, 368 pp, Quality PB, 978-1-58023-152-7 **$18.95**

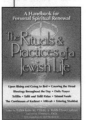

Jewish Ritual: A Brief Introduction for Christians
By Rabbi Kerry M. Olitzky and Rabbi Daniel Judson
5½ x 8½, 144 pp, Quality PB, 978-1-58023-210-4 **$14.99**

The Rituals & Practices of a Jewish Life: A Handbook for Personal Spiritual
Renewal *Edited by Rabbi Kerry M. Olitzky and Rabbi Daniel Judson*
6 x 9, 272 pp, Illus., Quality PB, 978-1-58023-169-5 **$18.95**

The Sacred Art of Lovingkindness: Preparing to Practice
By Rabbi Rami Shapiro 5½ x 8½, 176 pp, Quality PB, 978-1-59473-151-8 **$16.99**
(A book from SkyLight Paths, Jewish Lights' sister imprint)

Science Fiction/Mystery & Detective Fiction

Criminal Kabbalah: An Intriguing Anthology of Jewish Mystery &
Detective Fiction *Edited by Lawrence W. Raphael; Foreword by Laurie R. King*
All-new stories from twelve of today's masters of mystery and detective fiction—sure to delight mystery buffs of all faith traditions.
6 x 9, 256 pp, Quality PB, 978-1-58023-109-1 **$16.95**

Mystery Midrash: An Anthology of Jewish Mystery & Detective Fiction
Edited by Lawrence W. Raphael; Preface by Joel Siegel
6 x 9, 304 pp, Quality PB, 978-1-58023-055-1 **$16.95**

Wandering Stars: An Anthology of Jewish Fantasy & Science Fiction
Edited by Jack Dann; Introduction by Isaac Asimov
6 x 9, 272 pp, Quality PB, 978-1-58023-005-6 **$18.99**

More Wandering Stars: An Anthology of Outstanding Stories of Jewish Fantasy and
Science Fiction *Edited by Jack Dann; Introduction by Isaac Asimov*
6 x 9, 192 pp, Quality PB, 978-1-58023-063-6 **$16.95**

Inspiration

The Seven Questions You're Asked in Heaven: Reviewing and
Renewing Your Life on Earth *By Dr. Ron Wolfson*
An intriguing and entertaining resource for living a life that matters.
6 x 9, 176 pp, Quality PB, 978-1-58023-407-8 **$16.99**

Happiness and the Human Spirit: The Spirituality of Becoming the
Best You Can Be *By Rabbi Abraham J. Twerski, MD*
Shows you that true happiness is attainable once you stop looking outside yourself for
the source. 6 x 9, 176 pp, Quality PB, 978-1-58023-404-7 **$16.99**; HC, 978-1-58023-343-9 **$19.99**

A Formula for Proper Living: Practical Lessons from Life and Torah
By Rabbi Abraham J. Twerski, MD
Gives you practical lessons for life that you can put to day-to-day use in dealing
with yourself and others. 6 x 9, 144 pp, HC, 978-1-58023-402-3 **$19.99**

The Bridge to Forgiveness: Stories and Prayers for Finding God and Restoring
Wholeness *By Rabbi Karyn D. Kedar* 6 x 9, 176 pp, HC, 978-1-58023-324-8 **$19.99**

The Empty Chair: Finding Hope and Joy—Timeless Wisdom from a Hasidic Master,
Rebbe Nachman of Breslov *Adapted by Moshe Mykoff and the Breslov Research Institute*
4 x 6, 128 pp, Deluxe PB w/ flaps, 978-1-879045-67-5 **$9.99**

The Gentle Weapon: Prayers for Everyday and Not-So-Everyday Moments—
Timeless Wisdom from the Teachings of the Hasidic Master, Rebbe Nachman of Breslov
Adapted by Moshe Mykoff and S. C. Mizrahi, together with the Breslov Research Institute
4 x 6, 144 pp, Deluxe PB w/ flaps, 978-1-58023-022-3 **$9.99**

God Whispers: Stories of the Soul, Lessons of the Heart *By Rabbi Karyn D. Kedar*
6 x 9, 176 pp, Quality PB, 978-1-58023-088-9 **$15.95**

God's To-Do List: 103 Ways to Be an Angel and Do God's Work on Earth
By Dr. Ron Wolfson 6 x 9, 144 pp, Quality PB, 978-1-58023-301-9 **$16.99**

Jewish Stories from Heaven and Earth: Inspiring Tales to Nourish the Heart and
Soul *Edited by Rabbi Dov Peretz Elkins* 6 x 9, 304 pp, Quality PB, 978-1-58023-363-7 **$16.99**

Life's Daily Blessings: Inspiring Reflections on Gratitude and Joy for Every Day, Based on
Jewish Wisdom *By Rabbi Kerry M. Olitzky* 4½ x 6½, 368 pp, Quality PB, 978-1-58023-396-5 **$16.99**

Restful Reflections: Nighttime Inspiration to Calm the Soul, Based on Jewish Wisdom
By Rabbi Kerry M. Olitzky and Rabbi Lori Forman 4½ x 6½, 448 pp, Quality PB, 978-1-58023-091-9 **$15.95**

Sacred Intentions: Daily Inspiration to Strengthen the Spirit, Based on Jewish Wisdom
By Rabbi Kerry M. Olitzky and Rabbi Lori Forman 4½ x 6½, 448 pp, Quality PB, 978-1-58023-061-2 **$15.95**

Kabbalah/Mysticism

Ehyeh: A Kabbalah for Tomorrow
By Rabbi Arthur Green, PhD 6 x 9, 224 pp, Quality PB, 978-1-58023-213-5 **$16.99**

The Flame of the Heart: Prayers of a Chasidic Mystic
By Reb Noson of Breslov; Translated and adapted by David Sears, with the Breslov Research Institute
5 x 7¼, 160 pp, Quality PB, 978-1-58023-246-3 **$15.99**

The Gift of Kabbalah: Discovering the Secrets of Heaven, Renewing Your Life on Earth
By Tamar Frankiel, PhD 6 x 9, 256 pp, Quality PB, 978-1-58023-141-1 **$16.95**

Kabbalah: A Brief Introduction for Christians
By Tamar Frankiel, PhD 5½ x 8½, 208 pp, Quality PB, 978-1-58023-303-3 **$16.99**

The Lost Princess & Other Kabbalistic Tales of Rebbe Nachman of Breslov
The Seven Beggars & Other Kabbalistic Tales of Rebbe Nachman of Breslov
Translated by Rabbi Aryeh Kaplan; Preface by Rabbi Chaim Kramer
Lost Princess: 6 x 9, 400 pp, Quality PB, 978-1-58023-217-3 **$18.99**
Seven Beggars: 6 x 9, 192 pp, Quality PB, 978-1-58023-250-0 **$16.99**

Seek My Face: A Jewish Mystical Theology *By Rabbi Arthur Green, PhD*
6 x 9, 304 pp, Quality PB, 978-1-58023-130-5 **$19.95**

Zohar: Annotated & Explained *Translation & Annotation by Dr. Daniel C. Matt; Foreword by*
Andrew Harvey 5½ x 8½, 176 pp, Quality PB, 978-1-893361-51-5 **$15.99**
(A book from SkyLight Paths, Jewish Lights' sister imprint)

See also *The Way Into Jewish Mystical Tradition* in The Way Into... Series.

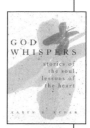

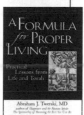

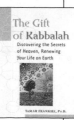

Theology/Philosophy/The Way Into... Series

The Way Into... series offers an accessible and highly usable "guided tour" of the Jewish faith, people, history and beliefs—in total, an introduction to Judaism that will enable you to understand and interact with the sacred texts of the Jewish tradition. Each volume is written by a leading contemporary scholar and teacher, and explores one key aspect of Judaism. The Way Into... series enables all readers to achieve a real sense of Jewish cultural literacy through guided study.

The Way Into Encountering God in Judaism
By Rabbi Neil Gillman, PhD

For everyone who wants to understand how Jews have encountered God throughout history and today.

6 x 9, 240 pp, Quality PB, 978-1-58023-199-2 **$18.99**; HC, 978-1-58023-025-4 **$21.95**

Also Available: **The Jewish Approach to God:** A Brief Introduction for Christians
By Rabbi Neil Gillman, PhD
5½ x 8½, 192 pp, Quality PB, 978-1-58023-190-9 **$16.95**

The Way Into Jewish Mystical Tradition
By Rabbi Lawrence Kushner

Allows readers to interact directly with the sacred mystical texts of the Jewish tradition. An accessible introduction to the concepts of Jewish mysticism, their religious and spiritual significance, and how they relate to life today.

6 x 9, 224 pp, Quality PB, 978-1-58023-200-5 **$18.99**; HC, 978-1-58023-029-2 **$21.95**

The Way Into Jewish Prayer
By Rabbi Lawrence A. Hoffman, PhD

Opens the door to 3,000 years of Jewish prayer, making anyone feel at home in the Jewish way of communicating with God.

6 x 9, 208 pp, Quality PB, 978-1-58023-201-2 **$18.99**

Also Available: **The Way Into Jewish Prayer Teacher's Guide**
By Rabbi Jennifer Ossakow Goldsmith
8½ x 11, 42 pp, PB, 978-1-58023-345-3 **$8.99**
Download a free copy at www.jewishlights.com.

The Way Into Judaism and the Environment
By Jeremy Benstein, PhD

Explores the ways in which Judaism contributes to contemporary social-environmental issues, the extent to which Judaism is part of the problem and how it can be part of the solution.

6 x 9, 288 pp, Quality PB, 978-1-58023-368-2 **$18.99**; HC, 978-1-58023-268-5 **$24.99**

The Way Into Tikkun Olam (Repairing the World)
By Rabbi Elliot N. Dorff, PhD

An accessible introduction to the Jewish concept of the individual's responsibility to care for others and repair the world.

6 x 9, 304 pp, Quality PB, 978-1-58023-328-6 **$18.99**; 320 pp, HC, 978-1-58023-269-2 **$24.99**

The Way Into Torah
By Rabbi Norman J. Cohen, PhD

Helps guide you in the exploration of the origins and development of Torah, explains why it should be studied and how to do it.

6 x 9, 176 pp, Quality PB, 978-1-58023-198-5 **$16.99**

The Way Into the Varieties of Jewishness
By Sylvia Barack Fishman, PhD

Explores the religious and historical understanding of what it has meant to be Jewish from ancient times to the present controversy over "Who is a Jew?"

6 x 9, 288 pp, Quality PB, 978-1-58023-367-5 **$18.99**; HC, 978-1-58023-030-8 **$24.99**

Theology/Philosophy

Jewish Theology in Our Time: A New Generation Explores the Foundations and Future of Jewish Belief *Edited by Rabbi Elliot J. Cosgrove, PhD* A powerful and challenging examination of what Jews can believe—by a new generation's most dynamic and innovative thinkers.
6 x 9, 272 pp, HC, 978-1-58023-413-9 **$24.99**

Maimonides, Spinoza and Us: Toward an Intellectually Vibrant Judaism
By Rabbi Marc D. Angel, PhD A challenging look at two great Jewish philosophers and what their thinking means to our understanding of God, truth, revelation and reason. 6 x 9, 224 pp, HC, 978-1-58023-411-5 **$24.99**

The Death of Death: Resurrection and Immortality in Jewish Thought
By Rabbi Neil Gillman, PhD 6 x 9, 336 pp, Quality PB, 978-1-58023-081-0 **$18.95**

Doing Jewish Theology: God, Torah & Israel in Modern Judaism *By Rabbi Neil Gillman, PhD*
6 x 9, 304 pp, Quality PB, 978-1-58023-439-9 **$18.99**; HC, 978-1-58023-322-4 **$24.99**

Ethics of the Sages: *Pirke Avot*—Annotated & Explained
Translation & Annotation by Rabbi Rami Shapiro 5½ x 8½, 192 pp, Quality PB, 978-1-59473-207-2 **$16.99***

Hasidic Tales: Annotated & Explained *Translation & Annotation by Rabbi Rami Shapiro*
5½ x 8½, 240 pp, Quality PB, 978-1-893361-86-7 **$16.95***

A Heart of Many Rooms: Celebrating the Many Voices within Judaism
By Dr. David Hartman 6 x 9, 352 pp, Quality PB, 978-1-58023-156-5 **$19.95**

The Hebrew Prophets: Selections Annotated & Explained
Translation & Annotation by Rabbi Rami Shapiro; Foreword by Rabbi Zalman M. Schachter-Shalomi
5½ x 8½, 224 pp, Quality PB, 978-1-59473-037-5 **$16.99***

A Jewish Understanding of the New Testament *By Rabbi Samuel Sandmel;*
Preface by Rabbi David Sandmel 5½ x 8½, 368 pp, Quality PB, 978-1-59473-048-1 **$19.99***

Jews and Judaism in the 21st Century: Human Responsibility, the Presence of God and the Future of the Covenant *Edited by Rabbi Edward Feinstein; Foreword by Paula E. Hyman*
6 x 9, 192 pp, Quality PB, 978-1-58023-374-3 **$19.99**; HC, 978-1-58023-315-6 **$24.99**

A Living Covenant: The Innovative Spirit in Traditional Judaism
By Dr. David Hartman 6 x 9, 368 pp, Quality PB, 978-1-58023-011-7 **$20.00**

Love and Terror in the God Encounter: The Theological Legacy of Rabbi Joseph
B. Soloveitchik *By Dr. David Hartman* 6 x 9, 240 pp, Quality PB, 978-1-58023-176-3 **$19.95**

The Personhood of God: Biblical Theology, Human Faith and the Divine Image
By Dr. Yochanan Muffs; Foreword by Dr. David Hartman
6 x 9, 240 pp, Quality PB, 978-1-58023-338-5 **$18.99**; HC, 978-1-58023-265-4 **$24.99**

A Touch of the Sacred: A Theologian's Informal Guide to Jewish Belief
By Dr. Eugene B. Borowitz and Frances W. Schwartz
6 x 9, 256 pp, Quality PB, 978-1-58023-416-0 **$16.99**; HC, 978-1-58023-337-8 **$21.99**

Traces of God: Seeing God in Torah, History and Everyday Life *By Rabbi Neil Gillman, PhD*
6 x 9, 240 pp, Quality PB, 978-1-58023-369-9 **$16.99**

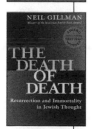

We Jews and Jesus: Exploring Theological Differences for Mutual Understanding *By Rabbi Samuel Sandmel; Preface by Rabbi David Sandmel* 6 x 9, 192 pp, Quality PB, 978-1-59473-208-9 **$16.99***

Your Word Is Fire: The Hasidic Masters on Contemplative Prayer
Edited and translated by Rabbi Arthur Green, PhD, and Barry W. Holtz
6 x 9, 160 pp, Quality PB, 978-1-879045-25-5 **$15.95**

I Am Jewish
Personal Reflections Inspired by the Last Words of Daniel Pearl
Almost 150 Jews—both famous and not—from all walks of life, from all around the world, write about many aspects of their Judaism.
Edited by Judea and Ruth Pearl 6 x 9, 304 pp, Deluxe PB w/ flaps, 978-1-58023-259-3 **$18.99**
Download a free copy of the *I Am Jewish Teacher's Guide* at www.jewishlights.com.

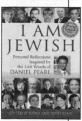

Hannah Senesh: Her Life and Diary, The First Complete Edition
By Hannah Senesh; Foreword by Marge Piercy; Preface by Eitan Senesh; Afterword by Roberta Grossman
6 x 9, 368 pp, b/w photos, Quality PB, 978-1-58023-342-2 **$19.99**

*A book from SkyLight Paths, Jewish Lights' sister imprint

Social Justice

There Shall Be No Needy
Pursuing Social Justice through Jewish Law and Tradition
By Rabbi Jill Jacobs; Foreword by Rabbi Elliot N. Dorff, PhD; Preface by Simon Greer
Confronts the most pressing issues of twenty-first-century America from a deeply Jewish perspective.
6 x 9, 288 pp, Quality PB, 978-1-58023-425-2 **$16.99**; HC, 978-1-58023-394-1 **$21.99**
Also Available: **There Shall Be No Needy Teacher's Guide**
8½ x 11, 56 pp, PB, 978-1-58023-429-0 **$8.99**

Conscience: The Duty to Obey and the Duty to Disobey
By Rabbi Harold M. Schulweis
This clarion call to rethink our moral and political behavior examines the idea of conscience and the role conscience plays in our relationships to government, law, ethics, religion, human nature, God—and to each other.
6 x 9, 160 pp, Quality PB, 978-1-58023-419-1 **$16.99**; HC, 978-1-58023-375-0 **$19.99**

Judaism and Justice: The Jewish Passion to Repair the World
By Rabbi Sidney Schwarz; Foreword by Ruth Messinger
Explores the relationship between Judaism, social justice and the Jewish identity of American Jews.
6 x 9, 352 pp, Quality PB, 978-1-58023-353-8 **$19.99**; HC, 978-1-58023-312-5 **$24.99**

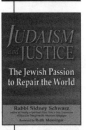

Spiritual Activism: A Jewish Guide to Leadership and Repairing the World
By Rabbi Avraham Weiss; Foreword by Alan M. Dershowitz
6 x 9, 224 pp, Quality PB, 978-1-58023-418-4 **$16.99**; HC, 978-1-58023-355-2 **$24.99**

Righteous Indignation: A Jewish Call for Justice *Edited by Rabbi Or N. Rose,*
Jo Ellen Green Kaiser and Margie Klein; Foreword by Rabbi David Ellenson, PhD
Leading progressive Jewish activists explore meaningful intellectual and spiritual foundations for their social justice work.
6 x 9, 384 pp, Quality PB, 978-1-58023-414-6 **$19.99**; HC, 978-1-58023-336-1 **$24.99**

Spirituality/Women's Interest

New Jewish Feminism: Probing the Past, Forging the Future
Edited by Rabbi Elyse Goldstein; Foreword by Anita Diamant
Looks at the growth and accomplishments of Jewish feminism and what they mean for Jewish women today and tomorrow.
6 x 9, 480 pp, HC, 978-1-58023-359-0 **$24.99**

The Divine Feminine in Biblical Wisdom Literature
Selections Annotated & Explained
Translation & Annotation by Rabbi Rami Shapiro
5½ x 8½, 240 pp, Quality PB, 978-1-59473-109-9 **$16.99**
(A book from SkyLight Paths, Jewish Lights' sister imprint)

The Quotable Jewish Woman: Wisdom, Inspiration & Humor from the Mind & Heart
Edited by Elaine Bernstein Partnow 6 x 9, 496 pp, Quality PB, 978-1-58023-236-4 **$19.99**

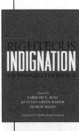

The Women's Haftarah Commentary: New Insights from Women Rabbis on the 54 Weekly Haftarah Portions, the 5 Megillot & Special Shabbatot
Edited by Rabbi Elyse Goldstein Illuminates the historical significance of female portrayals in the Haftarah and the Five Megillot.
6 x 9, 560 pp, Quality PB, 978-1-58023-371-2 **$19.99**

The Women's Torah Commentary: New Insights from Women Rabbis on the 54 Weekly Torah Portions
Edited by Rabbi Elyse Goldstein
Over fifty women rabbis offer inspiring insights on the Torah, in a week-by-week format.
6 x 9, 496 pp, Quality PB, 978-1-58023-370-5 **$19.99**; HC, 978-1-58023-076-6 **$34.95**

See Passover for *The Women's Passover Companion: Women's Reflections on the Festival of Freedom* and *The Women's Seder Sourcebook: Rituals & Readings for Use at the Passover Seder.*

Holidays/Holy Days

Who by Fire, Who by Water—Un'taneh Tokef
Edited by Rabbi Lawrence A. Hoffman, PhD
Examines the prayer's theology, authorship and poetry through a set of lively essays, all written in accessible language.
6 x 9, 272 pp, HC, 978-1-58023-424-5 **$24.99**

Rosh Hashanah Readings: Inspiration, Information and Contemplation
Yom Kippur Readings: Inspiration, Information and Contemplation
Edited by Rabbi Dov Peretz Elkins; Section Introductions from Arthur Green's These Are the Words
An extraordinary collection of readings, prayers and insights that will enable you to enter into the spirit of the High Holy Days in a personal and powerful way, permitting the meaning of the Jewish New Year to enter the heart.
Rosh Hashanah: 6 x 9, 400 pp, Quality PB, 978-1-58023-437-5 **$19.99**
Yom Kippur: 6 x 9, 368 pp, Quality PB, 978-1-58023-438-2 **$19.99**

Jewish Holidays: A Brief Introduction for Christians
By Rabbi Kerry M. Olitzky and Rabbi Daniel Judson
5½ x 8½, 176 pp, Quality PB, 978-1-58023-302-6 **$16.99**

Reclaiming Judaism as a Spiritual Practice: Holy Days and Shabbat
By Rabbi Goldie Milgram 7 x 9, 272 pp, Quality PB, 978-1-58023-205-0 **$19.99**

7th Heaven: Celebrating Shabbat with Rebbe Nachman of Breslov
By Moshe Mykoff with the Breslov Research Institute
5⅛ x 8¼, 224 pp, Deluxe PB w/ flaps, 978-1-58023-175-6 **$18.95**

Shabbat, 2nd Edition: The Family Guide to Preparing for and Celebrating
the Sabbath *By Dr. Ron Wolfson*
7 x 9, 320 pp, Illus., Quality PB, 978-1-58023-164-0 **$19.99**

Hanukkah, 2nd Edition: The Family Guide to Spiritual Celebration
By Dr. Ron Wolfson 7 x 9, 240 pp, Illus., Quality PB, 978-1-58023-122-0 **$18.95**

The Jewish Family Fun Book, 2nd Edition: Holiday Projects, Everyday Activities,
and Travel Ideas with Jewish Themes *By Danielle Dardashti and Roni Sarig; Illus. by Avi Katz*
6 x 9, 304 pp, 70+ b/w illus. & diagrams, Quality PB, 978-1-58023-333-0 **$18.99**

The Jewish Lights Book of Fun Classroom Activities: Simple and Seasonal
Projects for Teachers and Students *By Danielle Dardashti and Roni Sarig*
6 x 9, 240 pp, Quality PB, 978-1-58023-206-7 **$19.99**

Passover

My People's Passover Haggadah
Traditional Texts, Modern Commentaries
Edited by Rabbi Lawrence A. Hoffman, PhD, and David Arnow, PhD
A diverse and exciting collection of commentaries on the traditional Passover Haggadah—in two volumes!
Vol. 1: 7 x 10, 304 pp, HC, 978-1-58023-354-5 **$24.99**
Vol. 2: 7 x 10, 320 pp, HC, 978-1-58023-346-0 **$24.99**

Leading the Passover Journey: The Seder's Meaning Revealed,
the Haggadah's Story Retold *By Rabbi Nathan Laufer*
Uncovers the hidden meaning of the Seder's rituals and customs.
6 x 9, 224 pp, Quality PB, 978-1-58023-399-6 **$18.99**; HC, 978-1-58023-211-1 **$24.99**

The Women's Passover Companion: Women's Reflections on the Festival of Freedom
Edited by Rabbi Sharon Cohen Anisfeld, Tara Mohr and Catherine Spector; Foreword by Paula E. Hyman
6 x 9, 352 pp, Quality PB, 978-1-58023-231-9 **$19.99**; HC, 978-1-58023-128-2 **$24.95**

The Women's Seder Sourcebook: Rituals & Readings for Use at the Passover Seder
Edited by Rabbi Sharon Cohen Anisfeld, Tara Mohr and Catherine Spector
6 x 9, 384 pp, Quality PB, 978-1-58023-232-6 **$19.99**

Creating Lively Passover Seders: A Sourcebook of Engaging Tales, Texts & Activities
By David Arnow, PhD 7 x 9, 416 pp, Quality PB, 978-1-58023-184-8 **$24.99**

Passover, 2nd Edition: The Family Guide to Spiritual Celebration
By Dr. Ron Wolfson with Joel Lurie Grishaver 7 x 9, 416 pp, Quality PB, 978-1-58023-174-9 **$19.95**

Spirituality

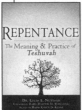

Repentance: The Meaning and Practice of *Teshuvah*
By Dr. Louis E. Newman; Foreword by Rabbi Harold M. Schulweis; Preface by Rabbi Karyn D. Kedar
Examines both the practical and philosophical dimensions of *teshuvah*, Judaism's core religious-moral teaching on repentance, and its value for us—Jews and non-Jews alike—today. 6 x 9, 256 pp, HC, 978-1-58023-426-9 **$24.99**

Tanya, the Masterpiece of Hasidic Wisdom
Selections Annotated & Explained
Translation & Annotation by Rabbi Rami Shapiro; Foreword by Rabbi Zalman M. Schachter-Shalomi
Brings the genius of *Tanya*, one of the most powerful books of Jewish wisdom, to anyone seeking to deepen their understanding of the soul.
5½ x 8½, 240 pp, Quality PB, 978-1-59473-275-1 **$16.99**
(A book from SkyLight Paths, Jewish Lights' sister imprint)

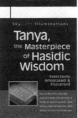

Aleph-Bet Yoga: Embodying the Hebrew Letters for Physical and Spiritual Well-Being
By Steven A. Rapp; Foreword by Tamar Frankiel, PhD, and Judy Greenfeld; Preface by Hart Lazer
7 x 10, 128 pp, b/w photos, Quality PB, Lay-flat binding, 978-1-58023-162-6 **$16.95**

A Book of Life: Embracing Judaism as a Spiritual Practice
By Rabbi Michael Strassfeld 6 x 9, 544 pp, Quality PB, 978-1-58023-247-0 **$19.99**

Bringing the Psalms to Life: How to Understand and Use the Book of Psalms
By Rabbi Daniel F. Polish, PhD 6 x 9, 208 pp, Quality PB, 978-1-58023-157-2 **$16.95**

Does the Soul Survive? A Jewish Journey to Belief in Afterlife, Past Lives & Living with Purpose *By Rabbi Elie Kaplan Spitz; Foreword by Brian L. Weiss, MD*
6 x 9, 288 pp, Quality PB, 978-1-58023-165-7 **$16.99**

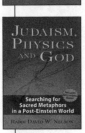

First Steps to a New Jewish Spirit: Reb Zalman's Guide to Recapturing the Intimacy & Ecstasy in Your Relationship with God *By Rabbi Zalman M. Schachter-Shalomi with Donald Gropman* 6 x 9, 144 pp, Quality PB, 978-1-58023-182-4 **$16.95**

Foundations of Sephardic Spirituality: The Inner Life of Jews of the Ottoman Empire
By Rabbi Marc D. Angel, PhD 6 x 9, 224 pp, Quality PB, 978-1-58023-341-5 **$18.99**

God & the Big Bang: Discovering Harmony between Science & Spirituality
By Dr. Daniel C. Matt 6 x 9, 216 pp, Quality PB, 978-1-879045-89-7 **$16.99**

God in Our Relationships: Spirituality between People from the Teachings of Martin Buber *By Rabbi Dennis S. Ross* 5½ x 8½, 160 pp, Quality PB, 978-1-58023-147-3 **$16.95**

The Jewish Lights Spirituality Handbook: A Guide to Understanding, Exploring & Living a Spiritual Life *Edited by Stuart M. Matlins*
What exactly is "Jewish" about spirituality? How do I make it a part of my life? Fifty of today's foremost spiritual leaders share their ideas and experience with us.
6 x 9, 456 pp, Quality PB, 978-1-58023-093-3 **$19.99**

Judaism, Physics and God: Searching for Sacred Metaphors in a Post-Einstein World
By Rabbi David W. Nelson 6 x 9, 352 pp, Quality PB, inc. reader's discussion guide,
978-1-58023-306-4 **$18.99**; HC, 352 pp, 978-1-58023-252-4 **$24.99**

Meaning and Mitzvah: Daily Practices for Reclaiming Judaism through Prayer, God, Torah, Hebrew, Mitzvot and Peoplehood *By Rabbi Goldie Milgram*
7 x 9, 336 pp, Quality PB, 978-1-58023-256-2 **$19.99**

Minding the Temple of the Soul: Balancing Body, Mind, and Spirit through Traditional Jewish Prayer, Movement, and Meditation *By Tamar Frankiel, PhD, and Judy Greenfeld*
7 x 10, 184 pp, Illus., Quality PB, 978-1-879045-64-4 **$16.95**

One God Clapping: The Spiritual Path of a Zen Rabbi *By Rabbi Alan Lew with Sherril Jaffe*
5½ x 8½, 336 pp, Quality PB, 978-1-58023-115-2 **$16.95**

The Soul of the Story: Meetings with Remarkable People
By Rabbi David Zeller 6 x 9, 288 pp, HC, 978-1-58023-272-2 **$21.99**

There Is No Messiah ... and You're It: The Stunning Transformation of Judaism's Most Provocative Idea *By Rabbi Robert N. Levine, DD*
6 x 9, 192 pp, Quality PB, 978-1-58023-255-5 **$16.99**

These Are the Words: A Vocabulary of Jewish Spiritual Life
By Rabbi Arthur Green, PhD 6 x 9, 304 pp, Quality PB, 978-1-58023-107-7 **$18.95**

Spirituality/Prayer

Making Prayer Real: Leading Jewish Spiritual Voices on Why Prayer Is Difficult and What to Do about It *By Rabbi Mike Comins*

A new and different response to the challenges of Jewish prayer, with "best prayer practices" from Jewish spiritual leaders of all denominations.

6 x 9, 320 pp, Quality PB, 978-1-58023-417-7 **$18.99**

Witnesses to the One: The Spiritual History of the *Sh'ma*
By Rabbi Joseph B. Meszler; Foreword by Rabbi Elyse Goldstein
6 x 9, 176 pp, Quality PB, 978-1-58023-400-9 **$16.99**; HC, 978-1-58023-309-5 **$19.99**

My People's Prayer Book Series: Traditional Prayers, Modern Commentaries *Edited by Rabbi Lawrence A. Hoffman, PhD*

Provides diverse and exciting commentary to the traditional liturgy. Will help you find new wisdom in Jewish prayer, and bring liturgy into your life. Each book includes Hebrew text, modern translations and commentaries from all perspectives of the Jewish world.

Vol. 1—The *Sh'ma* and Its Blessings
  7 x 10, 168 pp, HC, 978-1-879045-79-8 **$24.99**
Vol. 2—The *Amidah* 7 x 10, 240 pp, HC, 978-1-879045-80-4 **$24.95**
Vol. 3—*P'sukei D'zimrah* (Morning Psalms)
  7 x 10, 240 pp, HC, 978-1-879045-81-1 **$24.95**
Vol. 4—*Seder K'riat Hatorah* (The Torah Service)
  7 x 10, 264 pp, HC, 978-1-879045-82-8 **$23.95**
Vol. 5—*Birkhot Hashachar* (Morning Blessings)
  7 x 10, 240 pp, HC, 978-1-879045-83-5 **$24.95**
Vol. 6—*Tachanun* and Concluding Prayers
  7 x 10, 240 pp, HC, 978-1-879045-84-2 **$24.95**
Vol. 7—Shabbat at Home 7 x 10, 240 pp, HC, 978-1-879045-85-9 **$24.95**
Vol. 8—*Kabbalat Shabbat* (Welcoming Shabbat in the Synagogue)
  7 x 10, 240 pp, HC, 978-1-58023-121-3 **$24.99**
Vol. 9 Welcoming the Night: *Minchah* and *Ma'ariv* (Afternoon and
  Evening Prayer) 7 x 10, 272 pp, HC, 978-1-58023-262-3 **$24.99**
Vol. 10—Shabbat Morning: *Shacharit* and *Musaf* (Morning and
  Additional Services) 7 x 10, 240 pp, HC, 978-1-58023-240-1 **$24.99**

Spirituality/Lawrence Kushner

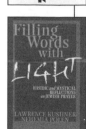

The Book of Letters: A Mystical Hebrew Alphabet
  Popular HC Edition, 6 x 9, 80 pp, 2-color text, 978-1-879045-00-2 **$24.95**
  Collector's Limited Edition, 9 x 12, 80 pp, gold-foil-embossed pages, w/ limited-edition silkscreened print, 978-1-879045-04-0 **$349.00**

The Book of Miracles: A Young Person's Guide to Jewish Spiritual Awareness
  6 x 9, 96 pp, 2-color illus., HC, 978-1-879045-78-1 **$16.95** *For ages 9–13*

The Book of Words: Talking Spiritual Life, Living Spiritual Talk
  6 x 9, 160 pp, Quality PB, 978-1-58023-020-9 **$16.95**

Eyes Remade for Wonder: A Lawrence Kushner Reader *Introduction by Thomas Moore*
  6 x 9, 240 pp, Quality PB, 978-1-58023-042-1 **$18.95**

Filling Words with Light: Hasidic and Mystical Reflections on Jewish Prayer
By Rabbi Lawrence Kushner and Rabbi Nehemia Polen
  5½ x 8½, 176 pp, Quality PB, 978-1-58023-238-8 **$16.99**; HC, 978-1-58023-216-6 **$21.99**

God Was in This Place & I, i Did Not Know: Finding Self, Spirituality and Ultimate Meaning 6 x 9, 192 pp, Quality PB, 978-1-879045-33-0 **$16.95**

Honey from the Rock: An Introduction to Jewish Mysticism
  6 x 9, 176 pp, Quality PB, 978-1-58023-073-5 **$16.95**

Invisible Lines of Connection: Sacred Stories of the Ordinary
  5½ x 8½, 160 pp, Quality PB, 978-1-879045-98-9 **$15.95**

Jewish Spirituality: A Brief Introduction for Christians
  5½ x 8½, 112 pp, Quality PB, 978-1-58023-150-3 **$12.95**

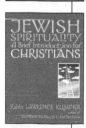

The River of Light: Jewish Mystical Awareness
  6 x 9, 192 pp, Quality PB, 978-1-58023-096-4 **$16.95**

The Way Into Jewish Mystical Tradition
  6 x 9, 224 pp, Quality PB, 978-1-58023-200-5 **$18.99**; HC, 978-1-58023-029-2 **$21.95**

About Jewish Lights

People of all faiths and backgrounds yearn for books that attract, engage, educate, and spiritually inspire.

Our principal goal is to stimulate thought and help all people learn about who the Jewish People are, where they come from, and what the future can be made to hold. While people of our diverse Jewish heritage are the primary audience, our books speak to people in the Christian world as well and will broaden their understanding of Judaism and the roots of their own faith.

We bring to you authors who are at the forefront of spiritual thought and experience. While each has something different to say, they all say it in a voice that you can hear.

Our books are designed to welcome you and then to engage, stimulate, and inspire. We judge our success not only by whether or not our books are beautiful and commercially successful, but by whether or not they make a difference in your life.

For your information and convenience, at the back of this book we have provided a list of other Jewish Lights books you might find interesting and useful. They cover all the categories of your life:

Bar/Bat Mitzvah	Life Cycle
Bible Study / Midrash	Meditation
Children's Books	Men's Interest
Congregation Resources	Parenting
Current Events / History	Prayer / Ritual / Sacred Practice
Ecology / Environment	Social Justice
Fiction: Mystery, Science Fiction	Spirituality
Grief / Healing	Theology / Philosophy
Holidays / Holy Days	Travel
Inspiration	Twelve Steps
Kabbalah / Mysticism / Enneagram	Women's Interest

Stuart M. Matlins, Publisher

Or phone, fax, mail or e-mail to: **JEWISH LIGHTS Publishing**
Sunset Farm Offices, Route 4 • P.O. Box 237 • Woodstock, Vermont 05091
Tel: (802) 457-4000 • Fax: (802) 457-4004 • www.jewishlights.com
Credit card orders: **(800) 962-4544** (8:30AM–5:30PM ET Monday–Friday)
Generous discounts on quantity orders. SATISFACTION GUARANTEED. Prices subject to change.

**For more information about each book,
visit our website at www.jewishlights.com**